PALM COUNTRY
·Cuisine·

Favorite Recipes and Photographs
from the Heart of Florida

BY THE
JUNIOR LEAGUE OF GREATER LAKELAND, FLORIDA

The purpose of the Junior League of Greater Lakeland, Florida, Inc. is to promote voluntarism; to develop the potential of its members for voluntary participation in community affairs; and to demonstrate the effectiveness of trained volunteers.

Proceeds from the sale of Palm Country Cuisine will be returned to the community through projects of the Junior League of Greater Lakeland, Inc.

To obtain additional copies, use the order form at the back of this book, or write:

Palm Country Cuisine
2020 Crystal Grove Drive
Lakeland, Florida 33801

Palm Country Cuisine may be obtained for fundraising projects or by retail outlets at special rates. Write to the above address for further information.

Cover Design and Graphics
Anne Powell

Illustrator
Gary Gessford

Photographer
Bud Lee

Creative Portions of Manuscript
Melinda Morris Knight

Copyright © 1987 by The Junior League of Greater Lakeland, Inc.
First Edition
First Printing: 10,000 copies, February, 1987
Second Printing: 10,000 copies, October, 1988

The Library of Congress Catalog Number: 86-082335
International Standard Book Number: 0-9617578-0-9

Printed by S.C. Toof and Company
Memphis, Tennessee

If your image of central Florida is a network of highways interlacing myriad tourist attractions, the Junior League of Greater Lakeland invites you to experience natural living in the heart of the South's great state. **PALM COUNTRY CUISINE** is your passport to the sights, savories and sensations of a lifestyle lived in the sunshine. Ours is a region of vast diversity, and both our recreation and our major industries are keyed to the outdoors.

The natural life in central Florida is a celebration for the senses. Fresh vegetables are grown year 'round. While much of the nation copes with winter, we celebrate the harvest season of ripe strawberries and succulent citrus. Our lakes, rivers and coastal waters offer abundant fish of great variety. Beef cattle graze in our countryside. Orange blossoms, jasmine and gardenias compete to own the air. The song of winter's migratory birds joins a chorus of crane and heron.

At the crossroads of a dozen cultures, delights for the palate emerge from the marriage of traditions and culinary heritages — North and South, creole and Cuban, French and "Florida cracker."

The diversity of our heritage and our partnership with nature encourage the custom of eating and entertaining outdoors. With **PALM COUNTRY CUISINE** and a little imagination, you can join us for a picnic by one of our many lakes, or a hearty bar-be-que at a ranch. Be with us for brunch on the patio, a tailgate lunch at Lakeland's annual EAA Fly-In air show, a backpack snack while canoeing, or a formal candlelit dinner by the pool. Come for elegant entertaining or casual cooking. Follow us home and discover Florida, naturally, in **PALM COUNTRY CUISINE**.

About the Artist

Anne Spears Powell has created the fresh and exciting appearance that sets this cookbook apart from the rest. A native of Florida, she attended Auburn University and University of Florida, earning a degree in graphic design. Her talents have earned her many awards including the "Addy" for excellence in advertising design and Best of Show.

At one time the Art Director for Nissen Advertising, and Pearson, Clarke and Sawyer Advertising, Anne now free-lances. Her logos and designs have appeared in magazines and newspapers, and she has worked with the Florida Citrus Commission, Food Machinery Corporation, Lakeland Regional Medical Center, Lykes-Pasco, and the Florida Phosphate Council.

About the Photographer

While searching Florida for a photographer for our cookbook, we found a diamond in our own back yard. His business card reads "Bud Lee, Picture Maker, Paris - London - Plant City." Not only does Bud have a sense of humor, he has a depth and diversity of talent and an excellent reputation known all over the United States and Europe.

Bud is a native of New York, and first worked in Florida under a grant from the National Endowment for the Arts. He fell in love with our southern ways, and moved to Plant City 10 years ago, where he and his wife Peggy are raising their four children.

His honors include *LIFE* Magazine Photographer of the Year, and his work appears in *The Best of LIFE*. He was a contract photographer for *Esquire Magazine* for 6 years. His work has appeared in *Fortune, Town and Country, Elle, Time, House and Garden, Newsweek, Vogue, Harpers Bazaar, New York Times Sunday Magazine, Yankee, Historic Preservation* and *Ambassador.*

Bud's photos are seen in books, including a *Time-Life Cooking Series.* In the future, his photos will tour the country in a collection entitled "Mothers and Daughters," sponsored by the Aperture Foundation.

Although he has photographed celebrities and news events, Bud says this cookbook was his most interesting and rewarding assignment. It opened up a new way of viewing life, of exploring the world as a child. Bud's assignment took him down the backroads of central Florida, to secluded cypress swamps and pristine springs. He now has a true sense of the land and of the people who live here.

PALM COUNTRY
·Cuisine·

Contents

Cookbook Committee

1984-85

Chairman
Beth Myers
Sustaining Advisor
Sue Coleman
Committee
Judy Harris
Susan Nichols
Judy Webb

1985-86

Chairman
Beth Myers
Assistant Chairman
Mary Stiles
Sustaining Advisor
Sue Coleman
Artistic Coordinator
Melinda Knight
Recipe Chairmen
Ann Caroline Bean
Cheryl Philpot
Committee
Susan Cox
Bonnie Edwards
Judy Harris
Jacki Hill
Debbie Hooks
Dotty Ivey
Jody Kane
Carole Little
Vicki Reddick
Mary Stephens
Judy Webb
Sharie Weeks

Special Acknowledgments

Lynda Buck
Carol Williams

1986-87

Chairmen
Susan Cox
Mary Stiles
Sustaining Advisor
Anne McLaughlin
Promotional Captain
Melinda Knight
Retail Captain
Betsy Watson
Wholesale Captain
Leslie Wallace
Committee
Moira Allsopp
Michelle Badcock
Ann Caroline Bean
Liz Daughtrey
Lin Docherty
Judy Harris
Felicia Hauseman
Marti Jones
Beth Myers
Betsy Phillips
Robin Smith
Peggy Stephens
Olinda Sykes
Sharie Weeks
Dana Woodsby

1987-88

Co-Chairmen
Susan Cox
Mary Stiles
Sustaining Advisor
Anne McLaughlin
Assistant Chairmen
Liz Daughtrey
Treasurer
Sharie Weeks
Computer
Robin Smith

Promotional Design
Melinda Knight
Sandra Blackman
Bonnie Edwards
Jennifer Morris
Olinda Sykes
Retail
Judy Fortin
Lin Docherty
Bev Mansfield
Jamie Robinson
Allison Williams
Wholesale
Leslie Wallace
Nancy Fisher
Debe Jordan
Suzanne Siegel
Debbie Tibbs

1988-89

Chairmen
Kim Ruthven
Robin Smith
Sustaining Advisor
Susie Carr
Sales Committee
Carol Bevis
Ginny Burris
Robyn Harrell
Suzy Little
Debbie Tibbs
Barbara Turner
Promotions Committee
Bonnie Edwards
Patty Fouts
Bev Hollis
Debe Jordan
Gigi Skipper
Nancy Fisher
Treasurer
Jackie Fowler

MENUS

Sunrise Breakfast

Mimosa Hawaiian
Canadian Egg Casserole
Florida Sunrise Breakfast Salad
Pecan Mini Muffins   Lemon Refreshers
Honey-Orange Butter

Most of the palms native to the United States are found in Florida, ranging from dwarf shrubby types to magnificent trees reaching 100 feet. Some are erect in growth, while others lean. Some have a single trunk, while others have numerous stems. Over 35 species flourish in central Florida, and the sabal palm is the state tree. Early settlers depended on the palm for both food and shelter. The young bud and heart were edible, and the straight fibrous trunk formed the walls of homes and forts. The fronds were woven into thatched roofs.

Photo: Kissimmee

Marth, Del and Marth, Martha J., Editors. *The Florida Almanac*. Gretna, Louisiana: Pelican Publishing Company. 1985.

Southern and Homecooked

Southern Baked Ham
Black-Eyed Peas and Rice   Okra and Tomatoes
Creamy Broccoli Salad
Best Buttermilk Biscuits
Cream Cheese Pound Cake with Fresh Peaches

The honeycombed aquifer under central Florida's swamps supplies our drinking water. The 870 square miles of the Green Swamp are protected as natural water storage. Swamps and wetlands contain unique varieties of trees, including the bald cypress. When the cypress stands in water, it develops a fluted, buttressed trunk. The roots send up "knees" which emerge from the water. These knees supply oxygen to the roots, and provide an anchor for the tree, which can reach a height of 170 feet and a diameter of 15 feet. A fun way to admire a tranquil cypress swamp is from a catwalk.

Photo: Fish Eating Creek

Feeding the Flock Buffet

Artichoke Dip
LYCC Southern Fried Chicken
Melon Mélange   Patio Peas and Cashews
Family Reunion Potato Salad
Whole Wheat Muffins
Pecan Pie Bars   Caramel Chocolate Brownies

Central Florida lies within a major flyway traveled by 150 species of migratory waterfowl and shore birds. Our lakes are the feeding and breeding ground for such water birds as the wood stork, heron, ibis, and egret. Our marshes host game birds including the mallard, pintail, snipe, woodcock, marsh hen, turkey, coot, and goose. Our sky belongs to the raptores including the eagle, hawk, and osprey, pictured here. We are vigilant in protecting our wild birds, and special building guidelines prevent construction from disrupting the bald eagle's habitat. Rescue volunteers heal wounded birds, help them regain flight skills, then release them into the wild.

Photo: The chain of lakes near Winter Haven

Sunny Day Picnic

Quick Spinach Dip
Heartland Ham Salad
Minestrone Salad   Disappearing Pickles
Strawberry Jam Loaf
Chocolate Pretzels   Peanut Butter Chocolate Chip Crispies
Fruity Iced Tea

In the early 1880's succulent strawberry crops were introduced to central Florida. When the railroad reached the area in 1884, millions of boxes were shipped to northern cities. For decades children were the main laborers, bending over the low plants. Some schools closed in December at the start of the season and did not open until late March. These "strawberry schools" were abolished in the 1950's. Plant City, west of Lakeland, is the nation's Winter Strawberry Capital. We love to take our families to the fields and fill our buckets with the fragrant ripe berries.

Photo: Plant City

Springtime Luncheon

Bleu Cheese Chicken Salad
Tomatoes and Hearts of Palm Vinaigrette
Strawberry-Pecan Congealed Salad
Pineapple Wheat Muffins
Frozen Lemon Pudding

Central Florida is honeycombed with artesian springs, and the 71°- 74° water is chilly and refreshing on sweltering summer days. Aquatic plants blanket the bottom, and white sand-boils indicate where the springs emit fresh water at thousands of gallons per minute. These sparkling waters are the source of rivers and streams, surrounded by hammocks of cool, dense forests. Many of us have enjoyed a lazy afternoon floating on an inner tube along a shady river. In the winter, gentle manatees swim inland to these warmer spring-fed rivers. The manatee is endangered, and conservation programs strive to protect these tame creatures.

Photo: Crystal Springs

Lakeside Luncheon

Cheese Bits   White Sangria
Shrimp Florentine
Fresh Fruit with Almond Whipped Cream
Carrots en Casserole
Standard Yeast Rolls
Mocha Meringue Pie

Henry David Thoreau said "The lake is earth's most beautiful and expressive feature." It is easy to understand why Lakelanders find so many ways to enjoy our 13 lakes. Recreation paths around the shores are a scenic setting for strolling, biking, jogging, and roller skating. In the spring, yellow lotus blossoms rise from the lily pads. Red-winged blackbirds balance on cattails, while egrets and blue herons wade among the reeds. The lakes are a playground for fishermen, sailors, and water skiers. World speed records are set on Lake Hollingsworth when the annual Orange Cup Regatta tests the skilled pilots of hydroplane racing boats. Also of renown is Florida Southern College on the north shore of Lake Hollingsworth. Its campus contains the world's largest collection of buildings designed by Frank Lloyd Wright.

Photo: Lake Hollingsworth in Lakeland

Sweet Sampling

Chocolate Chip Kisses   White Cranberry-Almond Fudge
Cookie Madam Butterscotch Cheesecake Bars
Brownie Spoon Cupcakes   Coconut Pound Cake
Angel Pie
Strawberry-Orange Punch   Coffee

These fallow sugar cane fields with their rich black soil have not changed much from their humble beginnings. Sugar cane was a staple of the Florida Cracker diet and an integral element of social life. Cane grinding brought families together, and news was exchanged as the syrup boiled. A banquet was spread on blankets and quilts. Each cook brought her specialty, and recipes were exchanged and handed down to new generations. Syrup making disappeared from central Florida in the early 1960's, but Florida still grows more sugar cane than any other state.

Photo: South central Florida

Afternoon Tea

Purple Plum Pecan Bread   Toasted Coconut Loaf
Party Cucumber Sandwiches
Cheese Straws   Salmon Mold
Chocolate Dipped Strawberries
Peppermint Party Brownies   Lime Bars
Champagne Punch with Fruit   Coffee Frappé

Although America's founding fathers signed the Declaration of Independence in 1776, Florida remained loyal to Great Britain. British rule was short-lived, but 180 years later Lakeland called upon the Crown of England for a favor. In our letter to Queen Elizabeth II, we described Lake Morton, one of our many bird sanctuaries. Her Majesty replied with a gift, a pair of royal mute swans. Today their descendants grace Lake Morton, along with other species of swans, ducks, and geese. A national historic district of 700 homes borders the lake, and the annual art festival, Mayfaire-by-the-Lake, is held on the shore.

Photo: Lake Morton in the center of Lakeland

Very Vegetarian

Vegetarian Lasagne
Green French Onion Salad
Red Onion Loaf
Apple Nut Cake
Red Sangria

The tradition of harvesting Florida's bounty from land and sea goes back to pre-history. European explorers discovered that Creek and Seminole Indians raised tobacco, vegetables, and citrus. White settlers raised rice and indigo for export crops in the 18th and 19th centuries. These were only a clue to our modern crop production, as Florida's sub-tropical climate and agricultural technology have made us the nation's winter vegetable producer. In fact, Florida produces more different kinds of vegetables than any other state, as well as flowers, ferns, and ornamental plants.

Photo: Turkey Creek

Hearty Round-Up

Beef Pecan Dip
Teriyaki Flank Steak on the Grill
Buttered Onions   Crock Pot Beans
Dutch Lettuce
Corny Cornbread
Hummingbird Cake

Our cattle population of more than two million began in 1521, when Juan Ponce de Leon sailed into Saint Augustine with six heifers and a bull. Spanish friars tended the early herds, which evolved into thousands of semi-wild cattle. As late as 1879, central Florida cattlemen exported these "scrub cows" to Cuba in exchange for gold Spanish doubloons. Tough cowboys controlled their herds with long whips, earning the nickname "Florida Crackers." Today Florida is a large exporter of breeding stock, like the Brahmans pictured here.

Photo: Brahman ranch near Bartow

Citrus Celebration

Company Cheese Ball

Citrus Center Chicken

Asparagus with Sautéed Mushrooms   Orange Rice

Valencia Ambrosia Cups

Bits of Sunshine

Classic Key Lime Pie

A legend says early explorers unknowingly sowed the official symbol of Florida by spitting out the seeds of their Spanish oranges. The Indians cultivated the seedlings and established the first orange groves. The grapefruit did not arrive from Spain until 1809, and the Marsh seedless grapefruit was developed in Lakeland in 1887. Citrus groves blanket the gently rolling hills of central Florida, and their sweet blossoms scent the air. At harvest time millions of oranges, tangerines, and grapefruit are picked by hand.

Photo: Near Lake Wales

Catch of the Day

Crab-Broccoli Soup
Catch of the Day Fish
Shoepeg Corn Pudding
Crunchy Picnic Slaw
Herb Cheese Loaf
Brownie Fudge Pie

Our abundant lakes and rivers provide excellent fishing. Unique to Florida are phosphate pits, prized as superb fishing holes. These long narrow pits are early phosphate excavations that have been reclaimed by nature. A fishing line dropped from a bridge, a boat, or a backyard dock may bring up speckled perch, large-mouth bass, bream, pikerel, or catfish. Fishermen also cast their lines into the salt waters of the Gulf of Mexico and the Atlantic Ocean. Central Floridians also visit the coast for reasons other than fishing. Only an hour from Lakeland, the Gulf entices us with its gentle azure tides. A casual stroll along soft white sands yields exquisite shells. The pounding Atlantic surf is two hours to the east of Lakeland. The higher waves are loved by surfers, and colorful coral reefs attract snorklers and scuba divers.

Photo: Longboat Key bridge

Cocktails on the Bank

Danish Wine Cooler
Crab-Stuffed Snow Peas
Hanky Pankies   Shrimp Butter
Spinach Balls   Mushroom Roll-Ups
Tower of Cheese
Pineapple Dip and Fruit
Cocoa Kisses   After Dinner Cookies

Florida is a relatively "new" state in geologic time. Thirty million years ago, central Florida poked out of the sea like a giant sandbar. The waters gradually receded, leaving a peninsula of limestone, sand, and clay. Captured between these layers were mastodons, rhinoceroses, camels, and huge sharks with teeth as big as a hand. Their fossils are unearthed in the course of mining one of the world's richest phosphate deposits. Florida had its own gold rush in the late 1880's. After phosphate was discovered in the banks of the Peace River, thousands of prospectors mined the river bed for the "white gold." A century later the river lives up to its name as it winds along the 106-mile course from the Green Swamp to the Gulf of Mexico.

Photo: Peace River near Bartow

Arabian Nights

Caviar Cream Cheese Spread
Beef Tenderloin
Best Potato Casserole   Company Carrots
Classic Caesar Salad
Popovers
Fudge Truffle Cake

Some American thoroughbreds can trace their roots back to 1539, when Hernando de Soto brought 225 head of royal Spanish stock to Florida. Over the years some horses escaped and ran wild through our awakening country. English colonists bred their stallions to the Spanish mares and developed the American quarter horse. American Indians prized their pinto ponies, also of Spanish origin. Floridians have always had a great interest in horses, and racing has been a popular sport since 1800. The Florida horse-breeding industry, however, is barely a generation old. Central Florida ranches, paddocks, and training tracks now produce Arabians, Quarter Horses, Standardbreds, Kentucky Derby winners, and pleasure and working horses.

Photo: Arabian ranch in Lakeland

Candlelight Dinner

Fresh Artichokes with Curry Dip
Butterfly Leg of Lamb on the Grill
Asparagus with Cashew Butter
Rice Casserole Extraordinaire
Mixed Green Salad with Parmesan Cheese Dressing
Whole Wheat Rolls
Stawberry Mousse

Travelers have always found that Florida is something to write home about. As early as 1765 visitors included naturalist William Bartram. He suffered many hardships, yet accepted his adventure with spirit and eagerness. In an exerpt from his *Travels*, he described his campsite. "I spread my skins and blanket by my cheerful fire under the protecting shade of the hospitable live oak. I listened, undisturbed, to the divine hymns of the feathered songsters of the groves, whilst the softly whispering breezes faintly died away. The sun now below the western horizon, the moon majestically rising in the east, again the tuneful birds become inspired." Over 200 years later a Florida sunset remains a serene and magical experience.

Photo: A pasture located between Lakeland and Plant City

Bartram, John. *John and William Bartran's America.* New York: Devin-Adair Co., 1957.

We give the following persons our sincere thanks for allowing us to photograph their property and guiding us to the most beautiful spots central Florida can offer.

Carl Allen
Mary and Wogan Badcock
Jean and David Bunch
Cypress Knees Museum
Dees Ski School
Nina and Peter Fing
Jean Gaffney
Sonny Griffin
Martha and Brand Laseter
Mina and Jules Leopold
Carolee and Pat Lyons
Mary and Snow Martin
Bobby Parkes
Ray Peek

References for Photo Captions

Bartram, John. *John and William Bartram's America.* New York: Devin-Adair Co., 1957.

Gill, Joan E. and Read, Beth R., Editors. *Born of the Sun.* Hollywood, Florida: Florida Bicentennial Commemorative Journal, Inc., a subsidiary of Worth International Communications Corporation, 1975.

Marth, Del and Marth, Martha J., Editors. *The Florida Almanac.* Gretna, Louisiana: Pelican Publishing Company, 1985.

APPETIZERS
& BEVERAGES

Artichoke Dip

1 (14-ounce) can artichoke hearts,
   drained
½ cup mayonnaise
1 teaspoon Worcestershire sauce
1-2 teaspoons onion, grated

1 cup Parmesan cheese, grated
3 slices bacon, cooked and
   crumbled
Red pepper
Melba round crackers

Mash artichoke hearts with fork and set aside. Combine mayonnaise, Worcestershire sauce, onion, and Parmesan cheese. Stir in artichokes and bacon. Chill. Before serving sprinkle with red pepper. Serve with melba round crackers.

Yield: 1 cup.

Flavor is enhanced when made a day ahead.

Fresh Artichokes with Curry Dip

1½ cups mayonnaise
1 teaspoon Worcestershire sauce
1 tablespoon curry powder
¼ teaspoon dry mustard
½ teaspoon Tabasco sauce
Seasoned salt to taste

Juice of ½ lemon
2 fresh artichokes
1 tablespoon onion flakes
1 bay leaf
1 lemon, sliced
½ teaspoon salt

Combine mayonnaise, Worcestershire sauce, curry powder, dry mustard, Tabasco sauce, seasoned salt, and lemon juice. Mix well and chill until ready to serve with artichokes. Wash and trim artichokes. Cover artichokes with water and season with onion flakes, bay leaf, lemon slices, and salt. Boil gently for 40 minutes. May serve artichokes warm or cold, with curry dip.

Yield: Approximately 20 servings.

Fresh and delicious!

Skinny Dip

1 cup mayonnaise
2 packages Hidden Valley
    Buttermilk dressing
32 ounces small curd cottage
    cheese

1 pound baby shrimp, cooked and
    cleaned, or 18 ounces frozen
    shrimp
Crackers or raw vegetables

Blend together mayonnaise and dressing mix and add to cottage cheese. Mix together well. Stir in shrimp. Refrigerate for several hours, to enhance flavor. Serve with crackers or raw vegetables.

Yield: 6 cups.

Doubles and triples easily. Keeps in refrigerator for several days. May also serve as a luncheon salad. To reduce calories you may substitute a low calorie mayonnaise and low fat cottage cheese.

Simple Shrimp Dip

16 ounces cream cheese
½ cup mayonnaise
1 clove garlic, minced
2 teaspoons onion, grated
2 teaspoons prepared mustard
2 teaspoons sugar

½ teaspoon seasoned salt
1 pound fresh shrimp, cooked and
    cleaned
6 tablespoons sauterne or dry wine
Chips or crackers

Over low heat, melt the cream cheese. Blend in mayonnaise, garlic, onion, mustard, sugar, and salt. Stir in shrimp and sauterne. Serve warm in a chafing dish with chips or crackers.

Yield: 12-15 servings.

Curry Dip for Vegetables

8 ounces cream cheese, softened
1 tablespoon onion, chopped
½ cup sour cream
¼ cup raisins
½ teaspoon curry powder
¼ teaspoon salt
Raw vegetables

Place cream cheese, onion, sour cream, raisins, curry powder, and salt in food processor. Mix well. Chill and serve with raw vegetables.

Yield: 1½ cups.

Lake Charles Dip

½ pint sour cream
1 package Good Seasons Italian
   dressing mix
1 tablespoon mayonnaise
Juice of ½ lemon
½ avocado, finely chopped
½ tomato, minced
Dash of Tabasco sauce
Raw vegetables or chips

Mix sour cream, dressing mix, mayonnaise, lemon juice, avocado, tomato, and Tabasco in a medium bowl. Refrigerate overnight. Serve with raw vegetables or chips.

Yield: Approximately 1 cup.

Marylee's Veggie Dip

1 cup mayonnaise
1 cup sour cream
½ teaspoon salt
2 tablespoons fresh dill, chopped
2 tablespoons fresh parsley, chopped
2 tablespoons onion salt or grated
   onion
1 clove garlic, crushed
Raw vegetables

Combine the mayonnaise, sour cream, salt, dill, parsley, onion, and garlic. Serve with fresh vegetables cut up for dipping.

Yield: Approximately 2 cups.

Quick Spinach Dip

1 (10-ounce) package frozen
   chopped spinach, thawed and
   well drained
1 cup sour cream
1 tablespoon mayonnaise

1 tablespoon onion, minced
1 (4-ounce) package Ranch Style
   Buttermilk dressing
Corn chips or raw vegetables

Mix together spinach, sour cream, mayonnaise, onion, and dressing. Chill. Serve with corn chips or assorted raw vegetables.

Yield: 1 cup.

This is attractive served in a hollowed-out loaf of rye bread.

Beef Pecan Dip

¾ cup pecans, chopped
2 teaspoons butter
¼ teaspoon salt
8 ounces cream cheese, softened
2 teaspoons milk
1 (4-ounce) package smoked
   chipped beef

1 small onion, grated
½ teaspoon garlic salt
¼ teaspoon pepper
½ cup sour cream
English water biscuits

Toast pecans with butter and salt. Set aside. Whip cream cheese and milk together. Chop beef and add to cream cheese. Add onion, garlic salt, pepper, and sour cream. Stir in ½ cup pecans. Pour into a buttered 2 cup soufflé dish or 9-inch pie plate. Sprinkle ¼ cup pecans on top. Bake at 350° for 20 minutes. Serve hot with water biscuits or other low-salt crackers.

Yield: Approximately 15 to 20 servings.

Tex-Mex Dip

1 large avocado, mashed
4 tablespoons picante sauce, mild
  or hot
1 cup sour cream
½ cup mayonnaise
1 package taco seasoning mix
2 (16-ounce) cans refried beans
  with chilies

1 bunch green onions, chopped
2 medium tomatoes, chopped
1 small can ripe olives, chopped
8 ounces sharp Cheddar cheese,
  grated
1 large bag Tostitos

Mix avocado with picante sauce and set aside. Mix together sour cream, mayonnaise, and taco mix and set aside. In a 9 x 13-inch dish, layer ingredients in the following order: refried beans with chilies, avocado mixture, sour cream mixture, onions, tomatoes, and olives. Top with cheese. Serve with traditional flavored Tostitos. Keeps up to three days in the refrigerator.

Yield: 8-10 servings.

Pineapple Dip

2 pints sour cream
2 tablespoons light brown sugar
12 coconut macaroons, crumbled
1 fresh pineapple

Fruit Fresh
Strawberries, grapes, apple slices,
  and other seasonal fruits

Mix sour cream, light brown sugar, and macaroons. Chill overnight or several days. Halve pineapple, remove fruit and cube. Sprinkle inside of pineapple and other fruits likely to brown with Fruit Fresh. Spoon dip into a pineapple half and arrange fruits around it.

Yield: 40 servings.

Amaretto Dip for Fruits

1 pint sour cream
4 tablespoons brown sugar

2 tablespoons Amaretto
Assorted fresh fruits

Mix sour cream, brown sugar, and Amaretto. Serve as dip for fresh fruits.

Yield: 1 pint.

A hollowed-out pineapple shell filled with melon balls, orange sections, strawberries, and other seasonal fruits makes a pretty presentation.

Shrimp Butter

5 tablespoons butter, softened
8 ounces cream cheese, softened
½ small onion, minced
4 teaspoons mayonnaise

1 (8-ounce) can shrimp, drained
Juice of ½ lemon
Dash of salt, pepper, and garlic salt
Crackers

Blend butter and cream cheese. Add onion, mayonnaise, shrimp, lemon juice, salt, pepper, and garlic salt. Blend well. Refrigerate for several hours to enhance flavor. Serve as a spread for crackers.

Yield: 2-2½ cups.

Shrimp Log

8 ounces cream cheese, softened
1 cup cooked shrimp, minced
2 tablespoons chili sauce
2 tablespoons stuffed olives,
   chopped

2 tablespoons green onion,
   chopped
1 teaspoon lemon juice
Stuffed olives, sliced
Crackers

Stir cream cheese until smooth. Blend in shrimp, chili sauce, olives, onion, and lemon juice. Shape into a log and decorate with sliced stuffed olives. Chill thoroughly. Serve with crackers.

Yield: 6-8 servings.

Tomato Cheese Spread

1 (10¾-ounce) can tomato soup
12 ounces cream cheese, softened
2 envelopes unflavored gelatin
¼ cup water
1 bell pepper, finely chopped

1 small onion, finely chopped
1 cup mayonnaise
⅛ teaspoon salt
Wheat crackers

Warm soup in saucepan over low heat. Add softened cream cheese and stir until blended. Combine gelatin and water and stir until dissolved. Pour gelatin into soup mixture and stir. Add bell pepper, onion, mayonnaise, and salt. Place mixture in a gelatin mold. Refrigerate until firm. Serve with wheat crackers.

Yield: Approximately 25 servings.

Chili Crabmeat

16 ounces cream cheese, softened
¼ cup onion, minced
1 tablespoon Worcestershire sauce
1 tablespoon mayonnaise
½ teaspoon garlic powder

1 (12-ounce) bottle chili sauce
2 (7½-ounce) cans crabmeat,
   drained
Fresh parsley, minced for garnish
Wheat or water crackers

Combine cream cheese, onion, Worcestershire sauce, mayonnaise, and garlic powder. Spread mixture evenly in the bottom of a 9-inch glass pie plate. Cover with chili sauce. Top with flaked crabmeat. Cover and chill thoroughly. Prior to serving, garnish heavily with parsley. Serve with wheat or water crackers. Best if chilled 24 hours ahead of time to blend flavors.

Yield: Approximately 3 cups.

Especially colorful for holiday entertaining.

Salmon Spread

2 (15½-ounce) cans salmon
1 medium onion
1 large dill pickle
1 cup mayonnaise

1 tablespoon lime juice
1 tablespoon dill pickle juice
Dill weed
Wheat crackers

Drain salmon and pick out bones. Spread salmon 1 inch thick on serving platter. In food processor chop onion and dill pickle. Transfer to mixing bowl and add mayonnaise, lime juice, and dill pickle juice. Mix together. Spread sauce over salmon and sprinkle with dill weed. May garnish with fresh parsley. Serve with wheat crackers.

Yield: 25 appetizer servings.

Caviar Cream Cheese Spread

19 ounces cream cheese, softened
1 cup mayonnaise
1 small onion, grated
1 tablespoon Worcestershire sauce
1 tablespoon lemon juice
Dash of Tabasco sauce

2 (3½-ounce) jars black caviar,
  drained
4 hard boiled eggs, finely chopped
1 cup chopped fresh parsley
Saltines

Beat cream cheese until smooth. Add mayonnaise, onion, Worcestershire sauce, lemon juice, and hot sauce. Mix well. Mound mixture into an oval shape on a large serving platter. Layer mixture with caviar, eggs and parsley. Arrange saltine crackers around outside edge of platter.

Yield: 18-20 servings.

An impressive and delicious addition to any party.

Salmon Mold

2 (7-ounce) cans salmon
½ cup salmon juice or water
1 package unflavored gelatin
2 tablespoons onions, diced
2 tablespoons lemon juice
½ cup mayonnaise
2 sprigs fresh dill or 1 teaspoon
    dried dill
½ teaspoon salt
¼ teaspoon white pepper
1 cup heavy cream
Fresh dill or parsley for garnish
Crackers

Drain salmon and reserve salmon juice. Bring salmon juice to a boil and remove from heat. Add gelatin, onions, and lemon juice. Place in blender on high speed for 30 seconds. Turn off and add mayonnaise, dill, salt, pepper, and salmon. Blend on high for 30 seconds. Remove blender cover and gradually add cream keeping blender on. Turn into an oiled one-quart mold. Chill. Garnish with fresh dill or parsley and serve with your favorite crackers. (Mold may be served with a dill sauce. To make sauce, mix sour cream, dill weed, and lemon juice to taste.)

Yield: 25 servings.

Tower of Cheese

½ pound Port Wine Cheddar
    cheese
1 cup chopped pecans
½ pound Havarti cheese
2 tablespoons coffee cream
1 bunch parsley, cleaned and
    chopped
½ pound sharp Cheddar cheese,
    grated
Pecan halves for garnish
Water crackers

Allow cheeses to come to room temperature. Line a 3½-cup crown mold with plastic wrap. Mold Port Wine Cheddar cheese in bottom. Top with chopped pecans about ¼ inch deep. Combine Havarti cheese and cream. Layer over pecans. Top with chopped parsley about ¼ inch deep. Layer softened Cheddar cheese over parsley. Cover with plastic wrap and chill overnight. Unmold on serving platter and garnish with more parsley and pecan halves. Serve with water crackers.

Yield: 24 servings.

Pavé Mold

12 ounces cream cheese	½ cup white raisins
½ cup butter	1 cup slivered almonds, toasted
½ cup sour cream	Grated rind of 2 lemons
½ cup sugar	Saltine crackers or Bremner Wafers
1 envelope unflavored gelatin	Grapes for garnish
¼ cup cold water	

Allow cream cheese, butter, and sour cream to come to room temperature then cream well with sugar. Soften gelatin in cold water. Dissolve in a double boiler over hot water. Add to cream cheese mixture. Then add raisins, slivered almonds, and lemon rind. Lightly coat a one quart mold with vegetable cooking spray. Pour mixture into mold and refrigerate. When firm, unmold onto serving platter and garnish with grapes. Serve with saltines or Bremner Wafers.

Yield: 20-25 servings.

Chicken Liver Paté

1 pound chicken livers	8 ounces cream cheese, softened
2 small onions, chopped	½ cup butter, softened
2 cloves garlic, chopped	4 teaspoons cognac
2 tablespoons paprika	Fresh parsley
1 teaspoon salt	Melba rounds
2 tablespoons sherry	

Wash chicken livers and remove yellow fat. Place in saucepan with onions, garlic, paprika, salt, and sherry. Cover with 2½ cups water and simmer for 2 hours, uncovered. Stir occasionally and add water if needed. Remove from stove, drain, and discard liquid. Place drained chicken livers in blender or food processor with cream cheese and butter. Blend until smooth; then add cognac and blend once more. Pour into a 4-cup mold and refrigerate. When firm, unmold and garnish with chopped parsley. Serve with melba rounds.

Yield: Approximately 30 servings.

Becky's Shrimp Mold

8 ounces cream cheese
1 (10¾ounce) can tomato soup
1½ envelopes unflavored gelatin
1 cup mayonnaise
1 teaspoon Worcestershire sauce
1 tablespoon fresh dill weed,
    chopped
1 teaspoon Tabasco sauce

1 tablespoon lemon juice
1 bell pepper, chopped
¾ cup celery, chopped
1 medium onion, chopped
2 (6½-ounce) cans small shrimp,
    drained
Crackers

In a double boiler, mix cream cheese and soup until smooth. Dissolve gelatin in ½ cup cold water. Add gelatin to soup mixture, and beat. Add mayonnaise, Worcestershire, dill, Tabasco, and lemon juice, mixing well. Fold in bell pepper, celery, onion, and shrimp. Pour into a 7-cup fish mold that has been lightly greased. Refrigerate for at least four hours or overnight. Serve with your favorite crackers.

Yield: Seven cups or 8 first course servings.

This makes an excellent first course. Pour into a loaf pan and refrigerate. When ready to serve, slice and serve on a bed of watercress and garnish with small shrimp.

Brie Appetizer Round

1 (2½ pound) round of Brie cheese
⅔ cup pecans, chopped

2-3 tablespoons brown sugar
Crackers

Trim rind from top of cheese leaving ¼ inch of the rind along the edge. Place cheese on an ungreased baking sheet. Sprinkle top of cheese with pecans and sugar. Broil away from heat 3-5 minutes until bubbly. Be careful not to burn. Serve with bland crackers.

Yield: 25 servings.

Easy, elegant, and excellent!

Chicken Chutney Ball

8 ounces cream cheese, softened
1 cup chicken or turkey, finely
  chopped
¾ cup toasted almonds, finely
  chopped
½ cup mayonnaise

2 tablespoons chutney, chopped
1 tablespoon curry powder
¼ teaspoon salt
Fresh chopped parsley or fresh
  coconut
Bland crackers

Combine cream cheese, chicken, almonds, mayonnaise, and chutney. Mix well.
Add curry powder and salt; continue to mix well. May have to knead like bread dough
to blend well. Shape into a ball and refrigerate. When ready to serve roll ball in
parsley or coconut. Will keep for several days in refrigerator. Serve with crackers.

Yield: 2 cups.

Everyone's favorite cheese ball!

Company Cheese Ball

16 ounces cream cheese, softened
½ - ¾ cup chutney, chopped
1½ teaspoons curry powder or to
  taste

½ teaspoon dry mustard
¾ cup toasted almonds, finely
  chopped
Wheatsworth crackers

Combine cream cheese, chutney, curry powder, dry mustard, and almonds. Mix
well and knead like bread dough. Shape into a ball and refrigerate. When ready
to serve remove and garnish with parsley. Will keep for several weeks in the refrigerator.
Serve with crackers.

Yield: 2 cups.

Hot Cheese Curls or Straws

½ cup butter, softened
1 pound sharp Cheddar cheese,
  grated
1½ cups flour

1 teaspoon baking powder
1 teaspoon red pepper
½ teaspoon salt

Mix softened butter and cheese. Sift together flour, baking powder, red pepper, and salt. Add dry ingredients to butter and cheese. Put through cookie press onto ungreased cookie sheet. Bake in preheated 325° oven for 12-15 minutes.

Yield: Approximately 5 dozen.

May roll dough into little balls and press with fork if cookie press not available.

Cheese Bits

1 cup butter, softened
2 cups Cheddar cheese, grated
2 cups flour

2 cups pecans or Rice Krispies
Cayenne pepper to taste

Mix together butter, cheese, flour, and nuts or Rice Krispies. Season with cayenne pepper and mix well. Roll into little balls. Place on a lightly greased cookie sheet and press with fork. Bake at 350° for 15 minutes. These will keep for weeks in a tin. May also freeze.

Yield: Approximately 5 dozen.

These are great anywhere and anytime!

Party Cucumber Sandwiches

8 ounces cream cheese, softened
¼ cup mayonnaise
1 seedless cucumber
1 loaf fresh sandwich bread (white
    or whole wheat)

1 (4½-ounce) can shrimp, rinsed
    and drained

Mix cream cheese and mayonnaise thoroughly and set aside. Wash cucumber and remove ends. Make rows of indentations on outside of cucumber with fork tines and then slice cucumber. Cut bread with biscuit cutters. Spread cream cheese mixture on bread rounds and top with a cucumber. Garnish each with a shrimp. Chill until ready to serve.

Yield: Approximately 40 open-faced sandwiches.

Crab-Stuffed Snow Peas

½ pound fresh snow peas
½ teaspoon salt
2 (6-ounce) packages frozen
    crabmeat, thawed and well
    drained

2 hard boiled eggs, finely chopped
3-4 tablespoons mayonnaise
1 tablespoon lemon juice
1 teaspoon capers
3 tablespoons celery, finely chopped

Wash and trim snow peas. Split on top side, leaving bottom intact to form a pocket. Blanch in boiling salted water for 10 seconds, then immerse in cold water for 1 minute. Drain and cool. (This can be done a day ahead.) For filling, combine crabmeat, eggs, mayonnaise, lemon juice, capers, and celery. Stir very gently until well mixed. Stuff each snow pea with about 1 teaspoon of crabmeat filling. Refrigerate until ready to serve. Snow peas can be stuffed up to 6 hours ahead.

Yield: 60 servings.

This appetizer will impress the most discerning guest!

Marinated Shrimp

5 pounds shrimp, cooked, shelled,
  and deveined
1 cup mayonnaise
1 cup chili sauce
1 teaspoon mustard
1 tablespoon Worcestershire sauce
2 cloves garlic, minced

½ teaspoon pepper
Dash of paprika
Juice of medium onion
Juice of lemon
2 tablespoons water
½ cup vegetable oil

Combine mayonnaise, chili sauce, mustard, Worcestershire sauce, garlic, pepper, and paprika. Mix well. Add onion juice, lemon juice, water, and oil. Blend well. Place cleaned shrimp in a large bowl and pour sauce over shrimp. Marinate in refrigerator for 24 hours.

Yield: Approximately 25 servings.

An elegant do-ahead hors d'oeuvre.

Glazed Pecans

1 cup sugar
½ cup water
1 teaspoon ground cinnamon

¼ teaspoon allspice
2 cups pecan halves
1 teaspoon vanilla extract

Combine sugar, water, ground cinnamon, and allspice in a large saucepan. Cook over medium heat for 5 minutes, stirring constantly. Add pecans and continue to cook for another 5 minutes, stirring constantly. Remove from heat and stir in vanilla. Place pecans individually on waxed paper. Cool completely.

Yield: 2 cups.

Roquefort Grapes

1 pound seedless grapes
8 ounces cream cheese, softened
4 ounces Roquefort or blue cheese,
  softened

2 tablespoons heavy cream
1 teaspoon lemon juice
8 ounces pecans, toasted, and finely
  chopped

Wash, stem, and dry grapes. Combine cream cheese, Roquefort cheese, and heavy cream. Mix until smooth. Add lemon juice and blend well. Cheese mixture will be thick and sticky. Gently stir grapes into cheese mixture, coating them evenly. Roll the cheese-coated grapes in the pecans. Place on a tray lined with wax paper. Chill until ready to serve.

Yield: Approximately 50 appetizers.

Leftover cheese mixture may be made into a salad dressing by adding sour cream and mayonnaise to taste.

Candied Wings

3 pounds chicken wings
Salt to taste
Pepper to taste
Paprika
½ cup honey

¼ cup soy sauce
4 tablespoons brown sugar
1 clove garlic, crushed
¼ cup catsup

Place chicken in a foil lined shallow baking pan. Sprinkle with salt, pepper, and paprika. Combine honey, soy sauce, brown sugar, garlic, and catsup. Pour over chicken wings. Bake at 350° for 35 minutes. Transfer to serving platter.

Yield: 20 servings.

Great for a crowd. Men love them!

Mushroom Turnovers

8 ounces cream cheese, softened
½ cup butter
1½ cups flour
3 tablespoons butter
½ pound fresh mushrooms, chopped

1 large onion, minced
1 teaspoon salt
⅛ teaspoon garlic powder
2 tablespoons flour
¼ cup sour cream
2-3 egg whites, beaten

With mixer on high speed, beat cream cheese, ½ cup butter, and flour. Wrap dough in wax paper and refrigerate at least one hour. In 3 tablespoons butter, sauté the mushrooms and onion. Stir in salt, garlic powder, 2 tablespoons flour, and sour cream. Remove dough from refrigerator. Roll out to ¼ inch thickness on a floured surface. Cut dough into 12 (2 ¾-inch) circles. Place a spoonful of filling in each circle and pinch to seal. Brush with beaten egg whites. Prick top. Bake on an ungreased cookie sheet at 450° for 12-15 minutes.

Yield: 12 appetizers.

Mushroom Roll-Ups

18 slices white bread, crusts removed
1 pound fresh mushrooms, chopped
3 teaspoons onion, finely chopped
1 tablespoon butter
3 ounces cream cheese, softened

⅛ teaspoon salt
⅛ teaspoon pepper
2 tablespoons sherry
1 teaspoon Worcestershire sauce
½ cup butter, melted

Flatten bread by placing between wax paper and rolling with rolling pin. Sauté mushrooms and onions in butter for 4 minutes. Blend in cream cheese. Remove pan from heat and add salt, pepper, sherry, and Worcestershire; mix well. Spread 1 tablespoon mixture on each slice of bread, and roll up as for a jelly roll. Refrigerate or freeze. Just before serving, cut each roll into 3 pieces. Place on a cookie sheet. Dot with melted butter. Broil for 4-5 minutes. Serve immediately.

Yield: Approximately 54 appetizers.

Favorite Asparagus Roll-Ups

18 slices thin-sliced bread
4 ounces Roquefort cheese
8 ounces cream cheese, softened
1 egg

1 tablespoon mayonnaise
1 (14½-ounce) can asparagus
   spears, drained
½ cup butter, melted

Cut crust from bread and roll each piece flat. Combine Roquefort cheese, cream cheese, egg, and mayonnaise. Spread cheese mixture on each slice of bread. Place an asparagus spear on each slice of bread and roll bread up. Cut each rolled slice into 3 pieces. Dip each piece into melted butter and place on an ungreased cookie sheet. Bake at 350° for 15 minutes or until browned.

Yield: 54 Roll-Ups.

Bacon Roll-Ups

6 ounces cream cheese with chives,
   softened
1 tablespoon mayonnaise
25 slices mixed-grain sandwich
   bread

25 slices bacon, cut in half
Parsley for garnish

Combine cream cheese and mayonnaise, stirring until spreading consistency. Remove crust from bread and cut bread in half. Spread one scant teaspoon of cream cheese mixture on each slice of bread and roll tightly. Wrap each roll-up with bacon half and secure with a toothpick. Place roll-ups on a broiler pan. Bake at 350° for 30 minutes, turning if necessary to prevent over browning. Garnish with parsley and serve.

Yield: 4 dozen.

Crab Puffs

1 lime	2 teaspoons Worcestershire sauce
2 (6-ounce) cans crabmeat, drained and flaked	1 cup water
	½ cup butter
1 cup sharp Cheddar cheese, grated	¼ teaspoon salt
6 green onions, chopped	1 cup all purpose flour
2 teaspoons dry mustard	4 eggs

Squeeze ½ lime over crabmeat. Combine crabmeat, Cheddar cheese, onion, dry mustard, Worcestershire sauce, and set aside. Combine water, butter, and salt in a medium saucepan; bring mixture to a boil. Reduce heat to low, add flour and stir vigorously until mixture leaves sides of the pan and forms a smooth ball. Remove pan from heat and allow mixture to cool slightly. Add eggs, one at a time, beating after each addition. Beat until batter is smooth. Add crab mixture, stir well. Drop batter by teaspoonfuls onto a lightly greased baking sheet. Bake at 400° for 15 minutes, reduce heat to 350° and bake an additional 10 minutes. Serve puffs hot.

Yield: 100 puffs.

May be frozen. Remove from freezer an hour before serving and heat 8-10 minutes.

Hot Crab Triangles

1 package English muffins	1 clove garlic, minced
½ cup butter	1 teaspoon Worcestershire sauce
1 jar Old English Cheddar cheese spread	1 (6-ounce) package crabmeat, thawed and drained
1 tablespoon mayonnaise	

Split muffins and slightly brown each side. In saucepan, melt butter and cheese together over low heat. Add mayonnaise, garlic, Worcestershire sauce, and crabmeat. Mix well. Spread mixture on top of each muffin. Cut each muffin into quarters and place on a cookie sheet. Broil until bubbly and slightly brown. Serve immediately. May freeze triangles before broiling. When ready to serve remove from freezer and heat at 375° for 10-15 minutes. Broil until brown and bubbly. Triangles will keep in the freezer for several months.

Yield: 48 triangles.

Quick, easy, and delicious!

Oriental Chicken Puffs

1 (7-ounce) package chicken-
 flavored rice mix
2 eggs, beaten
1½ tablespoons horseradish
1 teaspoon Worcestershire sauce
½ teaspoon dry mustard
¼ teaspoon salt

1 (5½-ounce) can chicken, finely
 chopped
⅔ cup Cheddar cheese, shredded
1 cup Rice Chex, finely crushed
Vegetable oil
Bottled duck sauce

Prepare rice mix as directed. Set aside and cool. Combine eggs, horseradish, Worcestershire sauce, mustard, and salt. Add chicken, cheese, and rice mix; blend thoroughly. Chill 2-3 hours. Shape into 1-inch balls and roll in Rice Chex. Heat vegetable oil to 375° in a skillet. Fry puffs until golden brown. Drain. Serve with warmed duck sauce as a dip.

Yield: 5 dozen.

May be prepared up to 2 days ahead. Reheat on lightly greased pan at 400° for 15 minutes.

Cheese Puffs

1 loaf unsliced bread
3 ounces cream cheese
4 ounces sharp Cheddar cheese

½ cup butter
2 egg whites, stiffly beaten

Trim crust from bread and cut into 1-inch cubes. Melt cheeses and butter in top of double boiler, stirring until well blended. Remove from heat. Fold in egg whites. Dip bread cubes into cheese mixture until well coated. Place on a greased cookie sheet and refrigerate overnight. Bake at 400° for 7 minutes until puffy and golden brown.

Yield: Approximately 10 dozen.

Onion Puffs

16 ounces cream cheese, softened
6 tablespoons mayonnaise
6 shakes Tabasco sauce
6 green onions, chopped

2 loaves white bread
Butter, softened
1 cup Parmesan cheese

Combine cream cheese, mayonnaise, Tabasco sauce, and green onions. Mix well and chill. Cut out bread rounds using a 1½-inch or 2-inch round cutter. Butter one side and broil bread rounds buttered side up. Spread the cream cheese mixture on the other side of bread rounds. Sprinkle with Parmesan cheese. Freeze. When ready to serve broil bread rounds 3-5 minutes.

Yield: Approximately 6 dozen.

Spinach Balls

2 (10-ounce) packages chopped
   frozen spinach
3 cups herb seasoned dressing
1 large onion, finely chopped
¾ cup butter, melted

½ cup Parmesan cheese
6 eggs, beaten
1 tablespoon pepper
½ teaspoon garlic salt
½ teaspoon thyme

Thaw and drain spinach very well. Mix together spinach, dressing, onion, butter, cheese, eggs, pepper, salt, and thyme. Make into small balls. Place on a lightly greased cookie sheet. Bake at 325° for 15-20 minutes.

Yield: 20 servings.

Hanky Pankies

1 pound ground chuck
1 pound hot pork sausage
1 teaspoon red pepper flakes
1 teaspoon oregano

½ teaspoon garlic salt
1 pound Velveeta cheese, cut into
   2-inch cubes
2 packages cocktail rye bread

In a skillet, brown chuck and sausage together. Drain well and return to skillet. Add the pepper, oregano, garlic salt, and cheese, mixing well over low heat. Spread mixture on bread and place on a cookie sheet to freeze. Place frozen Hanky Pankies in plastic bag, and return to freezer. Before serving broil 6 minutes or bake 12 to 15 minutes at 350°.

Yield: 40 servings.

Bacon Wraps

1 pound bacon
1 box Towne House crackers or
   saltine crackers

Cut each slice of bacon into three pieces. Wrap bacon piece around cracker and place on broiler pan. Bake at 325° for 20 minutes or until golden brown. Drain well. These are best when served warm.

Yield: Approximately 50 servings.

Quick and easy!

Strawberry-Orange Punch

6 cups fresh strawberries
1 cup sugar

1 gallon orange juice
1 quart ginger ale

Blend strawberries, sugar, and 1 cup orange juice in blender. (Do this in two batches to avoid overflowing). Add remaining orange juice and chill. When ready to serve, pour into a punch bowl and add ginger ale.

Yield: 1½ gallons.

Make this punch especially attractive with an ice ring made of orange juice and strawberries.

Slushy Punch

1 (3-ounce) box strawberry gelatin
1 cup sugar
3 cups boiling water
3 cups cold water
1 (6-ounce) can lemonade
   concentrate

1 (46-ounce) can pineapple juice
½ ounce almond extract
1 (28-ounce) bottle ginger ale

Dissolve gelatin and sugar in boiling water. Add cold water, lemonade, pineapple juice, and almond flavoring. Freeze. Before serving, defrost until slushy. Add ginger ale and serve.

Yield: 1½ gallons.

The flavor of the gelatin may be varied to change the color of the punch.

Frosted Banana Punch

2 cups sugar
3 cups water
6 bananas, mashed
1 (12-ounce) can frozen orange
   juice concentrate

1 (6-ounce) can frozen limeade
   concentrate
1 (46-ounce) can unsweetened
   pineapple juice
2 (32-ounce) bottles Sprite

Dissolve sugar in water over medium heat. Add bananas, orange juice concentrate, limeade concentrate, and pineapple juice to sugar mixture. Freeze. Two hours before serving, partially thaw the frozen mixture and put in punch bowl. Add Sprite and mix.

Yield: 56 (4-ounce) servings.

Cranberry Punch

2 pounds seedless green grapes
2 quarts cranberry juice cocktail
1 tablespoon grated orange rind
2 cups orange juice

½ cup sugar
5 whole cloves
1 (28-ounce) bottle ginger ale,
   chilled

Freeze bunch of grapes on cookie sheet overnight. Combine cranberry juice, orange rind, orange juice, sugar, and cloves in a Dutch oven. Bring to boil, reduce heat and simmer uncovered for five to ten minutes. Remove cloves and chill. Just before serving, place frozen grapes in the bottom of a large punch bowl. Pour cranberry mixture and ginger ale over grapes.

Yield: 3½ quarts.

Cranberry Frappé

1 quart cranberry juice or
  cranberry juice cocktail (chilled)
1 quart unsweetened pineapple
  juice (chilled)
1½ cups sugar, divided

1-2 teaspoons almond extract
½ gallon strawberry ice cream,
  softened
1 pint whipping cream
1 quart ginger ale (chilled)

Combine cranberry juice, pineapple juice, 1 cup sugar, almond extract, and ice cream; stir well. Beat cream until foamy, add ½ cup sugar, beating until soft peaks form. Fold whipped cream into ice cream mixture. Stir in ginger ale just before serving.

Yield: Approximately 5½ quarts.

Lime Fruit Frappé

1 (6-ounce) can frozen limeade
  concentrate
2 limeade cans filled with ginger ale
1 banana

2 slices of pineapple
Ice cubes
Lime slices for garnish

Combine limeade, ginger ale, banana, and pineapple in a blender. Blend at high speed. Add ice cubes and blend until the drink is the consistency of a frappé. Garnish with fresh lime slices.

Yield: 5 cups.

Lemonade may be substituted for limeade.

Coffee Frappé

1 gallon brewed triple strength
   coffee (3-ounce jar instant coffee)
2 cups sugar

5 gallons vanilla ice cream, softened
1 quart heavy cream (unwhipped)
Cinnamon

Make coffee in advance, add sugar and allow to cool in refrigerator. Combine coffee, ice cream, and heavy cream. Return to refrigerator (not freezer) for 30 minutes. To serve, pour in a large bowl and sprinkle with cinnamon.

Yield: 100-150 servings.

Fruity Iced Tea

4 small tea bags
1 quart boiling water
1 (6-ounce) can lemonade
   concentrate

1 (6-ounce) can orange juice
   concentrate
½ cup sugar

Steep tea bags in boiling water for 5 minutes. Remove tea bags and add lemonade concentrate, orange juice concentrate, and sugar. Pour into a one-gallon container and add enough water to fill container. Stir well before serving.

Yield: 1 gallon.

Tastes best if made the day before serving.

Wassail

6 cups water	6 cups orange juice
½ ounce tea leaves	2 cups grapefruit juice
1 teaspoon whole cloves	1 cup cranberry juice
2 sticks cinnamon	2 cups syrup (made by boiling 1 cup
1¼ gallons cider	water and 1 cup sugar together)

Boil water, pour over tea and let steep for 5-7 minutes. Remove tea leaves. Add cloves and cinnamon. Heat to boiling point and simmer 10 minutes. Remove cinnamon sticks. Mix tea mixture, cider, orange juice, grapefruit juice, cranberry juice, and syrup in a large turkey roaster covering two burners. Bring to boiling point, but do not boil. Allow to cool and store in refrigerator overnight. Refrain from boiling when reheating. Keeps 2-3 weeks in refrigerator.

Yield: 50 servings.

Fluffy Orange Eggnog

6 egg yolks	1 cup orange juice
Salt	2 cups heavy cream, whipped
9 tablespoons sugar	6 egg whites
1 cup heavy cream	Grated orange rind
2 cups milk	Nutmeg

Beat egg yolks with a pinch of salt and 3 tablespoons sugar until lemon colored. Beat in 1 cup cream and 2 cups milk. Slowly stir in orange juice. Fold in 2 cups whipped cream. In a separate bowl beat egg whites, a pinch of salt, and 6 tablespoons sugar until stiff. Fold into eggnog. Top with grated orange rind and nutmeg.

Yield: 12 cups.

Greg's "Nog"

6 eggs, separated
1 cup sugar
1½ cups Grand Marnier or cognac
½ cup light rum

1½ quarts milk
3 cups whipping cream, whipped
Freshly grated nutmeg to taste

Beat egg yolks until thick. Continue beating and gradually add sugar. Add Grand Marnier and rum, and beat until blended. Chill for one hour, stirring at 15-minute intervals. Gradually add milk; fold in whipped cream and beaten egg whites. (Egg whites should be stiff.) Store in a covered container in refrigerator. Stir before serving. Sprinkle with nutmeg. Best if made 24 hours in advance.

Yield: 20 servings.

Even people who usually do not like eggnog think this is wonderful.

Dark Darfuskie

3-4 strawberries
½ cup ice, crushed
1½ ounces dark rum

2 ounces orange juice
1½ ounces cream of coconut
2 strawberries for garnish

Place strawberries, crushed ice, rum, orange juice, and cream of coconut in blender. Blend until smooth. Serve immediately and garnish with extra berries.

Yield: 2 servings.

Peach Fuzz Froth

1 (6-ounce) can frozen pink
  lemonade concentrate
6 ounces vodka
6-8 ice cubes
1 (8-ounce) can sliced peaches

2 ounces reserved juice from
  peaches
1 ounce peach brandy
1 teaspoon sugar

Place lemonade and vodka in blender. Blend slightly. Add ice cubes and blend until smooth. Add drained peaches, peach juice, brandy, and sugar. Blend thoroughly and serve in chilled glasses.

Yield: 4 servings.

Tranquilizers

1 quart vodka
1 (46-ounce) can unsweetened
  pineapple juice
1 (15-ounce) can cream of coconut

3 (6-ounce) cans lemonade
  concentrate
Sprite, chilled

Mix together vodka, pineapple juice, cream of coconut, and lemonade concentrate. Freeze for 24 hours. Stir well and freeze again. To make drink, place 1 ice cream scoop of frozen mixture in a 6-ounce glass and fill with Sprite.

Yield: 30 servings.

Champagne Punch with Fruit

1 bunch grapes
Whole fresh pears
Whole lemons
Whole tangerines
Whole strawberries

4 cups fresh strawberries
½ cup sugar
1 bottle sauterne
1 cup cognac
4 bottles champagne, chilled

Freeze whole fruits for use as ice cubes. Sprinkle 4 cups of strawberries with sugar, add sauterne and cognac. Refrigerate to blend flavors. Just before serving, arrange frozen fruits in punch bowl. Pour in strawberry mixture. Slowly add champagne.

Yield: 36 (½) cup servings.

Mimosa Hawaiian

1 (12-ounce) can apricot nectar
1 (12-ounce) can pineapple juice
1 (6-ounce) can frozen orange juice
concentrate, thawed

¾ cup water
1 (25-ounce) bottle dry champagne,
chilled

Combine apricot nectar, pineapple juice, orange juice concentrate, and water. Stir well. Chill. Immediately before serving stir in chilled champagne.

Yield: 7½ cups.

Danish Wine Cooler

2 oranges, sliced
1 lemon, sliced
¼ cup sugar
¼ cup brandy

Ice
1 (26-ounce) bottle dry white wine,
   chilled
1 (12-ounce) bottle club soda

Place fruit in a tall pitcher and sprinkle with sugar. Press fruit to release flavor. Add brandy and chill for one to two hours. Add ice and wine. Stir to blend. Add club soda before serving.

Yield: 8 to 10 servings.

Sangria

Juice of 2 small limes
Juice of 1 lemon
Juice of 2 small oranges
¼ cup sugar
1 bottle inexpensive dry red wine

1 (28-ounce) bottle club soda,
   chilled
Orange slices for garnish
Lime slices for garnish

Combine lime juice, lemon juice, orange juice, sugar, and wine. Chill. Before serving add club soda, and garnish.

Yield: 12 servings.

Men will love this one because it's not too sweet.

White Sangria

1 cup sugar
1 cup hot water
3 liters white wine
1 quart ginger ale

1 cup apricot or orange brandy
1 (6-ounce) can frozen limeade
Sliced fruit: apples, oranges,
    grapes, lemons, strawberries, etc.

Dissolve sugar in hot water. Combine with wine, ginger ale, brandy, limeade, and sliced fruit. Serve over ice.

Yield: 1 gallon.

Red Wine Sangria

½ cup sugar
1 cup water
1 lemon, thinly sliced
1 lime, thinly sliced

1 orange, thinly sliced
1 bottle red wine
2-4 ounces Cointreau or brandy
12-16 ice cubes

Combine sugar and water and bring to a boil over medium heat, stirring constantly. Remove from heat. Add slices of lemon, lime, and orange. Marinate at least 4 hours. To serve, fill large pitcher with marinated fruit and ½ cup of sugar-water syrup. Pour in wine, Cointreau or brandy, and ice cubes.

Yield: 1 quart.

Peaches add a special flavor to this versatile recipe.

Kahlúa

4 cups water	½ cup boiling water
8 cups sugar	2 vanilla beans (split lengthwise)
4-ounce jar instant or Espresso coffee	1 quart inexpensive vodka

Bring water and sugar to a boil. Stir until sugar dissolves. Cool. Dissolve coffee in ½ cup boiling water and add to sugar syrup. Mix well. Add vodka and vanilla beans. Pour into a 1 gallon container and cap tightly. Store for 30 days before using.

Yield: Approximately 1 gallon.

Irish Creme Liqueur

4 eggs	½ teaspoon almond extract
1 (14-ounce) can sweetened condensed milk	2 tablespoons chocolate syrup
1 cup light cream, or whole milk	2 teaspoons instant coffee
	1 teaspoon vanilla extract

In a blender, combine eggs, condensed milk, cream, almond extract, chocolate syrup, coffee, and vanilla extract. Blend until smooth. Store in refrigerator, tightly covered. Serve with Irish whiskey, rum, or brandy.

Yield: 1 quart.

This special liqueur will keep for 1 month refrigerated.

SOUPS
& SANDWICHES

French Onion Soup

4-5 large cooking onions, sliced
  ¼-inch thick
4 tablespoons butter
¼ cup dry sherry
⅛ teaspoon white pepper
1 bay leaf

3 (10¾-ounce) cans beef consommé
3 (10¾ ounce) cans chicken broth
1 (6-ounce) box croutons
8 tablespoons Parmesan cheese
8 slices Swiss cheese
8 slices Provolone cheese

Sauté onions in butter until translucent. Add sherry, pepper, and bay leaf. Cook 1 minute. Add beef consommé and chicken broth. Bring to a boil; lower heat and simmer 30 minutes. Remove bay leaf. Ladle soup into 8 crocks. Top each with a handful of croutons, 1 tablespoon Parmesan cheese, 1 slice Swiss cheese, and 1 slice Provolone cheese. Place under broiler until cheese is bubbly and slightly browned.

Yield: 8 servings.

Zucchini Soup

1 medium onion, chopped
2 tablespoons butter
1 pound fresh zucchini, sliced not
  peeled

2 (10¾-ounce) cans chicken broth
Salt to taste
Pepper to taste
¼ cup sour cream

Sauté onion in butter in a Dutch oven. Add zucchini and chicken broth. Salt and pepper to taste. Simmer, uncovered, 15-20 minutes. Remove from heat and purée in a blender or food processor. This will require dividing mixture into several loads. Return to Dutch oven and reheat. Stir in sour cream and remove from heat. Serve immediately for a hot soup, or refrigerate and serve cold later.

Yield: 4 servings.

Vichyssoise

3 medium leeks, white part only
1 medium onion, finely chopped
4 medium carrots, grated
2 tablespoons butter
4 medium potatoes, peeled and
   grated

4 cups chicken stock, clarified
1-2 cups heavy cream
¼ teaspoon mace
Salt to taste
Pepper to taste
Watercress or chives, chopped

Sauté leeks, onion, and carrots for 3 minutes in melted butter. Add potatoes and chicken stock; simmer, covered, for 15 minutes, or until tender. Purée in blender until smooth. Allow to cool. Fold in cream, mace, salt, and pepper. Garnish with watercress or chives.

Yield: 6-8 servings.

A delicious choice for a first course.

Gazpacho

1½ cups V-8 juice
1 (10¾-ounce) can tomato soup
1 (10¾-ounce) can water
1 tablespoon red wine vinegar
1 tablespoon Italian dressing
½ cup celery, chopped
¼ cup cucumber, chopped
½ cup zucchini, chopped

½ cup green pepper, chopped
1 cup tomatoes, chopped
½ cup onion, chopped
½ teaspoon Tabasco sauce, or more
Garlic salt to taste
Salt to taste
Pepper to taste

Mix V-8 juice, tomato soup, and water in a large refrigerator container. Add wine vinegar, Italian dressing, celery, cucumbers, zucchini, green pepper, tomatoes, and onion to container. Season with Tabasco, garlic salt, salt, and pepper to taste. Refrigerate several hours. Serve well-chilled.

Yield: 8 servings.

May be served in glasses with a celery stalk as a stirrer.

Cream of Broccoli Soup

4 cups water
2 cups fresh or frozen broccoli, chopped
2 cups cooked ham, chopped
1 medium onion, chopped
1 medium potato, chopped
3 tablespoons butter

1½ teaspoons whole, dried basil
½ teaspoon pepper
1 chicken bouillon cube
½ teaspoon dried thyme leaves
½ teaspoon salt
1 cup milk
Fresh Parmesan cheese, grated

Combine water, broccoli, ham, onion, potato, butter, basil, pepper, bouillon cube, thyme, and salt in a large Dutch oven. Bring to a boil. Reduce heat and simmer 30 minutes or until broccoli is tender, stirring occasionally. Spoon ⅓ of the broccoli mixture into blender container and blend 20 seconds. Continue until all mixture is blended. Pour mixture back into Dutch oven, stir in milk, and simmer 20 minutes. Sprinkle lightly with Parmesan cheese before serving.

Yield: 7 cups.

Broccoli Chowder Supreme

1 pound fresh broccoli
1 quart chicken broth
1 small onion, chopped
2 stalks celery, chopped
4 sprigs parsley, chopped
1 large carrot, diced

1 teaspoon salt
¼ teaspoon cayenne pepper
2 tablespoons cornstarch
2 tablespoons water
1 cup sour cream
1 tablespoon chives

Wash and trim broccoli. Chop florets. Peel and slice stalks. Place in large pot with broth, onion, celery, parsley, carrot, salt, and pepper. Simmer 20 minutes. Mix cornstarch with 2 tablespoons cold water and add to soup. Simmer and stir until thickened. Pureé in blender until smooth. At this point, recipe may be frozen. Soup may be served hot or cold. If serving cold, add sour cream just before serving. If serving hot, heat before adding sour cream. Garnish with chives.

Yield: 6-8 servings.

Crab Broccoli Soup

1 pound fresh broccoli, chopped, or
   2 (10-ounce) packages frozen
   chopped broccoli
4 stalks celery, chopped
1 large onion, chopped
6 tablespoons butter, divided
½ - 1 pound fresh mushrooms,
   sliced

4 tablespoons flour
2 cups light cream
1 pound crabmeat, cooked and
   flaked
Salt to taste
Pepper to taste

Cook broccoli in salted water until tender. Drain and set aside. Sauté celery and onions in 2 tablespoons butter. Add mushrooms and continue cooking until tender. Set aside. Using a Dutch oven, melt 4 tablespoons butter; stir in flour. Slowly pour in cream, stirring constantly. Add celery, onions, mushrooms, and broccoli. Stir in crabmeat and season with salt and pepper. Serve immediately.

Yield: 6-8 servings.

Collard Green Soup

½ cup dried northern beans
2 quarts water
1 small ham bone
1 small ham hock
½ - 1 pound beef short ribs
1 bay leaf
1 teaspoon salt

2 potatoes, peeled and diced
1 bunch fresh collard greens, or 2
   packages frozen, finely chopped
2 tablespoons oil
½ onion, chopped
½ green pepper, chopped
6 small chorizos, chopped

Soak beans overnight. Drain and reserve beans. In a large pot place 2 quarts water, ham bone, ham hock, short ribs, bay leaf, and salt. Bring to boil and remove foam. Lower heat and simmer for 30 minutes. Add beans and simmer on low until tender. Add potatoes and collard greens. In large skillet sauté onion, green pepper, and chorizos in oil until soft. Add to soup and bring to boil. Cook uncovered for 10 minutes; cover pot and simmer until potatoes and greens are done.

Yield: 6-8 servings.

Turnip Green Soup

1½ cups dried navy beans
1 ham hock
4 slices bacon, diced
1½ cups onion, chopped
¾ cup celery with leaves, chopped
¾ cup green pepper, chopped
2 cloves garlic, minced
1 bay leaf

1½ pounds fresh turnip greens, or 2
   (10-ounce) packages frozen
   turnip greens
3 cups potatoes, peeled and diced
1½ cups canned tomatoes, drained
   and chopped
Salt and pepper to taste

Cover beans with water; bring to boil. Remove from heat and let stand, covered, for 1 hour. Remove and dice rind from ham hock. Cook rind and bacon in a 6-quart Dutch oven over low heat until bacon is browned. Remove rind and bacon with slotted spoon; drain on paper towels. Heat fat left in pan until hot but not smoking. Add onion, celery, green pepper, and garlic. Cook, stirring often, until onions turn yellow. Add ham hock; return rind and bacon to pan. Add water almost to cover hock. Add bay leaf. Simmer, covered, for 30 minutes. Add beans and any water they may not have absorbed in soaking. If necessary, add enough water to make the level about ½-inch above beans. Cover; simmer about 45 minutes or until beans soften but aren't completely tender. Add turnip greens and potatoes. If necessary, add more water to cover vegetables. Simmer, covered, 30 minutes or until all vegetables are tender. Remove ham hock, cut off meat, dice, and return to soup. Discard bone and rind. At this point, soup may be cooled, covered, and refrigerated. To serve, add tomatoes, salt, and pepper to taste, and reheat.

Yield: 12 servings.

Beefy Minestrone

1 pound ground beef
2 carrots, cut into strips
1 medium onion, chopped
1 cup celery, chopped
8 cups water
8 beef bouillon cubes
½ teaspoon basil
½ teaspoon oregano

3 ounces vermicelli
1 (10-ounce) package frozen leaf
  spinach, thawed and cut-up
1 (15-ounce) can garbanzo beans
2 tablespoons Parmesan cheese
Salt to taste
Pepper to taste

Cook beef in Dutch oven over medium heat until lightly brown. Add carrots, onion, and celery to ground beef, cooking until vegetables are tender. Discard pan drippings. Dissolve 8 bouillon cubes in 8 cups water and add to Dutch oven. Add basil and oregano. Simmer, uncovered, for 45 minutes. Break up vermicelli and add to soup. Add spinach; bring to a boil and cook until vermicelli is tender. Add undrained garbanzo beans, Parmesan cheese, salt, and pepper. Stir and cook until heated.

Yield: 10 servings.

Italian Vegetable Soup

½ cup olive oil
3 tablespoons butter
1 cup onion, thinly sliced
1 cup carrots, diced
1 cup celery, diced
2 cups potatoes, peeled and diced
1½ cups canned great northern
  beans

2 cups zucchini, diced
1 cup fresh green beans, diced
3 cups cabbage, shredded
6 cups chicken broth
⅔ cup canned Italian style tomatoes
Fresh Parmesan cheese, grated

Melt olive oil and butter in a Dutch oven and sauté onion, carrots, and celery. Add potatoes, canned beans, zucchini, green beans, cabbage, chicken broth, and tomatoes. Cook until vegetables are tender (about 2 hours). Add grated cheese to individual servings.

Yield: 8-10 servings.

Excellent with cracked-wheat crackers.

Italian Sausage Soup

½ pound hot Italian sausage
1 pound mild (sweet) Italian
   sausage
2 onions, chopped
1 green pepper, chopped
4 cups beef broth
1½ cups red wine
1 (8-ounce) can tomato sauce
1 (28-ounce) can tomato pureé

1 teaspoon garlic powder
1 tablespoon oregano
1 tablespoon basil
1 tablespoon parsley
Salt to taste
Pepper to taste
1 (8-ounce) box corkscrew pasta
Parmesan cheese

Remove skin from sausage. Crumble and sauté in a large pot until brown. Drain. Add onions and green pepper; sauté until tender. Add broth and wine; bring to a boil. Add tomato sauce, tomatoes, garlic powder, oregano, basil, parsley, salt, and pepper to taste. Bring to a boil; reduce heat and cook, uncovered, for 1 hour. Pasta may be added the last 15 minutes. If a thinner soup is desired, precook pasta and add just before serving. Serve with grated Parmesan.

Yield: 6-8 servings.

Very thick and hearty!

H-H-Hot Chili

1 tablespoon butter
2 cloves garlic, pressed
1½ pounds ground chuck
2 teaspoons salt
2 (16-ounce) cans kidney beans

1 (10-ounce) can tomatoes and
   green chilies
1 (16-ounce) can tomato juice
2 tablespoons (or less) hot chili
   powder

Melt butter in a large skillet or Dutch oven. Sauté garlic briefly. Add ground chuck and brown. Drain; discard drippings. Add salt, beans, tomatoes and green chilies, and tomato juice. Season with chili powder. Bring to a boil; lower heat, and simmer for 30 minutes or more. Stir occasionally.

Yield: 6-8 servings.

Very hot and spicy!

Black Beans

1 pound black beans
1 medium onion, chopped
½ green pepper, chopped
4 ounces tomato sauce
2 cloves garlic, crushed
2 tablespoons olive oil
1 ham hock
1 chorizo, sliced
1 bay leaf

½ tablespoon salt
2 tablespoons wine vinegar
¼ teaspoon cumin
Generous dashes of oregano,
   rosemary, thyme, Tabasco sauce,
   and black pepper
Hot cooked rice
Additional chopped onion and wine
   vinegar

Wash beans and place in a Dutch oven. Add enough water to cover beans and to reach a 2-inch level above beans. Soak overnight. Using same water, bring beans to a boil. Reduce heat. Add onion, green pepper, tomato sauce, garlic, oil, ham, chorizo, bay leaf, salt, wine vinegar, cumin, oregano, rosemary, thyme, Tabasco, and black pepper. Cook over low heat until beans are tender and soup appears to be thickened. If a thicker soup is preferred, remove about 1 cup of beans and broth to blender and pureé. Add to soup. Serve over white or yellow rice. Top with chopped onion and additional wine vinegar, if desired. Additional salt may be added.

Yield: 6-8 servings.

Navy Bean Soup

1 (12-ounce) bag dried navy beans
1 ham hock, cut into chunks
Dash salt
Dash cayenne pepper
Dash black pepper

1 medium onion, chopped
Dash garlic powder
2 medium potatoes, peeled and
   chopped
2-3 stalks celery, chopped

Soak beans overnight in 6-8 cups water. Combine beans and their remaining liquid, ham hock, salt, peppers, onion, garlic powder, potatoes, and celery. Cook until beans are tender.

Yield: 8 servings.

Very Southern and so easy to prepare.

Southern Corn Chowder

6 ears fresh corn
2 tablespoons butter or bacon fat
½ cup onion, chopped
2 tablespoons flour
1 quart milk
½ cup celery, thinly sliced
2 teaspoons sugar

1½ teaspoons salt
⅛ teaspoon ground white pepper
2 eggs
¼ cup parsley, chopped
3 slices bacon, crisply cooked and
    crumbled
Celery leaves

Remove husks and silks from corn. Cut kernels from corn, making about 3 cups; set aside. Melt butter or fat in large pot. Add onion and sauté for 1 minute. Stir in flour; cook and stir for 1 minute. Blend in milk; cook and stir until mixture comes to a boil and thickens. Stir in celery, sugar, salt, white pepper, and reserved corn. Cover and simmer over low heat for 10 minutes. Lightly beat eggs in bowl. Stir 1 cup hot mixture into eggs; return to chowder. Heat, but do not boil. Stir in parsley. Sprinkle with crumbled bacon and garnish with celery leaves, if desired.

Yield: 6-8 servings.

This chowder needs constant attention, but is worth the effort.

Golden Cheese Chowder

3 cups water
4 potatoes, peeled and chopped
1 cup celery, chopped
1 cup carrots, chopped
½ cup onion, chopped
2 teaspoons salt
¼ teaspoon pepper

½ cup butter
½ cup flour
4 cups milk
1 pound Cheddar cheese, shredded
2 cups cooked ham, cubed
Tabasco sauce to taste

Bring water to a boil in a large pan with a cover. Add potatoes, celery, carrots, onion, salt, and pepper. Cover. Lower heat and simmer 10 minutes. In large skillet, melt butter and blend in flour. Gradually stir in milk. Cook over medium heat, stirring until liquid boils. Boil one minute. Add cheese and stir until melted. Stir cheese mixture into vegetables. Add ham and Tabasco to taste. Stir well, but do not boil.

Yield: 6-8 servings.

Fish Chowder

1 cup potatoes, diced
1 cup carrots, sliced
½ cup celery, diced
½ teaspoon salt
2 tablespoons butter
1 medium onion, finely chopped
1-2 pounds snapper, grouper,
   snook, or other firm-meat fish,
   skinned, boned and cut into
   1-inch pieces

1 teaspoon Worcestershire sauce
1 teaspoon salt
¼ teaspoon pepper
1½ cups milk
1½ cups cream
¼ cup sherry

Place potatoes, carrots, celery, and salt in a large Dutch oven. Add just enough water to cover vegetables. Cook until almost tender. In a large skillet, melt butter and sauté onion until soft. Add fish and Worcestershire sauce; cook for 2 minutes, stirring frequently. Transfer fish to Dutch oven and cook gently 10 minutes. Add salt, pepper, milk, and cream. Heat slowly to boiling. Add sherry and serve.

Yield: 6-8 servings.

This chowder is great with toasted pita bread.

She-Crab Soup

½ cup butter
3 cups milk
1 cup half and half
2 (10¾-ounce) cans cream of celery
   soup
2 hard cooked eggs, chopped
½ teaspoon Worcestershire sauce

¼ teaspoon garlic salt
¼ teaspoon pepper
½ teaspoon Old Bay Seasoning
1 cup fresh or frozen crabmeat
¼ cup sherry
Parsley to garnish

Combine butter, milk, half and half, soup, eggs, Worcestershire, garlic salt, pepper, and Old Bay Seasoning in a large Dutch oven. Bring to a boil, slowly. Add crabmeat and cook over medium-low heat, stirring occasionally, until heated. Add sherry and cook only until hot. Sprinkle with parsley and serve.

Yield: 2 quarts

Easy-To-Do Oyster Stew

6 tablespoons butter	2 teaspoons Worcestershire sauce
½ pint select oysters	2 cups cream, or half and half
½ teaspoon celery salt	Paprika

Using a double boiler, combine 4 tablespoons butter, oysters, celery salt, and Worcestershire sauce. Cook over medium-high heat, stirring constantly. When oysters begin to curl around edges, pour in cream. Continue stirring until heated thoroughly, but not boiling. Remove from heat. Pour into individual bowls and top with ½ tablespoon butter and a dash of paprika.

Yield: 4 servings.

Serve the oyster stew with a loaf of crusty bread and a bottle of wine for a Sunday supper.

Puerto Penasco Fish Chowder

4 tablespoons butter or oil	6 ounces clam juice
2 medium onions, chopped	2 pounds boneless, skinned fish
1 clove garlic, minced	(red snapper, halibut, swordfish,
½ pound fresh mushrooms, sliced	sea bass, turbot, sole, or shrimp)
1 tablespoon lemon juice	1 (6½-ounce) can clams, chopped
2 red or green peppers, seeded and	½ cup parsley, minced
thinly sliced	Salt to taste
2 (10¾-ounce) cans chicken broth	Pepper to taste
2 potatoes, peeled and cubed	Lemon wedges
1 (28-ounce) can tomatoes	White cheese (Gruyère or
½ cup dry white wine	Parmesan)

Melt butter or oil in a Dutch oven. Add onions, garlic, mushrooms, lemon juice, and peppers. Cook on medium-high heat, stirring until vegetables are tender, about 5 minutes. Add broth, potatoes, tomatoes, wine, and clam juice. Bring to a boil; cover and simmer about 15 minutes, or until potatoes are tender. Cut fish into bite-size chunks. Add fish, clams, and parsley to soup. Return to boil; cover and simmer 5 minutes or until fish flakes. Season to taste and serve with lemon wedges and grated cheese.

Yield: 6-8 servings.

English Club Sandwiches

4 English muffins
8 slices turkey breast
8 slices cooked ham

8 slices tomato
8 broccoli spears, cooked

Split muffins and lightly toast. Layer turkey, ham, tomato, and broccoli on toasted muffin halves. Top with hollandaise sauce and serve.

Blender Hollandaise

5 egg yolks
2 tablespoons lemon juice
¼ teaspoon salt

Pinch of pepper
1 cup butter, melted and sizzling

Blend egg yolks, lemon juice, salt, and pepper in blender. With blender on, pour in hot butter. Continue until thoroughly blended.

Yield: 8 open-faced sandwiches.

Crab Tomato Sandwiches

1 egg, slightly beaten
3 ounces cream cheese, softened
1 teaspoon lemon juice
2 tablespoons fresh parsley,
  chopped

2 tablespoons Parmesan cheese
3 tablespoons mayonnaise
½ cup fresh or frozen crabmeat
2 English muffins, split
4 slices tomatoes

Combine egg, cream cheese, lemon juice, parsley, Parmesan, and mayonnaise. Stir in crabmeat and set aside. Lightly toast muffins. Top with tomato slice and spread with crab mixture. Broil until sandwich is bubbly. (Crab mixture may be made ahead and refrigerated).

Yield: 4 open-faced sandwiches.

Gyro Sandwiches

½ cup plain yogurt
½ cup sour cream
½ cup cucumber, shredded
¾ pound veal, ground
1 pound lamb, ground
1 teaspoon teriyaki sauce

1 egg
½ teaspoon basil
Salt and pepper to taste
4 pita bread pockets
Tomatoes, lettuce, and onions,
    chopped

To make sauce, combine yogurt, sour cream, and cucumber; refrigerate. For filling, mix veal, lamb, teriyaki sauce, egg, basil, salt, and pepper. Place meat mixture between two large pieces of waxed paper and flatten with rolling pin, about ⅛-inch thick. Once flattened, slice into strips 6-8 inches long by 2-inches wide. Place on baking sheet and cook for 10 minutes, or until brown, in a 375° preheated oven. To prepare pita, place bread in a heavy skillet coated with vegetable spray. Brown both sides over medium-high heat. To serve, cut opening in pita pocket. Into each pocket place several strips of meat, tomatoes, lettuce, and onions. Top with sauce.

Yield: 4 pita sandwiches.

Ham and Cheese Delights

1 package Pepperidge Farm party
    rolls
½ small onion, grated
½ cup butter
2 teaspoons poppy seeds

2 teaspoons Dijon mustard
½ pound boiled ham, sliced
½ pound Swiss cheese, grated or
    sliced

Keeping rolls in one group, remove from tray. Slice horizontally through entire group making a top and bottom section. (Electric knife makes slicing easier.) Sauté onion in butter. Add poppy seeds and mustard. Spread top and bottom sections of rolls with butter mixture. Add ham and cheese to bottom half of rolls. Replace tops and put entire group back in foil tray. Slice along joint lines to make individual rolls. May be frozen at this point. (Slicing is easier if rolls are partially frozen.) Wrap in foil before baking. Bake at 400° for 15 minutes, or at 350° for 20 minutes, if frozen.

Yield: 20 bite-size rolls.

Easy Burritos

1½ pounds ground chuck
1 small onion, chopped
1 (16-ounce) can refried beans
1-2 tablespoons water
1 (1¼-ounce) package taco
    seasoning mix

8 large flour tortillas
1 large tomato, chopped
1 cup sour cream
1 cup picante salsa

Brown beef and onion in large skillet. Drain well. Add refried beans, water, and seasoning mix. Cover and simmer 15-20 minutes, stirring occasionally. When ready to serve, spoon meat mixture down center of tortilla, which has been heated according to package directions. Sprinkle tomato on top of meat and top with 3-4 teaspoons sour cream. Spoon 2-3 teaspoons of salsa over top. Roll up sides of tortilla and serve.

Yield: 8 burritos.

Tortillas can be heated in microwave oven, 15 seconds for 1, or 45 seconds for 4. Meat filling may be made ahead and reheated in microwave.

Curried Cheese Halves

1½ cups sharp cheese, grated
½ cup mayonnaise
1 (4½-ounce) can chopped ripe
    olives

3 spring onions, chopped
½ - 1 teaspoon curry powder
4 tablespoons butter
4 English muffins, lightly toasted

Mix cheese, mayonnaise, olives, onions, and curry powder together. Lightly butter toasted English muffin halves. Spread with cheese mixture and broil until cheese melts.

Yield: 8 open-faced sandwiches

Shrimply Delicious Croissandwiches

1 (10-ounce) package frozen
  spinach
1 (4¼-ounce) can shrimp
¼ cup onion, minced
⅓ cup mayonnaise
1-2 tablespoons Dijon mustard

¼ - ⅓ cup macadamia nuts, chopped
¼ teaspoon celery salt
¼ teaspoon Cavender's seasoning
½ teaspoon fresh dill, chopped
3 croissants
3 slices Swiss cheese

Cook spinach according to package directions; drain well. Combine shrimp, onion, mayonnaise, mustard, nuts, celery salt, Cavender's seasoning, and dill. Mix well to make shrimp salad filling. Slice croissants in half lengthwise. Spread bottom half of each with spinach. Top spinach with shrimp salad. Place a slice of cheese on top of shrimp mixture. Replace the tops of croissants. Bake at 350° for 5-10 minutes or until cheese melts completely and croissants are lightly browned. (If using frozen croissants, bake completed sandwich according to package directions).

Yield: 3 croissants.

This is wonderful for ladies' luncheons!

SALADS
& DRESSINGS

Molded Peaches and Cream

1 (3-ounce) package peach gelatin
1 cup boiling water
¾ cup cold water
3 cups fresh peaches, peeled and
   sliced
1 banana, sliced
1 envelope unflavored gelatin
3 tablespoons cold water
½ cup half and half, scalded
½ pint whipping cream
8 ounces cream cheese, whipped
½ cup plus two tablespoons sugar
1 cup peaches, pureéd

Dissolve peach gelatin in boiling water. Add cold water and chill until slightly thickened. Stir in 3 cups sliced peaches and banana. Pour into a lightly oiled 8-cup mold and chill until firm. Soften unflavored gelatin in 3 tablespoons cold water. Blend in scalded half and half. Set aside. Whip cream and add cream cheese, sugar, and pureéd peaches. Add cream cheese mixture to the gelatin. Spread over congealed peach gelatin layer in mold and chill until firm. Just before serving, unmold.

Yield: 10-12 servings.

Select greenery and tiny fresh flowers from your garden to decorate your serving plate.

Party Apricot Salad

2 (17-ounce) cans apricots,
   undrained
8 ounces of cream cheese, softened
2 tablespoons lemon juice
3 (3-ounce) packages lemon gelatin
2½ cups boiling water
1 cup mayonnaise
Pinch of salt
Dash of Tabasco sauce

Combine apricots, cream cheese, and lemon juice in blender or food processor. Blend until smooth. Dissolve gelatin in boiling water and combine with apricot mixture in a large bowl. Pour into a 9 x 13-inch dish. Chill until firm. Mix mayonnaise with salt and Tabasco. Cut congealed salad into squares and top each with a dollop of mayonnaise mixture.

Yield: 10-12 servings.

Chopped nuts may be added to the gelatin mixture for a crunchy texture. For a unique tropical variation, substitute 2 (17-ounce) cans mangoes for apricots.

Holiday Eggnog Ring

1 (3-ounce) package lemon gelatin
1 cup boiling water
¼ cup cold water
¼ teaspoon rum extract
¾ cup eggnog
1 (11-ounce) can mandarin oranges

1 (8-ounce) can pears, diced
1 (3-ounce) package cherry gelatin
1 cup boiling water
Candied green and red cherries
    (optional)
Pecan halves (optional)

Dissolve lemon gelatin in boiling water. Add cold water and rum extract. Measure out ¾ cup gelatin mixture and add eggnog. Mix well. Pour into a lightly oiled 6-cup ring mold. Chill until partially set. Drain oranges and pears, reserving ¾ cup juice. Dissolve cherry gelatin in boiling water. Stir in ¾ cup juice from fruit and remaining lemon gelatin. Chill until slightly thickened. Add pears and spoon mixture over eggnog gelatin in mold. Arrange oranges in gelatin, pressing gently. Refrigerate until firm. Just before serving, unmold and garnish with cherries and pecans.

Yield: 10 servings.

Frosted Raspberry Noel

1 (6-ounce) package raspberry
    gelatin
2 cups boiling water
1 (12-ounce) package frozen
    raspberries
2½ cups applesauce
⅓ cup sugar

¼ cup pineapple juice
1 egg, slightly beaten
4 ounces cream cheese, softened
6 ounces frozen whipped topping,
    thawed
Lettuce leaves

Dissolve gelatin in boiling water. Stir in raspberries until thawed. Carefully add applesauce. Pour into an 8 x 8-inch dish and chill until firm. Combine sugar, pineapple juice and egg in a saucepan and cook over medium heat until thickened. Remove from heat. Beat cream cheese until smooth and blend into cooked mixture. Fold in whipped topping. Spread on top of congealed salad. Chill until ready to serve. Cut into squares and serve on leaves of crisp lettuce.

Yield: 6-8 servings.

Garnish with slivers of candied orange peel or nuts — or omit the topping for an equally delightful but less sweet version.

Blueberry Cream Cheese Salad

1 (6-ounce) package grape or
blackberry gelatin
2 cups boiling water
1 (8-ounce) can crushed pineapple,
undrained
1 (21-ounce) can blueberry pie
filling

8 ounces cream cheese, softened
½ cup sugar
8 ounces sour cream
1 teaspoon vanilla extract
Lettuce leaves

Dissolve gelatin in boiling water. Combine with pineapple and pie filling, blending thoroughly. Pour into a 9 x 13-inch dish and refrigerate until firm. Beat cream cheese and sugar. Add sour cream and vanilla extract, stirring until smooth. Spread on top of congealed salad. Chill until ready to serve. Cut into squares and serve on leaves of crisp lettuce.

Yield: 12 servings.

Fresh summer blackberries are an elegant final touch. This rich salad also doubles as a sumptuous dessert.

Sunny Orange Fluff

1 (15¼-ounce) can crushed
pineapple, undrained
1 (6-ounce) package orange gelatin
2 cups buttermilk
1 cup pecans, chopped

1 cup coconut (optional)
1 (12-ounce) container frozen
whipped topping, thawed
Fresh mint and orange slices for
garnish

In a saucepan bring undrained pineapple to a boil. Remove from heat and blend in dry gelatin until dissolved. Stir in buttermilk, pecans, and coconut. Cool thoroughly and fold in whipped topping. Pour into a 9 x 13-inch dish and chill until firm. Garnish with fresh mint and orange slices.

Yield: 12 servings.

Strawberry gelatin is a delicious alternative in the summer when strawberries for garnishing are plentiful.

Strawberry Pecan Congealed Salad

1 (6-ounce) package strawberry
  gelatin
1 cup boiling water
2 (10-ounce) packages frozen
  strawberries

1 (20-ounce) can crushed
  pineapple, drained
1 pint sour cream
3 medium bananas
1 cup pecans, chopped

Dissolve gelatin in boiling water. Add strawberries and stir until thawed. Add pineapple. Pour half of the gelatin mixture in a 9 x 13-inch dish and chill until firm. Spread with half of the sour cream and slice bananas on top. Spread with remaining sour cream and sprinkle with pecans. Pour remaining gelatin mixture on top and refrigerate until firm.

Yield: 12 servings.

Melon Mélange

2 medium melons (cantaloupe or
  honeydew)
1⅔ cups seedless grapes, halved
1⅔ cups berries (sliced
  strawberries, blueberries,
  blackberries, or raspberries)
1⅔ cups fresh pineapple chunks

½ cup cherry, cranberry, or orange-
  flavored brandy
8 ounces sour cream
¼ cup light brown sugar, firmly
  packed
3 coconut macaroons, crumbled
  (optional)

Cut melons in half and remove seeds. Scallop edges and chill. Combine grapes, berries, and pineapple. Pour brandy over fruit and marinate in refrigerator 2 hours. Blend sour cream with brown sugar. Just before serving, pour half of the sauce over the fruit and mix thoroughly. Fill melon halves with fruit. Top with remaining sauce and garnish with crumbled macaroons.

Yield: 4 servings.

Fresh Fruit With Almond Whipped Cream

1 fresh pineapple, cut into bite-size
    chunks
1-2 pints strawberries, capped and
    halved
2 red apples, unpeeled and cut into
    bite-size pieces

2 oranges, sectioned
2 grapefruit, sectioned
1 cup seedless grapes, halved
2 kiwis, peeled and sliced
2 bananas
Fruit Fresh

Prepare fruit, except bananas. Sprinkle pineapple chunks and apple pieces with Fruit Fresh to prevent browning. Combine all fruit except bananas in a large bowl and refrigerate. Just before serving, add bananas to fruit mixture. Spoon almond whipped cream over each serving and sprinkle with pecans and/or coconut.

Almond Whipped Cream

2 tablespoons lemon juice
½ cup sugar
2 tablespoons butter or margarine
1 teaspoon almond extract

2 eggs, beaten
½ pint whipping cream
¾ cup pecans, finely chopped
¾ cup flaked coconut (optional)

Mix lemon juice, sugar, butter, almond extract, and beaten eggs in a saucepan. Cook over medium heat until thickened. Allow to cool. Whip cream and fold into cooled mixture. Chill.

Yield: 10-12 servings.

Peaches, melons, berries — any fresh fruit can be used in this seasonal specialty.

Florida Sunrise Breakfast Salad

4 red apples, unpeeled and diced
Fruit Fresh
3 grapefruit, sectioned
3 oranges, sectioned

1¾ cups pitted dates, each date cut
  into quarters
1 cup walnuts, coarsely chopped

Sprinkle diced apples with Fruit Fresh if salad will not be served immediately. Combine apples, grapefruit, oranges, and dates. Spoon strawberry topping onto each serving and sprinkle with chopped nuts.

Strawberry Topping

¾ cup whipping cream
½ cup yogurt

2 tablespoons powdered sugar
¾ cup strawberries, mashed

Whip cream and fold in yogurt, sugar, and strawberries.

Yield: 8 servings.

Prepare all but the apples the night before. Topping will keep one week in refrigerator. The strawberry topping is lovely to have on hand — matchless on any fresh fruit medley.

Tipsy Tropical Fruit

1 cup watermelon balls
1 cup cantaloupe balls
1 cup honeydew balls
1 cup fresh pineapple chunks

1 cup fresh strawberries
½ cup sugar
½ cup dry sherry

Combine fruit, sugar, and sherry. Refrigerate at least 2 hours.

Yield: 10 servings.

Present this warm weather treat in a hollowed watermelon basket or pineapple boat.

Tangy Cranberry Relish

1 pound cranberries	1 (3-ounce) package lemon gelatin
½ cup water	½ cup celery, chopped
2 cups sugar	½ cup pecans, chopped

Combine cranberries and water in a saucepan and bring to a rolling boil. When all cranberries have popped, blend in sugar and remove from heat. Stir in dry gelatin and allow to cool 15 minutes. Add celery and pecans. Store in refrigerator up to 6 weeks.

Yield: 1 quart; 12 servings.

A thoughtful Christmas gift to share with a special friend.

Valencia Ambrosia Cups

6 oranges (Valencias or Navels)	1 cup strawberries, capped and
2 tablespoons grated orange rind	sliced
½ cup whipping cream	½ cup coconut
2 tablespoons lemon juice	Nutmeg
3 tablespoons sugar	6 whole strawberries
½ pound seedless red grapes, halved	

Cut a ½-inch slice from tops of oranges. Remove and reserve pulp, discarding seeds and membranes. Refrigerate orange shells. Add grated orange rind to whipping cream and chill. Whip cream until soft peaks form. Stir in lemon juice and sugar. Fold in orange pulp, grapes, sliced strawberries, and coconut. Spoon into orange cups. Garnish each with nutmeg and a strawberry.

Yield: 6 cups

Green French Onion Salad

Dressing

1 (0.7 ounce) package Italian
   dressing mix

1 (8-ounce) carton sour cream
1 (8-ounce) bottle Italian dressing

Blend dry Italian dressing mix into sour cream. Add bottle of dressing and stir well.

Salad

1 head iceberg lettuce
1 head romaine
5 scallions, chopped

1 (2.8-ounce) can French fried
   onions, coarsely crumbled

In a large salad bowl combine iceberg lettuce and romaine, torn into bite-size pieces. Add scallions and toss. Just before serving, pour dressing over salad and toss. Add crumbled French fried onions and toss again.

Yield: 8 servings.

The creamy Italian dressing is extraordinary on any crisp green salad.

Dutch Lettuce

6 strips bacon, cooked and
   crumbled
2 tablespoons bacon drippings
½ cup vinegar
¼ cup water
1½ teaspoons salt

⅛ teaspoon pepper
¼ cup sugar
1 large head lettuce, torn into bite-
   size pieces, at room temperature
1 medium onion, sliced

Combine bacon drippings, vinegar, water, salt, pepper, and sugar. Bring to a boil and pour over combined lettuce and onion. Sprinkle with crumbled bacon and serve immediately.

Yield: 4-6 servings.

Mandarin Spinach Salad

10 ounces spinach, stems removed,
   torn into bite-size pieces
¼ small red onion, thinly sliced
Salt to taste
1 cup sour cream
1 (0.7-ounce) package garlic-cheese
   dressing mix

2-4 teaspoons lemon juice
1 (11-ounce) can mandarin oranges,
   drained
6 slices bacon, cooked and
   crumbled

Combine spinach, onion, and salt. Thoroughly blend sour cream, dressing mix, and lemon juice. Just before serving, toss salad with dressing. Add mandarin oranges and toss again. Sprinkle with crumbled bacon.

Yield: 6 servings.

Strawberry and Spinach Salad

10 ounces spinach, stems removed,
   torn into bite-size pieces
1 pint strawberries, halved
2 tablespoons sugar
1 large lemon, juiced

1 egg yolk, slightly beaten
Pinch of salt
Ground pepper to taste
6 tablespoons vegetable oil

Combine spinach and strawberries. Mix sugar, lemon juice, egg yolk, salt, and pepper. Add vegetable oil, one tablespoon at a time, blending until creamy. Just before serving, toss salad with dressing.

Yield: 4-6 servings.

Red Delicious Spinach Salad

1 pound spinach, stems removed,
   torn into bite-size pieces
2 hard cooked eggs, sliced
1 red apple, unpeeled and diced

1 medium onion, thinly sliced
4 ounces bleu cheese, crumbled
1 cup mayonnaise
1 cup sour cream

Combine spinach, eggs, apple, onion, and bleu cheese. Blend mayonnaise with sour cream. Just before serving, pour dressing over salad and toss.

Yield: 6-8 servings.

LYCC Famous Caesar Salad

2 cloves garlic, crushed
1 teaspoon anchovy paste
1 cup mayonnaise
2 tablespoons cream cheese,
   softened
1 teaspoon Worcestershire sauce

6 cups romaine, torn into bite-size
   pieces
2-3 tablespoons Parmesan cheese,
   freshly grated
1-2 tablespoons bread crumbs

Mix garlic and anchovy paste. Add mayonnaise, cream cheese, and Worcestershire sauce. Toss with romaine, coating well. Add cheese and bread crumbs. Mix thoroughly and serve on chilled salad plates.

Yield: 4-6 servings.

The Lakeland Yacht and Country Club generously shares its renowned Caesar salad recipe with you. It is certain to bring praise to your kitchen, as it has to theirs.

Classic Caesar Salad

1 large head romaine	1½ teaspoons Worcestershire sauce
1 clove garlic, halved	6 anchovy fillets, drained
½ cup vegetable oil	¼ cup bleu cheese, crumbled
1 cup cubed French bread	1 egg
¼ teaspoon dry mustard	⅓ cup Parmesan cheese, grated
½ teaspoon black pepper, freshly ground	2 tablespoons lemon juice

Trim core from romaine, separate leaves, and rinse under cold running water. Dry thoroughly, place in plastic bag, and refrigerate several hours or overnight. Several hours before serving, halve garlic. Reserve one half. Crush the remaining half and combine with oil in a jar with a tight-fitting lid. Refrigerate at least one hour. Heat 2 tablespoons oil-garlic mixture in a skillet. Add bread cubes and sauté until browned. To remaining oil-garlic mixture, add mustard, pepper, Worcestershire sauce, anchovies, and bleu cheese. Blend 30 seconds in food processor and refrigerate. Bring 2-inch depth of water to a boil in a small saucepan. Turn off heat, lower egg into water, let stand one minute. Remove egg from water and refrigerate. Just before serving, rub inside of a large wooden salad bowl with reserved ½ clove garlic. Discard garlic. Remove coarse ribs from romaine and tear into bite-size pieces in salad bowl. Shake dressing well and pour over romaine. Sprinkle with Parmesan cheese and toss until romaine is thoroughly coated. Break egg over center of salad. Pour lemon juice directly over egg and toss again. (Egg may be mixed with lemon juice and then added to salad for a smoother blend of egg and lemon juice.) Sprinkle bread cubes over salad, toss, and serve immediately.

Yield: 6 servings.

All preparations except the final combining of ingredients in the salad bowl may be done a day in advance.

Tomatoes and Hearts of Palm Vinaigrette

6 large tomatoes, sliced
1 (14-ounce) can hearts of palm,
    drained and cut in ½-inch pieces
¼ cup fresh parsley, chopped
1 clove garlic, crushed
¼ cup plus 2 tablespoons olive oil
2 tablespoons red wine vinegar
1½ teaspoons fresh basil, minced
    (or ½ teaspoon dried basil,
    crushed)

1 teaspoon sugar
1 teaspoon salt
⅛ teaspoon pepper
2 teaspoons prepared mustard
Lettuce leaves

Arrange tomatoes and hearts of palm in a serving bowl. Sprinkle with parsley. Combine garlic, oil, vinegar, basil, sugar, salt, pepper, and mustard in a tightly covered jar and shake vigorously. Pour over tomatoes and hearts of palm. Chill at least 3 hours. Serve on a bed of crisp lettuce leaves.

Yield: 8 servings.

White asparagus and artichokes combine beautifully with the colors and textures of this attractive salad.

Marinated Mushroom Medley

1 pound fresh mushrooms
1 (6-ounce) can pitted ripe olives,
    drained
1 (14-ounce) can hearts of palm,
    drained and cut into ½-inch
    pieces

1 medium red onion, thinly sliced
8 ounces Caesar salad dressing
1 medium head of lettuce, torn into
    bite-size pieces
1 cup walnuts, chopped

Marinate mushrooms, olives, hearts of palm and onion in salad dressing 5-6 hours. Just before serving, toss with lettuce and chopped walnuts.

Yield: 6-8 servings.

Family Reunion Potato Salad

Dressing

3 cups mayonnaise
1-2 teaspoons dry mustard
2 tablespoons onion juice
2 tablespoons lemon juice

1 tablespoon sugar
Garlic salt to taste
Pepper to taste

Combine mayonnaise, mustard, onion juice, lemon juice, sugar, garlic salt, and pepper. Blend until smooth.

Salad

1 (5-pound) bag potatoes, peeled
6 hard cooked eggs, chopped

2 cups celery, chopped
¾ cup sweet pickle relish

Cut potatoes into bite-size pieces and boil in salted water until tender. Drain and cool. In a large bowl combine potatoes, eggs, celery, and pickle relish. Gently toss with dressing and chill until ready to serve.

Yield: 16 servings.

Crunchy Picnic Slaw

6 cups (1 head) cabbage, finely
   shredded
2 cups apples, unpeeled and diced
2 cups cucumber, peeled and diced
½ cup raisins
1½ cups carrot, grated
1 cup mayonnaise

1½ tablespoons lemon juice
1 tablespoon vinegar
1 teaspoon salt
¼ teaspoon sugar
½ cup honey roasted peanuts,
   coarsely chopped

In a large bowl combine cabbage, apples, cucumber, raisins, and carrot. Blend mayonnaise, lemon juice, vinegar, salt, and sugar. Pour mayonnaise dressing over cabbage mixture and toss to coat well. Refrigerate. Just before serving, sprinkle with chopped peanuts.

Yield: 12 servings.

Antipasto Toss

1 (15-ounce) can garbanzo beans, drained
1 (6-ounce) jar marinated artichoke hearts
½ cup Italian or other herb-garlic dressing
½ cup pitted ripe olives, halved
2 heads romaine, torn into bite-size pieces
1 head leaf lettuce, torn into bite-size pieces
1 cup pepperoni, sliced
1 cup Monterey Jack cheese, cubed
Freshly ground pepper

Combine beans, artichoke hearts with liquid, dressing, and olives. Cover and refrigerate. Just before serving, toss with romaine, lettuce, pepperoni, cheese, and pepper.

Yield: 8 servings.

Crispy Vegetable Salad

1 pound fresh broccoli, cut into bite-size pieces
1 small head cauliflower, cut into bite-size pieces
2-3 large carrots, sliced
2 small zucchini, sliced
2 small onions, sliced and separated into rings
⅔ cup mayonnaise
⅓ cup oil
⅓ cup apple cider vinegar
¼ cup sugar
1 tablespoon salt

Combine well-drained vegetables in a large bowl. Blend mayonnaise, oil, vinegar, sugar, and salt. Toss with vegetables, coating well. Chill several hours. Just before serving, toss again. Drain excess liquid or serve with slotted spoon.

Yield: 8-10 servings.

Strata Salad Superb

1 head lettuce, torn into bite-size
   pieces
½ cup scallions, chopped
½ cup celery, chopped
½ cup carrots, grated
1 (8-ounce) can sliced water
   chestnuts, drained
1 cup fresh mushrooms, sliced

1 (10-ounce) package frozen peas,
   thawed
1½ cups mayonnaise
½ cup Parmesan cheese
6 hard cooked eggs, chopped
5 tomatoes, cut in wedges
½ pound bacon, cooked and
   crumbled

In a large clear glass bowl layer lettuce, scallions, celery, carrots, water chestnuts, mushrooms, and peas. Spread with mayonnaise, covering completely. Sprinkle with Parmesan cheese. Cover and refrigerate several hours or overnight. Prior to serving, garnish with eggs, tomatoes, and bacon.

Yield: 15 servings.

Fresh Garden Galore

2 cups fresh broccoli, very finely
   chopped
1½ cups cauliflower, very finely
   chopped
1 cup carrots, finely shredded
1½ cups zucchini, finely diced
1 cup yellow squash, finely chopped
½ cup red seedless grapes,
   quartered; or ½ cup fresh
   pineapple, diced

1¼ teaspoons onion salt
¼ teaspoon white pepper
1¼ cups mayonnaise
2½ teaspoons rice vinegar
Red leaf lettuce
¼ cup red seedless grapes, whole

Combine broccoli, cauliflower, carrots, zucchini, squash, and grapes. Sprinkle with onion salt and white pepper. Blend in mayonnaise and rice vinegar. Line salad bowl with lettuce leaves, add salad, and garnish with whole red grapes.

Yield: 8 servings.

The secret here is to chop the vegetables as finely as possible. The texture should be slaw-like.

Minestrone Salad

1 cup cooked elbow macaroni
1 cup cooked rice
1 cup cooked green beans, cut into
   1-inch pieces
2 cups cabbage, shredded
2 medium carrots, thinly sliced
2 stalks celery, chopped
1 medium zucchini, diced
1½ cups canned garbanzo beans,
   drained
1 cup cherry tomatoes

2 scallions, cut into ¼-inch pieces
¾ cup olive oil
¼ cup red wine vinegar
1 clove garlic, minced
¼ cup fresh basil leaves, chopped
Freshly ground pepper
Salt to taste
Salad greens
¼ cup Parmesan cheese, freshly
   grated

Combine macaroni, rice, green beans, cabbage, carrots, celery, zucchini, beans, tomatoes, and scallions. Combine olive oil, vinegar, garlic, basil, and pepper. Mix well. Pour over salad. Refrigerate several hours or overnight. Just before serving, add salt and toss. Serve on salad greens and sprinkle with Parmesan cheese.

Yield: 8 servings.

Add tofu for a hearty vegetarian entreé. For even more lively color and crunch, add some red and green peppers.

Patio Peas and Cashews

1 (10-ounce) box frozen peas,
   thawed
6-8 scallions, sliced

4 ounces cashews
⅓ - ½ cup sour cream
Bibb lettuce leaves

Mix peas, scallions, cashews, and sour cream, coating thoroughly. Serve on bibb lettuce leaves in an attractive bowl or on individual salad plates.

Yield: 6 servings.

Add the cashews just before serving, if you mix and chill salad early in the day.

Commodore's Cauliflower Salad

1 large head lettuce, torn into bite-size pieces
1 head cauliflower, cut into bite-size pieces
3 scallions, chopped

2 cups mayonnaise
¼ cup sugar
⅓ cup Parmesan cheese, grated
1 pound bacon, cooked and crumbled

Layer lettuce, cauliflower, scallions, mayonnaise, sugar and Parmesan cheese in a covered 3-quart clear glass dish. Refrigerate several hours or overnight. Toss before serving and sprinkle with crumbled bacon.

Yield: 12 servings.

Broccoli is an equally tasty substitute for the cauliflower.

Creamy Broccoli Salad

6 ounces cream cheese, softened
1 egg
2 tablespoons vinegar
2 tablespoons sugar
2 tablespoons vegetable oil
1 teaspoon prepared mustard
¼ teaspoon garlic salt

6 cups fresh raw broccoli, chopped
¼ cup onion, finely chopped
⅓ cup golden raisins
Lettuce leaves
6 strips bacon, cooked and crumbled

Combine cream cheese, egg, vinegar, sugar, oil, mustard, and garlic salt in blender and process two minutes or until smooth. Toss broccoli with onion and raisins. Mix with cream cheese dressing, coating thoroughly, and chill at least 3 hours. Line one large or 6 individual salad bowls with lettuce leaves and add salad. Just before serving, sprinkle with crumbled bacon.

Yield: 6 servings.

Cucumbers German Style

2 medium cucumbers, peeled and
   sliced
1 medium onion, sliced thinly
¼ teaspoon salt

⅓ cup sugar
½ cup tarragon vinegar
½-¾ cup sour cream

Combine cucumbers and onions. Sprinkle with salt and sugar. Stir in vinegar and chill 1-2 hours. Drain well and blend in sour cream. Refrigerate. Serve as a salad or relish.

Yield: 4-6 servings.

Add an experimental dash of fresh dill or your favorite windowsill herb as a special accent.

Sensational Sauerkraut Salad

2½ cups sauerkraut, drained
½ cup vinegar
½ cup vegetable oil
1 cup celery, chopped

1 cup green pepper, chopped
1 onion, chopped
⅔ cup sugar
Caraway seeds (optional)

Combine sauerkraut, vinegar, oil, celery, green pepper, onion, and sugar. Refrigerate 24 hours. Just before serving, sprinkle with caraway seeds.

Yield: 6 servings.

Accentuate the tart crunchiness with a finely chopped crisp red apple.

Midsummer Salad Niçoise

Dressing

1 cup olive oil or vegetable oil
1 cup red wine vinegar
2 cloves garlic, crushed
1 tablespoon prepared mustard

1 tablespoon parsley, chopped
1 teaspoon onion, minced
1 teaspoon salt
Freshly ground pepper

Combine oil, vinegar, garlic, mustard, parsley, onion, salt, and pepper. Mix until blended well.

Salad

5 medium potatoes, boiled and
   sliced
1 pound green beans, cooked
1 large head romaine
1 red onion, sliced into rings
1 green pepper, sliced into rings
4 hard cooked eggs, sliced
8 pitted ripe olives, sliced

2 large tomatoes, cut into wedges
2 (9¼-ounce) cans tuna, drained
   and broken into chunks
1 (2-ounce) can anchovy fillets,
   drained
2-3 tablespoons capers (optional)
¼ cup parsley

Dribble ¾ cup dressing over potato slices and ¼ cup over green beans. Let stand 30 minutes or more. Line a large salad bowl with romaine leaves. Break remaining romaine into bite-size pieces and place in bottom of bowl. Layer potatoes, beans, onion rings, and green pepper slices over romaine. Arrange eggs and olives around edge of bowl. Place tomato wedges in a petal pattern in center. Mound tuna on top. Roll anchovies and place on top of egg slices. Garnish with capers and parsley. Pass remaining dressing.

Yield: 8 servings.

Shrimp and Artichoke Salad

1 (8-ounce) package chicken
  flavored Rice-a-Roni
1 pound shrimp, cooked, shelled
  and deveined
4 scallions, chopped
½ green pepper, chopped
12 pimiento-stuffed olives, sliced

2 (6-ounce) jars marinated
  artichoke hearts, sliced,
  liquid reserved
¾ teaspoon curry powder
½ cup mayonnaise
Lettuce leaves

Prepare Rice-a-Roni according to package directions and cool. Add shrimp, scallions, green pepper, olives, and artichoke hearts. Combine reserved artichoke liquid, curry powder and mayonnaise. Blend into rice mixture and refrigerate. Serve on crisp lettuce leaves.

Yield: 8 servings.

Try substituting chicken for shrimp, or add one cup finely chopped raw cauliflower and two chopped hard-cooked eggs for an even more substantial fare.

Salmon Seashell Salad

Dressing

¾ cup vegetable oil
½ cup lemon juice
3 tablespoons white vinegar

1½ teaspoons dill, crumbled
1½ teaspoons celery seed
¾ teaspoons salt

Combine oil, lemon juice, vinegar, dill, celery seed, and salt. Blend well.

Salad

1 (15½-ounce) can pink salmon
4 cups large shell macaroni, cooked
1 cup celery, sliced
1 cup cooked green peas

¾ cup carrots, diced
½ cup parsley, chopped
¼ cup scallions, chopped
Crisp lettuce leaves

Drain salmon and chill. Combine macaroni, celery, peas, carrots, parsley, and scallions. Pour dressing over macaroni mixture and toss well. Refrigerate. Before serving, break salmon into chunks and fold into macaroni mixture. Spoon into a salad bowl lined with crisp lettuce leaves.

Yield: 6 servings.

Shrimp Salad With Feta Cheese

1½ pounds shrimp, cooked and
  deveined
½ pound feta cheese
1 bunch scallions, minced
2 tomatoes, cut into wedges
2 hard cooked egg yolks
¼ cup olive oil

¼ cup vegetable oil
1½ teaspoons white vinegar
1 tablespoon lemon juice
¼ teaspoon salt
Dash of pepper
Fresh dill to taste
Romaine leaves

Mix shrimp, cheese, scallions and tomatoes. Blend yolks, oils, vinegar, lemon juice, salt, pepper and dill. Pour over salad. Toss and serve on romaine leaves.

Yield: 4 servings.

This dieters' delight has only 375 calories per serving. Garnish with olives or radish roses for an even more colorful display.

Seaside Crab and Avocado Salad

2 cups crabmeat, flaked
2 avocados, peeled and diced
1½ teaspoons lime juice
2 hard-cooked eggs, chopped
2 tablespoons onion, minced
1 tablespoon capers
½ cup celery, chopped

½ teaspoon salt
Dash of pepper
½ cup mayonnaise
1 clove garlic, pressed
3 tablespoons chili sauce
Lettuce leaves

Combine crabmeat and avocados in bowl and sprinkle with lime juice. Add eggs, onion, capers, celery, salt, and pepper. Blend mayonnaise, garlic, and chili sauce. Pour over salad and toss lightly. Serve on lettuce leaves.

Yield: 6 servings.

This delicate salad makes an excellent filling for pita bread.

Elegante Crab Louis

Dressing

½ cup mayonnaise
½ cup yogurt
⅓ cup chili sauce

1 tablespoon onion grated
Dash of Tabasco sauce
⅓ cup whipping cream, whipped

Combine mayonnaise, yogurt, chili sauce, onion, Tabasco, and whipped cream. Chill.

Salad

Lettuce leaves
1½ cups lettuce, shredded
1½ pounds cooked crabmeat

24 ripe olives
4 hard-cooked eggs, quartered
½ cup walnuts, chopped (optional)

Arrange lettuce leaves on individual salad plates. Top with shredded lettuce and the crab. Surround with olives and eggs. Spoon dressing over crab. If desired, garnish with chopped nuts.

Yield: 4 servings

Shrimp makes an elegant substitution for the crabmeat.

Suncoast Shrimp and Vermicelli Salad

6 (4¼-ounce) cans shrimp, drained
  and deveined
5 hard-cooked eggs, chopped
6 stalks celery, chopped
¼ cup onion, chopped
6 tablespoons sweet pickle relish

1 (12-ounce) package vermicelli,
  cooked and drained
1½ - 2 cups mayonnaise
Salt and pepper to taste
Lettuce leaves

Combine shrimp, eggs, celery, onion, and pickle relish. Add vermicelli, mayonnaise, salt and pepper. Mix well and refrigerate. Serve on lettuce leaves.

Yield: 10-12 servings.

Fresh shrimp may be used with delicious results. Seashell macaroni may be substituted for the vermicelli for a nice change.

Cantonese Seafood Salad

Dressing

3 tablespoons dry white wine
2 tablespoons unsweetened
  pineapple or orange juice
2 tablespoons lemon juice
2 tablespoons light brown sugar,
  firmly packed

1½ tablespoons curry powder
2 teaspoons soy sauce
1 teaspoon onion powder
Pinch of garlic powder
2 cups mayonnaise

Combine wine, pineapple or orange juice, lemon juice, brown sugar, curry powder, soy sauce, onion powder, and garlic powder in a non-aluminum bowl and stir until brown sugar dissolves. Add mayonnaise and blend until smooth.

Salad

1¾ cups snow peas, each cut
  diagonally into thirds
1¾ pounds crabmeat, lobster, or
  shrimp, cooked, shelled,
  deveined, and sliced
1½ (8-ounce) cans water chestnuts,
  drained and sliced
1 bunch scallions, chopped

1¾ cups zucchini, finely chopped
1¾ cups carrot, grated
1 head iceberg lettuce, torn into
  bite-sized pieces
¼ cup fresh cilantro
1 cup celery, chopped
1¾ cups chow mein rice noodles
¼ cup sliced almonds

Blanch snow peas 1 minute in boiling water. Combine crabmeat, lobster, or shrimp with snow peas, water chestnuts, scallions, zucchini, and carrot. In a glass salad bowl, toss lettuce, cilantro, and celery. Spread noodles evenly over top. Spoon seafood mixture over noodles. Add dressing and toss well. Garnish with almonds.

Yield: 8 servings

Prepare the dressing, seafood, and vegetables early in the day and assemble just prior to presentation. Chicken is a pleasant seafood substitute.

Oriental Chicken Salad

Sesame Soy Dressing

¼ cup vegetable oil
¼ cup white or rice vinegar
2 tablespoons soy sauce

3 tablespoons light brown sugar
2 tablespoons sesame seeds, toasted
¼ - ½ teaspoon crushed red pepper

Thoroughly blend oil, vinegar, soy sauce, brown sugar, sesame seeds, and red pepper.

Salad

3 cups chicken, cooked and
    shredded
1 (20-ounce) can pineapple tidbits,
    drained
1 (8-ounce) can sliced water
    chestnuts, drained

1 cup celery, chopped
½ cup carrots, shredded
⅓ cup scallions, sliced
½ cup salted peanuts
1 cup chow mein noodles

Combine chicken, pineapple, water chestnuts, celery, carrots, and scallions. Toss salad with dressing. Just before serving, mix in peanuts and chow mein noodles.

Yield: 8 servings.

Curried Turkey Salad

4 cups turkey, cooked and diced
1 (11-ounce) can mandarin oranges,
    drained, juice reserved
1½ cups seedless grapes, halved
1 cup celery, chopped
1 (8-ounce) can sliced water
    chestnuts, drained

½ cup pecans, chopped
1½ cups mayonnaise
2 tablespoons juice from mandarin
    oranges
2 teaspoons curry powder
2 teaspoons soy sauce
Lettuce leaves

Combine turkey, oranges, grapes, celery, water chestnuts, and pecans. Blend mayonnaise, juice from oranges, curry powder, and soy sauce. Mix thoroughly with salad and chill. Serve on crisp lettuce leaves.

Yield: 6-8 servings.

May substitute with diced chicken. Delicious!

Bleu Cheese Chicken Salad

Dressing

½ cup mayonnaise
½ cup sour cream
3 tablespoons milk

2 tablespoons lemon juice
½ teaspoon seasoned salt
⅔ cup bleu cheese, crumbled

Blend mayonnaise, sour cream, milk, lemon juice, and seasoned salt in blender or food processor 30 seconds. Add bleu cheese and blend 3-5 seconds. Chill several hours or overnight.

Salad

4 cups cooked white meat of
  chicken, diced
1 (14-ounce) can hearts of palm,
  drained and sliced into ½-inch
  pieces

Lettuce leaves
24 pitted black olives
3 tomatoes, cut into wedges
½ pound bacon, cooked and
  crumbled

Toss chicken and hearts of palm with dressing. Chill several hours. To serve salad, arrange lettuce leaves on individual salad plates and top with chicken mixture. Garnish with olives and tomatoes. Just before serving sprinkle with crumbled bacon.

Yield: 6 servings.

Vineyard Chicken Salad

2 cups cooked chicken, cut into
small pieces
1½ cups celery, diced
1½ cups seedless grapes, halved
¼ cup carrots, coarsely grated
½ cup almonds, toasted

½ cup mayonnaise
¼ cup sour cream
1-2 teaspoons curry powder
1 tablespoon lemon juice
½ teaspoon salt

Combine chicken, celery, grapes, carrots, and almonds. Blend mayonnaise with sour cream, curry powder, lemon juice, and salt. Toss salad with dressing. Chill several hours.

Yield: 6 servings.

Choose red leaf lettuce to line individual chilled salad plates or a large serving bowl for additional visual merit.

Lobster Salad With Curried Chutney Dressing

½ cup mayonnaise
¼ cup light cream
2 tablespoons chutney
1-3 teaspoons curry powder

2 cups (1½ pounds) cooked lobster,
chopped
1 cup celery, chopped
Lettuce leaves

Combine mayonnaise, cream, chutney, and curry powder. Blend well. Mix lobster and celery. Combine with dressing mixture and chill thoroughly. Serve on chilled salad plates lined with lettuce leaves.

Yield: 4-6 servings.

This salad is very attractive presented on a bed of unpeeled cucumber slices garnished with tomato and avocado wedges.

Shrimp Mimosa

Dressing

1¼ cups mayonnaise
¼ cup chili sauce
2 tablespoons chives, chopped

2 tablespoons parsley, chopped
½ teaspoon dried tarragon
White pepper to taste

Blend mayonnaise, chili sauce, chives, parsley, tarragon, and pepper. Chill.

Salad

2 cups lettuce, shredded
2 tomato slices, ½-inch thick
2 artichoke bottoms, cooked,
coarsely chopped (may use
canned)
3 hard cooked eggs, sieved

1 pound shrimp, cooked, deveined,
coarsely chopped
(Reserve 6 whole shrimp for
garnish)
1 carrot, grated
1 stalk celery, finely chopped

Place one cup of lettuce on two chilled salad plates. Top each with tomato slice and chopped artichoke. Sprinkle sieved egg on lettuce. Fold chopped shrimp, carrot, and celery into dressing. Spoon seafood mixture over artichoke. Garnish with whole shrimp.

Yield: 2 main course salads.

Six appetizer servings may be served from this recipe. Crabmeat may be used instead of shrimp.

Tostado Salad

1 pound ground beef
1 (1¼-ounce) package taco
   seasoning
1 (15-ounce) can kidney beans,
   drained
1 head lettuce, torn into bite-size
   pieces
4 tomatoes, quartered

1 cup Cheddar cheese, grated
1 small onion, chopped
¼ cup black olives, sliced
1 large avocado, peeled and sliced
   (optional)
8-12 ounces prepared ranch
   dressing
1 cup taco flavored chips, crushed

Brown ground beef with taco seasoning. Drain and add beans. Simmer ten minutes. Mix lettuce, tomatoes, cheese, onion, olives, avocado, dressing, and chips. Add warm meat mixture and serve immediately.

Yield: 10 servings.

Heartland Ham Salad

2 cups cooked ham, diced
2 cups frozen peas, thawed
1 cup celery, diced
2 cups cottage cheese
¼ cup mayonnaise
2 teaspoons Worcestershire sauce
Dash of Tabasco

2 tablespoons capers
3 tablespoons chives, chopped
2 tablespoons parsley, chopped
Lettuce leaves
Paprika
½ cup dry roasted sunflower seeds

Combine ham, peas, and celery. In a separate bowl, mix cottage cheese, mayonnaise, Worcestershire sauce, and Tabasco. Blend capers, chives, and parsley into cottage cheese mixture. Fold in ham mixture. Chill. Serve on individual salad plates lined with lettuce leaves. Sprinkle each serving with paprika and garnish with sunflower seeds.

Yield: 6 servings.

Carrot curls add the perfect color complement.

Park Place Café Tortellini Salad

1 (12-ounce) package of meat or
cheese-filled tortellini
2 cups of any of the following raw
vegetables, chopped into bite-
sized pieces:
Broccoli
Carrots
Cauliflower
Celery
Scallions
Yellow squash
Zucchini
8 ounces small salad shrimp,
cooked
8 ounces crabmeat, cooked
Black olives for garnish
Tomato wedges for garnish

Cook tortellini according to package directions. Mix with choice of vegetables, shrimp, and crabmeat. Chill. Shortly before serving, add pesto and toss well. Serve on a bed of salad greens. Garnish with black olives and tomato wedges.

Pesto

2 cloves garlic
¼ cup fresh basil or parsley, stems
removed
½ cup walnuts or pine nuts
¾ cup olive oil
¼ cup Parmesan cheese

Process garlic, basil or parsley, and nuts in a food processor until they form a paste. While processor is running, add olive oil. Blend in Parmesan cheese.

Yield: 4-6 servings.

Provençal Beef Salad With Anchovy Vinaigrette

Vinaigrette

1½ cups vegetable oil	1 teaspoon sugar
½ cup white vinegar	1 teaspoon black pepper
1 teaspoon anchovy paste	¼ cup parsley, minced
2 cloves garlic, peeled	1½ teaspoons salt

Combine oil, vinegar, anchovy paste, garlic, sugar, pepper, parsley, and salt. Blend well.

Salad

3 pounds new potatoes, unpeeled	1 (3¼-ounce) jar capers, drained
4 cups cooked tenderloin, sirloin or any tender roast beef, cut into ½-inch cubes	1 pint cherry tomatoes, stemmed
	⅓ cup parsley, minced
2 cups scallions, cut into ¼-inch slices	1 head romaine

Boil potatoes until tender. While still warm, cube potatoes and toss with dressing. Refrigerate 2-3 hours or overnight. Just before serving, toss potatoes and dressing with beef, scallions, capers, tomatoes, and parsley. Serve on a bed of romaine leaves.

Yield: 12 servings

Emerald Tofu Dressing

1 cup spinach leaves, stems
   removed
2 scallions, chopped
½ cup fresh parsley, chopped
1 teaspoon salt
¾ teaspoon dry mustard

2 tablespoons white vinegar
1 egg
2 tablespoons olive oil
1 cup vegetable oil
⅓ pound tofu

Combine spinach, scallions, parsley, salt, mustard, vinegar, and egg in blender or food processor and liquefy. Slowly add oils and blend until thick. Crumble tofu and fold into mixture. Refrigerate several hours or overnight.

Yield: 2 cups.

Serve this intriguing dressing on your favorite spinach, lettuce, or cucumber salad.

Bleu Cheese Buttermilk Dressing

2 cups mayonnaise
1 teaspoon lemon juice
1 teaspoon white vinegar
¼ cup buttermilk
½ cup sour cream

½ teaspoon salt
¼ teaspoon pepper
¼ teaspoon garlic powder
4 ounces bleu cheese, crumbled

Combine mayonnaise, lemon juice, vinegar, buttermilk, sour cream, salt, pepper, and garlic powder. Gently stir in bleu cheese. Cover tightly and refrigerate several hours or overnight.

Yield: 3 cups.

This is the ultimate bleu cheese dressing!

Ever Popular Poppy Seed Dressing

1 cup vegetable oil
¾ cup plus 3 tablespoons sugar
6 tablespoons white vinegar

4 teaspoons poppy seeds
1½ teaspoons salt
1½ teaspoons prepared mustard

Combine oil, sugar, vinegar, poppy seeds, salt, and mustard in food processor or blender. Blend on high speed for 30 seconds. Cover and chill several hours or overnight. Serve over fresh fruit.

Yield: 1½ cups.

Favorite Green Salad Dressing

1 cup vegetable oil
¼ cup red wine vinegar
¼ cup sour cream
1½ teaspoons salt
½ teaspoon dry mustard

2 tablespoons sugar
2 teaspoons parsley, minced
2 cloves garlic, crushed
Coarse black pepper to taste

Combine oil, vinegar, sour cream, salt, mustard, sugar, parsley, garlic, and pepper until well blended.

Yield: 1½ cups

Dijon Mustard Dressing

½ cup Dijon mustard
1 cup white vinegar
1 teaspoon garlic powder
1 teaspoon onion powder
1½ tablespoons parsley

1½ tablespoons dried basil
1½ tablespoons oregano
¼ cup sugar
1 cup vegetable oil

Combine mustard, vinegar, garlic powder, onion powder, parsley, basil, oregano, sugar, and oil in a jar with tight-fitting lid. Shake until thoroughly blended.

Yield: 2 cups

Parmesan Cheese Dressing

1 clove garlic, minced
1 egg
½ cup vegetable oil
½ teaspoon salt

Dash of Tabasco
2 tablespoons lemon juice
1 (3-ounce) can Parmesan cheese
1 tablespoon wine vinegar

Whisk garlic and egg. Slowly add oil, continuing to whisk until thickened. Blend in salt, Tabasco, and lemon juice. Gradually mix in Parmesan cheese. Beat in vinegar. Chill until ready to serve.

Yield: 1 cup.

This is a glorious dressing for spinach, watercress, or fresh mushroom salads.

Honey-Lime Fruit Sauce

1 (6-ounce) can frozen limeade,
    thawed and undiluted
¾ cup vegetable oil

½ cup honey
3 teaspoons poppy seeds

Combine limeade, oil, honey, and poppy seeds in blender and mix 15 seconds or until smooth.

Yield: 2 cups.

Present this light and unusual sauce in a clear glass bowl with strawberries, cantaloupe, blueberries, bananas, and watermelon.

VEGETABLES
& FRUITS

Asparagus with Cashew Butter

3 pounds fresh asparagus or 3
  (10-ounce) packages frozen
4 tablespoons butter
6 tablespoons lemon juice

½ teaspoon dried marjoram
½ cup salted cashew nuts, coarsely
  chopped

Cook asparagus in salted water until tender. Drain and arrange on heated platter. While asparagus cooks, melt butter. Add lemon juice, marjoram, and nuts. Simmer over low heat about 3 minutes. Pour over asparagus and serve.

Yield: 8-10 servings.

Asparagus with Sautéed Mushrooms

4 small green onions, chopped
2 cups fresh mushrooms, sliced
6 tablespoons butter

Salt to taste
3 pounds fresh asparagus

Sauté onions and mushrooms in butter until tender, but not brown. Add salt to taste. Keep warm. Cook asparagus spears until tender. Drain. Place on serving platter and spoon sautéed mushrooms on top. Serve immediately.

Yield: 8-10 servings.

Artichoke Hearts Casserole

3 (8½-ounce) cans artichoke hearts, quartered
1 cup mayonnaise
1 (6-ounce) can black olives, cut into halves
½ cup Parmesan cheese, grated
½ cup breadcrumbs
1 tablespoon vegetable oil

Mix artichoke hearts, mayonnaise, olives, and Parmesan cheese together. Place in a 1½-quart casserole. Combine breadcrumbs and oil; sprinkle on top of casserole. Bake at 375° for 40 minutes.

Yield: 8 servings.

Black-Eyed Peas with Rice

2 slices bacon
1 medium onion, chopped
1 (15-ounce) can black-eyed peas, drained
1 (14½-ounce) can stewed tomatoes, undrained, chopped
1 cup cooked rice
¼ teaspoon salt
¼ teaspoon pepper

Cook bacon in a large skillet until crisp. Reserve 2 tablespoons drippings in skillet. Crumble bacon and set aside. Sauté onion in drippings until tender. Add black-eyed peas, tomatoes, rice, salt, and pepper. Spoon mixture into a 1½-quart casserole. Bake at 350° for 30 minutes. Garnish with crumbled bacon.

Yield: 6 servings.

Barbequed Lima Beans

1 pound dried lima beans
6 slices bacon
1 cup onion, chopped
½ cup green pepper, chopped

1 (15-ounce) can tomato sauce with
    tomato pieces
1 cup barbeque sauce
¾ teaspoon salt

Wash beans and place in a Dutch oven. Cover with water and soak overnight. Bring beans to a boil; reduce heat and simmer 1 hour, or until tender. Pour off excess water. Fry bacon until crisp; drain, reserving 2 tablespoons of drippings. Crumble bacon and set aside. Sauté onion and green pepper in bacon drippings until tender. Stir in beans, tomato sauce, barbeque sauce, and salt. Spoon mixture into a 3-quart casserole. Bake uncovered at 350° for 30 minutes. Sprinkle with bacon.

Yield: 10-12 servings.

A wonderful change from baked beans!

Crock Pot Beans

8 slices bacon
4 onions, sliced into rings
1 cup firmly packed brown sugar
1 teaspoon dry mustard
½ teaspoon garlic powder
1 teaspoon salt
½ cup vinegar

2 (15-ounce) cans great northern
    beans, drained
1 (16-ounce) can green lima beans,
    drained
1 (15-ounce) can red kidney beans,
    drained
1 (28-ounce) can pork and beans

Cut bacon into 1-inch strips and fry until crisp. Drain, reserving drippings; crumble, and set aside. In crock pot, place bacon drippings, onions, brown sugar, mustard, garlic powder, salt, and vinegar. Cover pot and place on high setting for 20 minutes. Add northern beans, lima beans, kidney beans, pork and beans, and bacon. Stir to combine. Cover crock pot and cook on low setting 4-6 hours. Beans cannot cook too long.

Yield: 10-12 servings.

Beans may be baked for 2-3 hours in a 325° oven.

Lemon Broccoli

1½ pounds fresh broccoli, cut up
6 tablespoons butter
½ cup green onions, chopped with
tops

½ cup celery, chopped
2-3 tablespoons lemon juice
½ teaspoon lemon peel, finely
grated

Steam broccoli and drain well. Melt butter in a saucepan and sauté onions and celery until tender, but not brown. Stir in lemon juice and heat thoroughly. To serve, place broccoli in a serving dish and spoon lemon-vegetable mixture over top. Sprinkle with lemon peel and serve immediately.

Yield: 6-8 servings.

Company Carrots

¼ cup Port wine
¼ cup Chablis
8 ounces fresh mushrooms
3 tablespoons olive oil
1½ pounds thin carrots, peeled and
sliced diagonally
5 green onions, chopped (including
tops)

2 large cloves garlic, minced
Pinch of salt
Freshly ground black pepper to
taste
2 tablespoons parsley, chopped

Combine Port and Chablis. Add mushrooms and marinate for 2 hours. Drain mushrooms; reserve ¼ cup liquid. Chop mushrooms and set aside. Heat oil in a large skillet. Add carrots, onions, garlic, and salt. Cover and cook over medium heat for 5 minutes, stirring frequently. Stir in chopped mushrooms and reserved liquid. Continue cooking another few minutes, stirring periodically. Season with pepper and cook until desired crispness. Sprinkle with parsley and serve.

Yield: 4-6 servings.

Serve with beef tenderloin or roast for a delicious combination.

Glazed Carrots With Raisins

1½ pounds fresh carrots
4 tablespoons butter or margarine
⅓ cup dry white wine

½ teaspoon nutmeg
⅔ cup raisins
3 tablespoons light brown sugar

Peel and cut carrots into ¼-inch slices. Put carrots in saucepan with butter, wine, and nutmeg. Cover and cook over low heat until carrots are tender. Stir in raisins and sugar. Cook 3-4 minutes longer until raisins are plump and carrots are glazed.

Yield: 6 servings.

Carrots en Casserole

1 pound carrots, sliced
½ cup onion, finely chopped
1 cup Cheddar cheese, grated
¼ teaspoon salt
¾ cup mayonnaise

1 teaspoon sugar
½ (8-ounce) package cornbread
    stuffing
½ cup hot water
¼ cup margarine, softened

Steam carrots until tender and drain. Mix carrots, onion, cheese, salt, mayonnaise, and sugar together. Pour into a greased 9 x 13-inch casserole. Combine stuffing mix with water and margarine. Spread over carrot mixture. Bake at 350° for 20 minutes.

Yield: 4 servings.

Curried Cauliflower

1 head cauliflower
1 (10¾-ounce) can cream of chicken
   soup
⅓ cup mayonnaise
¼ teaspoon curry powder

¾ cup Cheddar cheese, grated
Salt to taste
Pepper to taste
Fresh parsley, chopped

Steam cauliflower until tender. Break into bite size pieces. In 2-quart casserole, stir undiluted soup, mayonnaise, curry powder, and cheese. Add cauliflower and mix well. Season with salt and pepper. Sprinkle with chopped parsley. Bake at 350° for 30 minutes or until hot and bubbly.

Yield: 8-10 servings.

Cauliflower Supreme

2 heads cauliflower, broken into
   florets
4 tablespoons butter
4 tablespoons flour
1½ cups milk
½ cup dry white wine

1 cup Havarti cheese, shredded and
   divided
1 teaspoon salt
½ teaspoon white pepper
½ cup breadcrumbs

Steam cauliflower until just tender. Drain and place in a greased casserole. Melt butter in a saucepan over low heat. Stir in flour and slowly add milk. Continue stirring; cook until sauce thickens. Mix in wine, ¾ cup cheese, salt, and pepper. Pour sauce over cauliflower and sprinkle with breadcrumbs. Top with remaining ¼ cup cheese. Bake at 350° for 35 minutes.

Yield: 8-10 servings.

For a creamier version, you might wish to make 1½ times sauce recipe.

Corn Zucchini Bake

1 pound zucchini, cut into ½-inch
   slices
¼ cup onion, chopped
1 tablespoon butter
2 cups fresh corn, cooked
2 eggs, beaten
1 cup Swiss cheese, shredded

¼ - ½ teaspoon salt
¼ cup breadcrumbs
2 tablespoons Parmesan cheese,
   grated
1 tablespoon butter, melted
Cherry tomatoes
Parsley

Cook zucchini in a small amount of salted water until just tender. Drain and mash. Set aside. Sauté onion in butter until tender. Combine zucchini, onion, corn, eggs, Swiss cheese, and salt. Mix well and pour into a greased 1-quart casserole. Combine breadcrumbs, Parmesan cheese, and melted butter. Sprinkle over zucchini mixture. Bake at 350° for 40 minutes. Garnish with tomatoes and parsley.

Yield: 4-6 servings.

Shoepeg Corn Pudding

1 (16-ounce) package frozen
   shoepeg corn
½ cup butter, melted
2 eggs
1 cup sour cream

1 cup Monterey Jack cheese, diced
¼ cup corn meal
1½ teaspoons salt
1 (4-ounce) can green chilies, diced

Preheat oven to 350°. Grease a 2-quart casserole dish. Purée half of corn with melted butter and eggs in food processor or blender. Mix remaining corn, sour cream, cheese, corn meal, salt, and chilies in a bowl. Add puréed mixture and mix well. Pour into prepared casserole. Bake uncovered at 350° for 50-60 minutes.

Yield: 6-8 servings.

Eggplant Pie

1 large eggplant, approximately 1
   pound
¾ teaspoon salt
⅛ teaspoon pepper
2 medium tomatoes, sliced
1 medium green pepper, cut into
   rings
1 onion, thinly sliced

2 teaspoons olive oil
1 clove garlic, minced
1 teaspoon dried oregano or basil
4-6 ounces Mozzarella cheese,
   sliced
½ cup Parmesan cheese, freshly
   grated

Peel and cut eggplant into ¼-inch slices. Arrange sliced eggplant in a single layer on a baking sheet. Sprinkle with ½ teaspoon salt and ⅛ teaspoon pepper. Broil 6 inches from heat until lightly browned. Remove eggplant from oven. Reduce heat to 375°. Line a 10-inch pie plate with eggplant slices, browned side down. Overlap slices in a circular pattern. Arrange tomato slices, green pepper rings, and onion slices in layers over eggplant. Drizzle with oil. Sprinkle with garlic, oregano, and ¼ teaspoon salt. Layer Mozzarella cheese on top. Sprinkle Parmesan over all. Bake at 375° for 25 minutes (until cheese is golden brown).

Yield: 4-6 servings.

"I Can't Believe It's Eggplant" Casserole

1 medium eggplant, peeled
½ teaspoon salt
4 tablespoons butter
3 eggs
½ teaspoon baking powder

½ cup milk
½ cup saltine crackers, crumbled
2 ounces cream cheese, softened
½ cup sharp Cheddar cheese,
   grated

Cut eggplant into small pieces. Place in a saucepan with enough water to cover. Add salt and cook until tender. Drain. Mash eggplant with a fork while adding butter, eggs, baking powder, milk, and crackers. Add cream cheese and ¼ cup Cheddar cheese. Put mixture into a greased 1-quart casserole. Sprinkle remaining cheese on top. Bake at 350° for 1 hour.

Yield: 6 servings.

Famous Amos Mushroom Casserole

1 pound fresh mushrooms, sliced
6 tablespoons butter
½ cup celery, chopped
½ cup onion, chopped
½ cup green pepper, chopped
½ cup mayonnaise
6 slices bread, buttered

1 (10¾-ounce) can cream of
   mushroom soup
½ cup water
2 eggs, beaten
Buttered breadcrumbs
Swiss cheese, grated

Sauté mushrooms in butter until tender. Add celery, onion, green pepper, and mayonnaise. Cut each buttered bread slice into 20 pieces. In a 2-quart casserole, layer one-third of bread pieces and one-third of mushroom mixture. Repeat layers twice more. Mix together soup, water, and eggs and pour over layers. Let stand 1 hour. Sprinkle with breadcrumbs, then cheese. Bake at 325° for 55 minutes.

Yield: 6 servings.

Good substitute for Thanksgiving dressing.

Mushrooms Divine

¼ cup onion, chopped
2 tablespoons butter
2 tablespoons olive oil
1 clove garlic, minced
1 pound fresh mushrooms, sliced
¼ cup lemon juice

1 teaspoon ground nutmeg
½ teaspoon salt
Dash of pepper
¼ cup fresh parsley, chopped
3 slices buttered toast, crusts
   removed and cut into 4 triangles

Sauté onions in butter and oil in a 10-inch skillet. Add garlic and mushrooms; cook until tender. Gently stir in lemon juice, nutmeg, salt, and pepper. Simmer 5 minutes. Stir in parsley and serve over toast triangles.

Yield: 6 servings.

Buttered Onions

5 pounds Vidalia onions, peeled
4 tablespoons butter
¼ cup water

Quarter onions and place in a casserole dish. Dot with butter and add water. Cover tightly. Bake at 350° for 3 hours.

Yield: 8 servings.

Delicious accompaniment to steak.

Okra And Tomatoes

1 pound okra, cleaned
3 slices bacon
1 large onion, chopped
1 medium green pepper, finely
  chopped

1 (16-ounce) can tomatoes,
  chopped
¼ teaspoon salt
¼ teaspoon pepper

Slice okra into ½-inch slices and set aside. Fry bacon in a Dutch oven until crisp. Drain and reserve 2 tablespoons drippings. Cook okra in drippings 5 minutes, or until lightly browned. Add onion and green pepper. Cook, stirring occasionally, until tender. Stir in tomatoes, salt, and pepper. Cover and simmer 20 minutes. Stir in bacon and heat thoroughly.

Yield: 6 servings.

Petit Pois Français

1 (10-ounce) package frozen peas
¼ cup butter, softened
1 tablespoon parsley, chopped
½ teaspoon dried chervil

1 cup lettuce, shredded
3 medium tomatoes, halved
  crosswise

Cook peas according to package directions. Drain. Stir in butter, parsley, and chervil. Add lettuce and toss gently. Set aside. Scoop out centers of tomatoes. Fill with pea mixture and bake at 350° for 15 minutes.

Yield: 6 servings.

Red Potato Bake

2½ pounds small red potatoes
Juice 1 large lemon
Peeling of 1 lemon, grated
½ cup butter
½ cup olive oil
1 teaspoon nutmeg

2 tablespoons chives
1 pinch onion salt
Salt to taste
Pepper to taste
2 tablespoons parsley, chopped
Paprika to taste

Wash potatoes and slice thinly, leaving peels on. Cook until crisp-tender. Drain and place in a 1½-quart casserole. Make sauce by combining lemon juice, lemon peel, butter, olive oil, nutmeg, chives, onion salt, salt, and pepper. Pour mixture over potatoes. Bake at 350° for 30 minutes. Sprinkle with parsley and paprika before serving.

Yield: 6 servings.

Caviar New Potatoes

12 small new potatoes
¼ cup sour cream or plain yogurt
3 tablespoons butter, softened
1 tablespoon chives, minced

Salt to taste
Pepper to taste
1 (2-ounce) jar caviar

Put potatoes into a casserole; add 2 tablespoons water. Cover and microwave 8-10 minutes until tender. Cut a slice off top of potato and scoop out center of potato leaving ¼-inch thick shell. Put potato pulp in small bowl. Stir in sour cream, butter, chives, salt, and pepper. Put mixture back in potato shells. Microwave on high 1-2 minutes until just hot. Top with caviar. Serve immediately.

Yield: 6 servings.

Shrimp Stuffed Potatoes

4 large baking potatoes	2 tablespoons parsley
2 egg yolks, beaten	2 tablespoons chives
Approximately ⅓ cup half and half	1 cup cooked shrimp
4 tablespoons butter	½ cup Cheddar cheese, grated
Salt to taste	Paprika
Pepper to taste	

Bake potatoes for 1 hour or until tender. Do not turn off oven. Cut thin slice from each potato. Scoop out pulp, leaving ¼-inch thick shell. Place pulp in medium size mixing bowl. Add egg yolks. Beat with electric mixer until smooth. Beat in enough cream to make mixture light and fluffy. Add butter, salt, and pepper. Fold in parsley, chives, and shrimp. Spoon mixture into shells. Sprinkle with cheese and paprika. Bake at 350° until cheese is melted and golden.

Yield: 4 servings.

Best Potato Casserole

6-8 potatoes	Salt to taste
1 cup sour cream	Pepper to taste
1 cup cottage cheese	Garlic powder to taste
6-8 green onions, chopped	1 cup cheese, grated

Cook, drain, peel, and dice potatoes. Mix potatoes, sour cream, cottage cheese, onions, salt, pepper, and garlic powder. Spoon into a greased 1½-quart baking dish. Top with your favorite cheese. Bake at 350° for 30 minutes.

Yield: 6-8 servings.

Greek Spinach Casserole

1 pound Feta cheese
7 eggs, beaten
7 tablespoons flour
½ cup butter
2 pounds cottage cheese
12 ounces Cheddar cheese, grated

3 (10-ounce) packages frozen
   spinach, thawed and drained
1 large onion, minced
1 teaspoon garlic, minced
1½ teaspoons oregano

Butter a 9 x 14-inch casserole. Rinse Feta cheese to remove salty liquid and crumble. Beat eggs with flour and combine with Feta cheese. Add butter, cottage cheese, Cheddar cheese, spinach, onion, garlic, and oregano. Pour into casserole and bake at 350° for 1 hour.

Yield: 12-14 servings.

Casserole freezes well after baking.

Spinach Madeline

2 (10-ounce) packages frozen
   chopped spinach
4 tablespoons butter
2 tablespoons chopped onion
2 tablespoons flour
½ cup spinach liquid
½ cup evaporated milk

½ teaspoon salt
¾ teaspoon garlic salt
½ teaspoon pepper
¾ teaspoon celery salt
1 (6-ounce) roll Jalapeños cheese
1 teaspoon Worcestershire sauce
Breadcrumbs

Cook spinach, drain and reserve liquid. Melt butter in a saucepan; add onion and cook until tender. Add flour and cook until smooth. Stir in spinach liquid and milk slowly and cook until smooth. Season with salt, garlic salt, pepper, celery salt, cheese, and Worcestershire sauce. Stir until cheese melts. Mix in spinach. Pour into greased casserole dish, and top with breadcrumbs. Bake at 325° for 30-40 minutes.

Yield: 6 servings.

Make this casserole a day ahead for improved flavor.

Squash-Tomato Sauté

1 pound yellow squash, julienned
1 pound zucchini, julienned
1 clove garlic, minced
3 tablespoons butter or margarine
½ teaspoon oregano

⅛ teaspoon pepper
1 teaspoon salt
2 medium tomatoes, cut into
 wedges

Sauté yellow squash, zucchini, and garlic in butter until crisp-tender. Sprinkle with oregano, pepper, and salt. Add tomato wedges; cover and cook until just heated. Do not overcook.

Yield: 8-10 servings.

A very colorful side dish.

Ratatouille

2 tablespoons olive oil
1 clove garlic, crushed
1 medium onion, coarsely chopped
1 green pepper, coarsely chopped
1½ teaspoons salt
½ teaspoon basil

½ teaspoon oregano
⅛ teaspoon pepper
1 large zucchini, sliced
1 medium eggplant, coarsely
 chopped
3-4 tomatoes, chopped

Heat oil in a 4-quart Dutch oven. Sauté garlic and onion until almost tender. Add green pepper and sauté until tender. Stir in salt, basil, oregano, pepper, zucchini, eggplant, and tomatoes. Cover and reduce heat to low. Cook 30 minutes, stirring occasionally. Remove cover and cook off excess liquid. Serve hot or cold.

Yield: 6-8 servings.

Spinach Stuffed Tomatoes

2 (10-ounce) packages frozen
  chopped spinach
8 ounces cream cheese, softened
½ cup butter

Salt to taste
Pepper to taste
6-8 tomatoes
3-4 tablespoons butter

Cook spinach according to package directions. Drain well. Blend cream cheese into hot spinach. Add butter, salt, and pepper. Set aside. Cut off tops of tomatoes and scoop out pulp. Fill with spinach mixture and dot with butter. Place in a baking dish with a small amount of water to prevent tomatoes from burning. Bake at 350° for 20-25 minutes.

Yield: 6-8 servings.

Zesty Tomato Pie

5 slices bacon
2 teaspoons onion, chopped
2 teaspoons green pepper, chopped
1 (28-ounce) can tomatoes, drained
  and mashed

1 cup croutons
1 tablespoon sugar
½ teaspoon salt
¼ teaspoon pepper
1 cup Cheddar cheese, grated

Fry bacon on one side only. Remove from pan and reserve. Lightly brown onion and green pepper in bacon drippings. Drain well. Combine onion, green pepper, tomatoes, croutons, sugar, salt, and pepper. Pour mixture into a 10-inch glass pie dish. Put bacon on top with fried side down. Bake at 400° for 20 minutes. Sprinkle with grated cheese and bake 15 minutes longer.

Yield: 4 servings.

Great side dish with steaks.

Zucchini-Yellow Squash Casserole

¾ pound yellow squash
¾ pound zucchini
4 tablespoons sour cream
½ cup Cheddar cheese, shredded
⅛ teaspoon nutmeg

1 teaspoon ground pepper
½ cup Swiss cheese, shredded
¾ cup Ritz crackers, crushed
2 tablespoons butter

Slice yellow squash and zucchini ¼-inch thick. Steam until just tender. Remove from heat and drain well. Allow to cool for 10 minutes. Place yellow squash and zucchini in a 1½-quart casserole. Add sour cream, cheddar cheese, and nutmeg. Lightly toss. Add pepper and toss again. Sprinkle with shredded Swiss cheese. Top with crackers and dot with butter. Bake at 375° for 20 minutes.

Yield: 6 servings.

Stuffed Zucchini

4 medium zucchini
1¾ cups soft breadcrumbs
½ cup mild Cheddar cheese, grated
¼ cup onion, chopped
2 tablespoons parsley, chopped
1¼ teaspoon salt

⅛ teaspoon pepper
2 eggs, beaten
¼ teaspoon salt
2 tablespoons butter
3 tablespoons Parmesan cheese, grated

Prepare zucchini by cutting off ends and slicing in half lengthwise. Steam until just tender. Carefully scoop out center of each half with spoon. Invert shell on paper towel to drain. Chop center part of zucchini and combine with breadcrumbs, grated cheese, onion, parsley, salt, pepper, and eggs. Place zucchini, hollow side up, in greased 13 x 9 x 2-inch baking pan. Sprinkle with salt. Fill with bread mixture. Dot with butter and sprinkle with Parmesan cheese. Bake at 350° for 35-45 minutes.

Yield: 8 servings.

Delectable Zucchini

½ cup butter
1 large onion, thinly sliced
2 pounds fresh zucchini, sliced
1 teaspoon garlic salt

½ pound fresh mushrooms, sliced
1 cup Parmesan cheese
1½ cups herb seasoned stuffing

Melt butter in a large pan. Add onion, zucchini, and garlic salt. Cook slowly until just done. Reserve 2 tablespoons of liquid. Place one-half of drained zucchini mixture in bottom of 2-quart casserole. Layer with one-half of mushrooms, one-half of cheese, and a 1-inch layer of stuffing. Drizzle stuffing layer with 1 tablespoon of liquid from zucchini. Repeat layers. Bake at 350° for 20-30 minutes.

Yield: 6-8 servings.

Stir-Fried Vegetables

2 tablespoons oil
4 cups celery, sliced diagonally
1 cup fresh mushrooms, sliced
1 cup snow peas, fresh or frozen
3 green onions, chopped
1 tablespoon cornstarch
¼ teaspoon ground ginger

¼ cup corn syrup
2 tablespoons soy sauce
2 tablespoons orange juice
1-2 teaspoons fresh orange peel, grated
¼ cup almonds, slivered

In a wok or large skillet, heat oil and sauté celery 3 minutes. Add mushrooms, snow peas, and onions. Stir fry 3 minutes. Combine cornstarch, ginger, corn syrup, soy sauce, and orange juice. Pour over vegetables. Continue stir frying over medium heat, stirring about 5 minutes. Sprinkle with orange peel and almonds. Serve immediately.

Yield: 8 servings.

Vegetable Casserole Supreme

1¼ cups dry stuffing mix
1 cup margarine, melted
2-3 carrots, coarsely grated
2 small onions, chopped
3-4 large yellow squash, zucchini, or a combination, sliced
1 cup sour cream
1 (10-ounce) can cream of celery soup, undiluted
Salt to taste
Pepper to taste
1 teaspoon summer savory
2 tablespoons margarine, melted
Paprika

Grease an 8 x 8-inch baking dish. Sprinkle ½ cup dry stuffing into bottom of dish. Combine ¼ cup stuffing mix with 1 cup melted margarine in a large bowl. Set aside. Steam carrots, onions, yellow squash, and zucchini until just tender. Drain off excess liquid. Mix steamed vegetables, sour cream, and soup with the reserved ¼ cup stuffing mix. Blend well. Season with salt, pepper, and summer savory. Pour mixture over stuffing in baking dish. Sprinkle with remaining dry stuffing, 2 tablespoons margarine, and paprika. Bake at 350° for 30 minutes.

Yield: 6-8 servings.

Broccoli may be substituted for either squash. Use ½ bunch fresh or 20 ounces frozen.

Calabacitas Guisada

8 medium zucchini, chopped into small cubes
2 tomatoes, chopped
½ onion, chopped
½ cup milk
1 tablespoon vegetable oil
½ pound Monterey Jack cheese, grated
Salt to taste
Pepper to taste

Combine zucchini, tomatoes, onion, milk, and vegetable oil in a sauce pan. Cover and cook for 10 minutes. Drain liquid. Add the cheese, salt, and pepper. Cook 5 minutes more.

Yield: 8 servings.

Wine Poached Apples

2 cups sugar
1 cup sherry
½ cup water

4 red Rome apples, halved, cored,
and peeled

Bring sugar, sherry, and water to a gentle boil. Add apples; reduce heat and cook 6 minutes. Gently turn apples over and cook 5 minutes more. Apples should still be firm. Transfer to a serving dish and pour syrup over top. Refrigerate until ready to serve.

Yield: 8 servings.

Curried Apples

4 large cooking apples, peeled,
cored, and cut-up
⅓ cup brown sugar, firmly packed

½ teaspoon curry powder
1 teaspoon grated orange peel
⅓ cup beer

Place apples in a 1½-quart casserole. Combine sugar, curry powder, orange peel, and beer. Pour over apples. Cover and bake at 350° for 40-45 minutes. Serve hot.

Yield: 6 servings.

Baked Pineapple

1 (20-ounce) can sliced pineapple,
drained and juice reserved
Maraschino cherries
2 eggs, beaten

2 tablespoons cornstarch
¾ cup sugar
1 tablespoon butter, melted
½ teaspoon ground cinnamon

Place pineapple rings in a greased shallow baking dish. Place a cherry in the middle of each ring. Set aside. Combine reserved pineapple juice, eggs, cornstarch, sugar, butter, and cinnamon. Pour mixture over pineapple rings. Bake at 350° for 40 minutes. Serve warm.

Yield: 6-8 servings.

Hot Sherried Fruit

1 (29-ounce) can peach halves, cut
  into thirds
1 (29-ounce) can pear halves, cut
  into thirds
1 (29-ounce) can pineapple chunks

¾ cup light brown sugar
½ cup butter, melted
¾ cup sherry
2½ cups coconut macaroons
  (chopped in blender)

One day in advance: Drain fruit well and place in a 2-quart baking dish. Sprinkle with brown sugar. Pour melted butter and sherry over all. Sprinkle coconut cookies over fruit. Store covered in refrigerator for 24 hours. Bake at 350° for 45 minutes or until hot and bubbly.

Yield: 12 servings.

Disappearing Pickles

12 pickling cucumbers
4 large onions
4 cups sugar
4 cups apple cider vinegar

½ cup salt
1¼ teaspoons turmeric
1¼ teaspoons celery salt
1¼ teaspoons mustard seed

Slice cucumbers and onions in ¼-inch slices. Layer cucumbers and onions in a 1-gallon jar. Combine sugar, cider vinegar, salt, turmeric, celery salt, and mustard seed. Pour over cucumbers and onions. Refrigerate. Enjoy after 1 week.

Yield: 1 gallon.

It is difficult to wait a whole week before tasting these crisp bread and butter pickles. Once you do, watch how quickly they disappear!

Holiday Cranberry Sauce

1 pound fresh cranberries
2 cups sugar
⅓ cup brandy

Spread cranberries in a baking dish in a single layer. Sprinkle with sugar. Cover with foil. Bake at 300° for 1 hour. Remove from oven and pour brandy over berries. Serve warm.

Yield: 2 cups.

Wonderful with turkey and game.

Cranberry Relish

3 cups fresh cranberries
Pinch of salt
2 red apples, cored

1 orange, seeded and quartered
1 cup sugar
⅓ cup Grand Marnier

Use a food processor to chop cranberries. Add salt and set aside. Chop apples and add to cranberries. Chop orange and combine with cranberries and apples. Add sugar and Grand Marnier. Mix well. Spoon into jars with lids and refrigerate.

Yield: 2 pints.

Leave the peel on the fruit for a colorful relish that makes a lovely gift.

EGGS, PASTA
& GRAINS

Vegetarian Lasagna

1 (8-ounce) package lasagna
  noodles
2 (10-ounce) bags of fresh spinach
  or 3 (10-ounce) packages frozen
  spinach
2 cups fresh mushrooms, sliced
1 cup carrots, grated
½ cup onion, chopped
1 tablespoon oil

1 (15-ounce) can tomato sauce
1 (6-ounce) can tomato paste
½ cup pitted ripe olives, chopped
1½ teaspoons dried oregano
2 cups cream-style cottage cheese,
  drained, or 2 cups Ricotta cheese
1 (16-ounce) package Monterey
  Jack cheese, grated
Parmesan cheese, freshly grated

Cook lasagna noodles according to package directions; drain. Rinse spinach well. Cook covered for 3-5 minutes without water, except for the drops that cling to the leaves. Stir occasionally. Sauté mushrooms, carrots, and onions in hot oil until tender, but not brown. Stir in tomato sauce, tomato paste, olives, and oregano. In a greased 13 x 9 x 2-inch baking dish, layer half each of the noodles, cottage cheese, spinach, Monterey Jack cheese, and sauce mixture; repeat layers. Top with additional grated Parmesan cheese. Bake at 375° for 30-40 minutes. Let stand 10 minutes before serving. If desired, pass Parmesan cheese.

Yield: 8-10 servings.

Simply delicious!

Tonnarelli

½ pound fresh mushrooms, sliced
2 tablespoons butter or margarine
1 (8-ounce) package kluski (very
  fine egg noodles)

1 cup cooked ham, slivered
1 cup frozen peas, thawed
½ cup Parmesan cheese, grated

Sauté mushrooms in butter or margarine. Cook noodles according to package directions and drain. Combine mushrooms, ham, peas, and cheese with the hot noodles. Toss until all ingredients are well coated with the cheese. Serve immediately.

Yield: 4 servings.

A good way to use leftover ham. Recipe may be doubled or tripled for a popular buffet dish.

Lasagna

1 pound lean Italian sausage
1 clove garlic, minced
1 tablespoon basil
1½ teaspoons salt
1 (16-ounce) can tomatoes
2 (6-ounce) cans tomato paste
1 (10-ounce) package lasagna
  noodles
2 eggs, beaten

3 cups Ricotta or cottage cheese
½ cup Parmesan or Romano cheese,
  grated
2 tablespoons parsley flakes
1 teaspoon salt
½ teaspoon pepper
1 pound mozzarella cheese, thinly
  sliced

Brown meat slowly and drain well. Add garlic, basil, salt, tomatoes, and tomato paste. Simmer uncovered 30 minutes, stirring occasionally. Cook noodles according to package directions. Drain. To beaten eggs, add Ricotta cheese, Parmesan cheese, parsley, salt, and pepper. In a 9 x 13-inch baking dish layer ingredients: one-half of the noodles, one-half of the Ricotta mixture, one-half of the sliced mozzarella, and one-half of the tomato sauce. Repeat layers. Bake at 375° for 30 minutes. Let stand 10 minutes before serving.

Yield: 8-10 servings.

Stew-Ghetti

1 (15½-ounce) jar homestyle
  spaghetti sauce
1 (2½-3 pound) chicken, cut-up and
  skinned
6 ounces fresh mushrooms, sliced
¾ cup water
1 large onion, thinly sliced

1 green pepper, sliced
2 cloves garlic, minced
1 teaspoon dried basil
1 medium zucchini, sliced
Salt to taste
1 (8-ounce) package spaghetti,
  cooked and drained

Combine spaghetti sauce, chicken, mushrooms, water, onion, green pepper, garlic, and basil in a heavy Dutch oven. Simmer covered for 30 minutes. Remove chicken; debone and cube. Return to pan. Add zucchini and simmer 5 minutes. Salt to taste. Spoon over cooked spaghetti.

Yield: 4 servings.

Cheese Lasagna

1 medium onion, chopped
3 small cloves garlic, minced
2 tablespoons oil
1 (28-ounce) can peeled tomatoes, chopped
2 (6-ounce) cans tomato paste
½ cup water
1 teaspoon salt
½ teaspoon oregano leaves, crushed

½ teaspoon dried basil
¼ teaspoon crushed red pepper
1 (8-ounce) box lasagna noodles
2 (15 or 16-ounce) cartons Ricotta cheese
1 (16-ounce) package mozzarella cheese, sliced
1 cup regular wheat germ
½ cup Parmesan cheese, grated

Sauté onion and garlic in oil until onion is tender. Add tomatoes, tomato paste, water, salt, oregano, basil, and red pepper. Simmer uncovered for 30 minutes. Cook noodles according to package directions. Drain. Cover bottom of a 13 x 9 x 2-inch pan with one-third of noodles. Spread one-third of Ricotta cheese over noodles. Arrange one-third of mozzarella cheese on top. Sprinkle one-third cup of wheat germ over mozzarella. Spread with one-third of tomato sauce mixture. Repeat layers two more times. Sprinkle Parmesan cheese on top. Bake at 375° for 25-30 minutes. Let stand 10 minutes before cutting.

Yield: 8-10 servings.

A wonderful meatless dish.

Pasta on the Side

1 (8-ounce) package spinach noodles
2 cups sour cream

2 (6-ounce) packages sliced natural Swiss cheese
Garlic salt to taste

Cook noodles according to package directions. Drain and rinse in very hot water; drain thoroughly. In greased 2-quart casserole, alternate layers of noodles, sour cream, and Swiss cheese. Sprinkle with garlic salt. Repeat layers. Bake in preheated 300° oven until cheese is melted.

Yield: 8 servings.

Mexican Lasagne

1 pound ground beef
1 (15-ounce) can tomato sauce
1 package taco seasoning mix
1 (4-ounce) can green chiles,
 drained and chopped
5 flour tortillas
1 (16-ounce) can refried beans
Guacamole (recipe follows)
1 small sweet onion, chopped

½ cup ripe olives, sliced
1 cup Monterey Jack cheese, grated
½ cup medium Cheddar cheese,
 grated
1 jalapeño pepper, seeded and
 sliced
Sour cream
Taco sauce

Brown ground beef, stirring to crumble. Drain well, and set aside. Combine tomato sauce and taco seasoning mix in a small saucepan. Bring to a boil, reduce heat, and simmer for 10 minutes. Remove from heat and reserve ¼ cup sauce mixture. Add ground beef and chiles to remaining sauce. Place a tortilla in a greased 8 or 9-inch cake pan or pie pan. Place ½ of the meat mixture on the tortilla. Layer as follows: another tortilla and refried beans; another tortilla and guacamole, chopped onion, sliced olives, and ½ of the Monterey Jack cheese; another tortilla and the remaining meat mixture. Top with a tortilla and ¼ cup reserved sauce. Sprinkle with remaining cheese. Bake at 350° for 40 minutes uncovered. Garnish with jalapeño pepper, if desired. Serve with sour cream and taco sauce. Cut into wedges to serve.

Guacamole

1 medium avocado
3 green onions, chopped
1 tablespoon lemon juice

4 tablespoons sour cream
2 tablespoons taco sauce

Mash avocado with a fork. Stir in chopped onion, lemon juice, sour cream, and taco sauce. Cover and refrigerate until needed.

Yield: 4 to 6 servings.

Chicken Vegetable Linguine

2 chicken breasts, poached and
   julienned
2 carrots, sliced
2 unpeeled zucchini, sliced
1 cup fresh mushrooms, sliced
2 medium tomatoes, cut into
   wedges

1 (8-ounce) package linguine
4 tablespoons butter
¾ cup Parmesan cheese, grated
1 egg, slightly beaten
1 (8-ounce) package Monterey Jack
   cheese, grated

Remove skin from poached chicken and cut in julienne strips. Arrange carrots in a vegetable steamer over 1 inch of boiling salted water; put zucchini on top of carrots, then layer mushrooms and tomatoes. Steam until vegetables are tender-crisp. Cook linguine according to package directions. Drain well. Toss with butter. Blend Parmesan cheese and egg; gently toss with linguine. Spread linguine in 2-quart buttered casserole. Layer steamed vegetables and chicken over linguine. Top with Monterey Jack cheese. Bake at 350° until cheese is melted and bubbly.

Yield: 4-6 servings.

Linguine with Clam Sauce I

½ cup butter
1 cup onion, chopped
4 cloves garlic, minced
½ cup parsley, chopped
2 (6½-ounce) cans minced clams
   with juice

1 (8-ounce) bottle clam juice
½-1 cup dry white wine
1 teaspoon salt
1 teaspoon dried basil or marjoram
Freshly ground pepper to taste
1 (16-ounce) package linguine

In a large Dutch oven, sauté onion, garlic, and parsley in melted butter until onion is almost tender. Add clams with juice, bottled clam juice, and wine. Stir in salt, basil, and pepper. Simmer covered. Cook linguine according to package directions. Drain. Serve clam sauce over linguine in shallow bowls.

Yield: 4-6 servings.

A crisp green salad and French bread accompany this pasta meal deliciously.

Linguine with Clam Sauce II

½ cup olive oil
2 anchovies
2 cloves garlic, minced
2 (6½-ounce) cans minced clams
    with juice
¼ cup fresh parsley, chopped

Fresh basil to taste
¼ cup black olives, chopped
Dash of red pepper
Salt to taste
1 (16-ounce) package linguine
4 ounces Romano cheese, grated

In a skillet, sauté anchovies in olive oil until they turn to liquid. Add garlic and sauté until tender. Add clams with juice, parsley, basil, olives, red pepper, and salt. Simmer on low heat until hot. (Clams will toughen if cooked too long.) Cook linguine according to package directions. Drain, rinse, and place in a large bowl. Toss with clam sauce and top with Romano cheese. Serve immediately.

Yield: 4-6 servings.

Linguine Primavera

1 cup Ricotta cheese
½ cup Romano cheese, grated
1 teaspoon salt
1 medium cauliflower, cut into
    florets
1 bunch fresh broccoli, cut into
    florets
1 cup olive oil

6 cloves garlic, minced
1 pound fresh mushrooms, thickly
    sliced
2 teaspoons salt
½ teaspoon crushed red pepper
1 (16-ounce) package linguine
Romano cheese, freshly grated

Combine cheeses and set aside. Place cauliflower and broccoli in a large pot of salted water. Bring to a boil and cook uncovered for about 7 minutes or until vegetables are just tender. Remove vegetables, reserving the liquid. Heat olive oil and garlic in a large skillet. Stir in mushrooms, salt, and red pepper. Sauté 5 minutes. Stir in broccoli and cauliflower and cook 10 minutes. (May need to add some of cooking liquid if vegetable mixture is dry.) Cook linguine according to package directions, using reserved liquid. Drain. Stir in hot vegetable mixture. Sprinkle with Romano cheese and serve immediately.

Yield: 6 servings.

Linguine with Vegetables

1 cup Ricotta cheese
½ cup Parmesan cheese, grated
1 teaspoon salt
1 small head cauliflower, cut into pieces
1 bunch of broccoli, cut into pieces

1 pound fresh mushrooms, sliced
1 clove garlic, minced
½ cup olive oil
Salt and pepper to taste
1 (16-ounce) package linguine
¼ cup Parmesan cheese, grated

Combine Ricotta and ½ cup Parmesan cheeses, set aside. Steam cauliflower and broccoli in salted water until vegetables are tender-crisp, about 7 minutes. Drain. Sauté mushrooms and garlic in oil; add salt and pepper. Cook linguine according to package directions. Drain. Combine cheeses with steamed vegetables and mushrooms. Gently toss with linguine. Place in a 9 x 13-inch casserole and top with ¼ cup grated Parmesan cheese. Bake at 350° for 20 minutes.

Yield: 6 servings.

For a colorful variation, substitute spinach egg noodles for linguine.

Linguine Con Piselli

2 tablespoons unsalted butter
1 tablespoon olive oil
1 large onion, finely chopped
½ pound prosciutto, julienned
2 tablespoons parsley, chopped
2 tablespoons fresh basil, chopped (or 2 teaspoons dried basil)
Pinch of nutmeg
½ teaspoon salt

½ teaspoon white pepper
1 cup strong chicken broth
1 cup heavy cream
1 (16-ounce) package linguine
1 (10-ounce) package frozen tiny peas, thawed and drained
¾-1 cup Parmesan cheese, freshly grated

In a large skillet, heat butter and oil together. Add onion and prosciutto and cook over medium heat until soft (about 5-7 minutes). Add parsley, basil, nutmeg, salt, and pepper. Stir in chicken broth and cook until smooth. Add cream; continue to cook until slightly thickened. Cook linguine according to package directions. Drain. Toss pasta with peas. Stir in prosciutto mixture. Sprinkle with Parmesan cheese and serve immediately.

Yield: 4-6 servings.

Main Dish Pasta

3 cups thin spaghetti, broken into
  pieces
2 tablespoons butter
½ pound fresh mushrooms, sliced
¾-1 cup celery, sliced
1½ cups cooked ham, cubed
3 cups cooked chicken or turkey,
  cubed

1 teaspoon salt
¼ teaspoon pepper
2 cups sour cream
2 cups small curd cottage cheese
2 cups sharp Cheddar cheese,
  grated

Cook spaghetti according to package directions. Drain and set aside. Melt butter and sauté mushrooms and celery. Mix with ham, chicken, salt, and pepper. Stir in sour cream and cottage cheese. Combine with spaghetti and toss well. Pour into a greased 13 x 9 x 2-inch casserole and top with Cheddar cheese. Bake at 350° for 30 minutes.

Yield: 8-10 servings.

Delicious combination of leftover ham, chicken or turkey!

Pasta Con Pescal

1 (16-ounce) package linguine
2-3 cloves garlic, minced
1 cup fresh mushrooms, sliced
1 cup unsalted butter, divided
1 large fresh tomato, peeled,
  seeded, and chopped

1 cup cooked lobster, chopped
1 cup cooked shrimp, chopped
1 cup crabmeat, flaked
2 tablespoons parsley, chopped

Cook pasta according to package directions. Drain. In large skillet, sauté garlic and mushrooms in 2 tablespoons butter until golden, about 3 minutes. Add tomato and cook about 1 minute. Add lobster, shrimp, crabmeat, and remaining butter. Heat until butter has melted. Pour sauce over hot, cooked pasta and toss well. Garnish with chopped parsley.

Yield: 6 servings.

Canneloni

Pasta

2 cups flour, unsifted	1 teaspoon salt
3 eggs	2 tablespoons salt
4 tablespoons water	

Place flour into a large bowl and make a well in center. Break eggs into center. Combine water and 1 teaspoon salt and mix thoroughly with flour. Form into a ball. On a lightly floured board, knead until dough is smooth and pliable, about 10 minutes. Let rest 20 minutes. Prepare pasta for cooking by dividing dough into 12-16 parts. On a lightly floured surface, roll each part into a 4½-inch square. Bring 4 quarts of water to a boil and add 2 tablespoons salt. Drop pasta squares, 3 at a time, into boiling water. The pasta will sink to the bottom then rise to the top. Cook for 3 minutes longer after pasta rises. Remove with slotted spoon and place on wooden board to dry.

Filling

1 pound ground chuck	¼ cup tomato paste
2 cloves garlic, crushed	½ cup dry sherry
2 tablespoons margarine	1 tablespoon salt
¼ cup purple onion, chopped	½ teaspoon thyme leaves
1 tablespoon parsley, chopped	1 teaspoon oregano
2 (8-ounce) cans tomato sauce	Dash red pepper (optional)

Combine ground chuck with garlic. Sauté onion and parsley in margarine until onion is golden, about 5 minutes. Stir in beef and garlic; cook until lightly brown. Drain. Add tomato sauce and tomato paste to this mixture. Stir in sherry, salt, thyme, oregano, and red pepper; cook until filling mixture is thickened, 15-20 minutes. Set aside.

Continued . . .

Sauce

⅓ cup olive oil
1½ cups purple onion, chopped
1 clove garlic, crushed
1 (2-pound 3-ounce) can Italian
    tomatoes
¼ cup tomato paste
2 tablespoons parsley, chopped

1 tablespoon salt
1 tablespoon sugar
1 teaspoon oregano
1 teaspoon basil
⅛ teaspoon black pepper
1½ cups water
½ cup Parmesan cheese, grated

Heat oil in a 2½-quart saucepan. Add onion and garlic and cook until golden, about 5 minutes. Stir in tomatoes, tomato paste, parsley, salt, sugar, oregano, basil, pepper, and water. Continue cooking, stirring constantly until sauce begins to boil. Reduce heat and simmer 1 hour. Place 2 tablespoons of filling in center of each pasta square. Roll up square. Arrange canneloni in a single layer in a greased 8 x 12-inch baking pan. Cover with half of the sauce and bake in a preheated 400° oven for 10 minutes. Add remaining sauce and top with Parmesan cheese. Cook 10 minutes longer.

Yield: 8 servings.

A sensational homemade pasta dish! Involve the family or friends in its preparation on a rainy weekend.

Spaghetti with Meatballs

Tomato Sauce

¾ cup onion, chopped
1 clove garlic, minced
3 tablespoons vegetable oil
2 (16-ounce) cans tomatoes, cut up
2 (6-ounce) cans tomato paste
2 cups water

1 teaspoon sugar
1½ teaspoons salt
½ teaspoon pepper
1½ teaspoons oregano, crushed
1 bay leaf

Sauté onions and garlic in oil until tender. Add tomatoes, tomato paste, water, sugar, salt, pepper, oregano, and bay leaf. Simmer, stirring occasionally for 1 hour. Remove bay leaf.

Meatballs

4 bread slices
½ cup water
2 eggs, beaten
1 pound lean ground beef
¼ cup Parmesan cheese, grated

2 tablespoons parsley, chopped
1 teaspoon salt
¼ teaspoon oregano, crushed
Dash pepper
2 tablespoons oil
1 (16-ounce) package spaghetti

Soak bread in water for 3 minutes. Add beaten eggs. Mix in ground beef, Parmesan cheese, parsley, salt, oregano, and pepper. Form mixture into small balls. Brown slowly in oil. Drain and add to sauce. Simmer meatballs and sauce, loosely covered, for an additional 30 minutes. Serve over spaghetti cooked according to package directions.

Yield: 8 servings.

Try these meatballs in a sandwich topped with mozzarella cheese!

Four Cheese Spaghetti

1 (12-ounce) package spaghetti
1½ teaspoons flour
3 tablespoons butter, melted
1 cup half and half
¾ cup Provolone cheese, shredded
¾ cup Swiss cheese, shredded
¾ cup Edam or Gouda cheese,
   shredded

¼ cup Parmesan cheese, grated
½ teaspoon salt
⅛ teaspoon white pepper
1 tablespoon fresh parsley or basil,
   chopped

Cook spaghetti according to package directions; drain, and keep warm. In a saucepan, stir flour into butter; cook over low heat, stirring constantly until bubbly. Gradually add half and half, stirring until smooth and thickened. Add cheeses, salt, and pepper to white sauce. Stir constantly until cheeses melt. Pour cheese mixture over spaghetti and toss well. Sprinkle with parsley. Serve immediately.

Yield: 6-8 servings.

Spaghetti à la Carbonara

3 eggs, slightly beaten
1 cup Parmesan cheese, grated and
   divided
½ cup whipping cream
¼ cup fresh parsley, chopped
¼ teaspoon dried whole basil

1 clove garlic, crushed
1 (16-ounce) package spaghetti
¼ cup butter
8 strips lean bacon, cooked and
   crumbled

Combine eggs and ½ cup Parmesan cheese in a bowl. Set aside. Heat whipping cream in heavy saucepan until scalded. Stir in parsley, basil, and garlic. Cook spaghetti according to package directions. Drain. Combine spaghetti, egg mixture, whipping cream, and butter. Toss until butter is melted. Sprinkle with bacon and top with remaining Parmesan cheese. Serve immediately.

Yield: 4-6 servings.

Fettuccine Alfredo

1 (16-ounce) package fettuccine
   noodles
½ cup butter
1 cup heavy whipping cream

1 cup sour cream
1 cup Parmesan cheese, grated
½ cup fresh or dried chives, minced

Cook fettuccine according to package directions until tender, but still firm. Drain. While noodles are cooking, melt butter in a medium saucepan. Add heavy cream and cook over medium heat. Reduce heat to low and add sour cream, stirring constantly. Do not allow cream sauce to boil. Toss noodles, cream sauce, Parmesan cheese, and chives until well blended. Serve immediately.

Yield: 6 servings.

Green Chili Pasta

6 strips lean bacon, diced
1 (8-ounce) package vermicelli
1 medium onion, chopped
1 (10½-ounce) can beef broth
1 (16-ounce) can Italian tomatoes,
   chopped

1 (4-ounce) can green chilies,
   chopped
2 tablespoons red wine vinegar
Salt to taste
Pepper to taste
Parmesan cheese, freshly grated

In a Dutch oven, cook bacon until crisp; set aside. Reserve ¼ cup of drippings. Break pasta into 2-inch pieces, about 2 cups, and stir into pan drippings. Add onions and sauté over medium heat, stirring until golden brown. Stir in broth, tomatoes, chilies, and vinegar. Salt and pepper to taste. Cover and simmer about 15 minutes until pasta is tender and most of liquid is absorbed. Sprinkle with bacon and pass the Parmesan cheese.

Yield: 6-8 servings.

Noodles Romanoff

1 (8-ounce) package egg noodles
2 cups sour cream
½ cup Parmesan cheese, grated and
   divided
1 tablespoon chives

1 teaspoon salt
⅛ teaspoon pepper
1 large clove garlic, crushed or ⅛
   teaspoon garlic powder
2 tablespoons butter

Cook noodles according to package directions. While noodles cook, combine sour cream, ¼ cup Parmesan cheese, chives, salt, pepper, and garlic. Drain noodles. Return to pan and add butter to noodles. Fold in sour cream mixture. Arrange on a warm serving platter and sprinkle with the remaining ¼ cup Parmesan cheese. Serve immediately.

Yield: 6-8 servings.

Macaroni and Cheese Supreme

1 (8-ounce) box macaroni
1 pound sharp Cheddar cheese,
   grated
1 (2.5-ounce) jar sliced mushrooms
   with liquid
1 (2-ounce) jar chopped pimentos
   with liquid

1 (10¾-ounce) can cream of
   mushroom soup
1 large onion, chopped
1 cup mayonnaise
Salt and pepper to taste
Crushed cheese crackers

Cook macaroni according to package directions and drain. Stir in grated cheese while macaroni is hot. Add mushrooms, pimentos, mushroom soup, onion, mayonnaise, salt, and pepper. Pour into an 8 x 12-inch baking dish. Top with crushed cheese crackers. Bake at 300° for 45 minutes to 1 hour.

Yield: 8 servings.

Crab Quiche

1 (9-inch) pie shell, unbaked
6 ounces Swiss cheese, shredded
1 (7½-ounce) can white crabmeat,
    drained, or ½ pound fresh
3-4 green onions with tops, minced
3 eggs, beaten

1 cup half and half
¼ teaspoon dry mustard
½ teaspoon lemon rind, grated
½ teaspoon salt
Pinch of mace
¼ - ½ cup slivered almonds

Sprinkle cheese over bottom of pastry shell. Layer crabmeat and green onions. Combine eggs, half and half, mustard, lemon-rind, salt, and mace. Pour over crabmeat and top with almonds. Bake at 350° for 45 minutes-1 hour, or until quiche sets in middle. Let stand about 15 minutes before slicing. Garnish as desired.

Yield: 6 servings.

Golden Shrimp Puff

6 eggs, beaten
3 cups milk
2 tablespoons parsley, minced
¾ teaspoon dry mustard
½ teaspoon salt

10 slices crustless white bread,
    cubed
2 cups sharp cheese, grated
2 cups cooked shrimp, shelled and
    deveined

Combine eggs, milk, parsley, mustard, and salt. Stir in bread cubes, cheese, and shrimp. Pour into a 7½ x 11½-inch baking dish. Bake uncovered 1 hour in a preheated 325° oven, or until center is set.

Yield: 8 servings.

An excellent choice for a late night get together or a brunch.

Bleu Cheese Soufflé

1 tablespoon butter, softened
6 eggs
½ cup heavy cream
1 teaspoon Worcestershire sauce
Dash of Tabasco sauce

¼ teaspoon pepper
Pinch of salt
¼ pound bleu cheese
11 ounces cream cheese

Butter a five cup soufflé dish or five individual baking dishes. Combine eggs, cream, Worcestershire sauce, Tabasco sauce, pepper, and salt into an electric blender. Whirl until smooth. Break bleu cheese into pieces and add each piece to blender. Do the same with the cream cheese. Blend well at high speed for five seconds. Pour into prepared dish. Bake at 375° for 45 minutes to get a soft liquidy center, or 50 minutes for a firm soufflé. (Bake individual soufflés for 15-20 minutes.) Serve immediately.

Yield: 5-6 servings.

Easy to prepare and very impressive to serve!

Chili Cheese Soufflé

1 pound sharp Cheddar cheese
1 pound mild Cheddar cheese
2 (7-ounce) cans green chilies, seeded and chopped

1 pound Monterey Jack cheese, grated
12 eggs, slightly beaten
1 pint sour cream

Grate each of the cheeses, keeping separate. Layer sharp Cheddar cheese in bottom of buttered 2-quart casserole. Layer ½ of the chilies, all of mild Cheddar cheese, and remaining chilies. Top with Monterey Jack cheese. Blend eggs with sour cream and pour over cheese and chilies. Bake at 350° until eggs are set.

Yield: 8 servings.

Canadian Egg Casserole

Cheese Sauce

2 tablespoons margarine
2½ tablespoons flour
2 cups milk
½ teaspoon salt

⅛ teaspoon pepper
4 ounces medium Cheddar cheese,
   shredded

Melt 2 tablespoons margarine over low heat in a saucepan. Blend in flour and cook 1 minute. Gradually add milk. Cook over medium heat until thickened, stirring constantly. Add salt, pepper, and cheese. Stir until cheese is melted and sauce is smooth.

¼ cup fresh mushrooms, sliced
¼ cup green onions, chopped
1 cup Canadian bacon, cubed
3 tablespoons margarine

12 eggs, beaten well
¼ cup margarine, melted
2¼ cups soft breadcrumbs
⅛ teaspoon paprika

Sauté mushrooms, green onions, and Canadian bacon in 3 tablespoons margarine in a large skillet until onion is cooked. Add beaten eggs and stir until softly scrambled. Remove from heat. Pour cheese sauce over egg mixture. Mix carefully. Spoon mixture into a greased 9 x 13-inch casserole. Combine ¼ cup margarine and breadcrumbs. Spread evenly over egg mixture. Sprinkle with paprika. Cover and chill overnight. Uncover and bake at 350° for 30 minutes, or until heated thoroughly.

Yield: 12-15 servings.

Easy Oven Eggs

8 eggs
1 cup sour cream
1 cup Cheddar cheese, shredded

Salt and pepper, to taste
1 tablespoon butter, melted

Beat eggs well and blend in sour cream. Stir in shredded cheese. Add salt and pepper. Pour into buttered 9 x 9-inch baking dish. Drizzle melted butter over top. Bake in preheated 325° oven on middle rack for 20 minutes or until center is almost firm.

Yield: 4-6 servings.

Ham Broccoli Strata

12 slices crustless white bread,
  cubed
1½ cups fresh broccoli, cooked,
  drained, and chopped
2 cups ham, diced

6 eggs
3 cups milk
1 tablespoon onion, diced
¼ teaspoon dry mustard
3 cups Cheddar cheese, grated

Spread bread in a 12 x 8 x 2-inch greased casserole. Layer cooked broccoli and top with ham. Combine eggs, milk, onion, mustard, and cheese. Pour over layered casserole. Cover and refrigerate overnight. Bake at 325° for one hour, uncovered.

Yield: 10 servings.

Delicious for brunch!

Country Grits and Sausage

2 cups water
½ teaspoon salt
½ cup quick grits, uncooked
4 cups extra sharp Cheddar cheese,
  shredded
4 eggs, beaten

1 cup milk
½ teaspoon dried thyme
⅛ teaspoon garlic salt
2 pounds mild pork sausage,
  cooked, drained, and crumbled

Bring water and salt to boil. Stir in grits. Return water to boil; reduce heat. Cook 4 minutes, stirring occasionally. Combine cooked grits and cheese. Stir until cheese melts. Combine eggs, milk, thyme, and garlic salt; mix well. Add a large spoonful of hot grits mixture to egg mixture and stir well. Blend in remaining egg mixture with the grits. Add sausage and mix well. Pour into an 8 x 12-inch baking dish and refrigerate overnight. Let stand 10 minutes before baking. Bake at 350° for 55 minutes.

Yield: 8 servings.

Make this delicious casserole the night before and pop it in the oven first thing in the morning.

Rice Casserole Extraordinare

1 (6-ounce) package long grain and
   wild rice
½ onion, chopped
1 tablespoon butter
¼ teaspoon garlic powder

2 teaspoons Worcestershire sauce
1 tablespoon parsley, chopped
1½ cups chicken broth
⅔ cup dry white wine
1 cup Cheddar cheese, cubed

Sauté rice and onion with butter until golden brown. Add garlic powder, Worcestershire sauce, parsley, chicken broth, and wine. Heat to boiling. Stir in cheese. Pour into a greased 1½-quart casserole. Bake in a preheated 350° oven for 2 hours covered tightly. Check after 1½ hours, and add more liquid if necessary.

Yield: 6 servings.

A rich rice casserole that is delicious with smoked turkey!

Fruited Rice

½ cup raisins
½ cup dried or canned apricots
¼ cup water
3 tablespoons brown sugar

¼ cup green onions, chopped
3 cups hot, cooked rice
Butter

In saucepan combine raisins, apricots, water, and brown sugar; cover and simmer 5 minutes. Drain. Add cooked rice along with green onions. Dot with butter and serve.

Yield: 4-6 servings.

Delicious accompaniment with chicken!

Orange Rice

1 cup orange juice	1 tablespoon orange peel
1 cup water	1 teaspoon salt
2 tablespoons butter	¾ cup uncooked white rice

Combine orange juice, water, butter, orange peel, and salt. Bring to a boil. Add rice. Cover and cook for 25 minutes on low heat until liquid is absorbed.

Yield: 4 servings.

Delicious with baked ham or wild game!

Rice and Sausage Supreme

1 pound mild, bulk sausage	½ cup green pepper, chopped
½ cup onion, chopped	1 (10¾-ounce) can mushroom soup
½ cup celery, chopped	1 (10½-ounce) can consommé soup
1 (8-ounce) can water chestnuts, diced with liquid	1 cup uncooked rice
	Toasted almonds

Brown sausage and onion. Drain well. Combine celery, water chestnuts and liquid, green pepper, mushroom soup, consommé, and rice. Pour into a greased 2-quart casserole with lid. Top with almonds. Bake at 350° for 2 hours, covered.

Yield: 6 servings.

Fried Rice

3 cups uncooked rice	¼ teaspoon garlic powder
6 tablespoons oil	2 onions, chopped
5 eggs, beaten	2 cups celery, sliced diagonally
6 tablespoons soy sauce	Salt to taste

Cook rice according to package directions. Heat oil in large skillet; pour in eggs. As they harden, cut up eggs with two knives. Add soy sauce and garlic powder. Stir in rice, onions, celery, and salt. Stir over low heat 3 to 5 minutes, until well-blended.

Yield: 12-14 servings.

Spicy Rice Casserole

1 cup uncooked rice
2 (3-ounce) cans green chilies,
  diced
3 cups sour cream
Salt to taste

Pepper to taste
¾ pound Monterey Jack cheese, cut
  into strips
1½ cups Cheddar cheese, grated

Cook rice according to package directions. Combine chilies, sour cream, salt, and pepper. Layer rice, sour cream mixture, then Monterey Jack strips into a 9 x 13-inch buttered casserole. Top with Cheddar cheese. Cover. Bake in a preheated oven at 350° for 30 minutes. Uncover last few minutes of cooking.

Yield: 6 servings.

Vegetable Rice Medley

1 (6-ounce) package long grain and
  wild rice
1 cup water
1½ cups chicken broth
4 tablespoons margarine

1½ cups fresh mushrooms, sliced
1 cup carrots, shredded
¼ cup onions, sliced
¼ cup parsley, chopped

Combine rice mixture, water, broth, and margarine. Bring to a boil. Stir in mushrooms, carrots, onions, and parsley. Cover and cook for 25 minutes on low heat until liquid is absorbed.

Yield: 6 servings.

Ranch Rice

½ cup margarine
1 cup uncooked rice
1 (10½-ounce) can beef consommé

1 (10½-ounce) can onion soup
1 (4-ounce) can sliced mushrooms

Melt margarine and stir in rice. Add beef consommé, onion soup, and mushrooms. Place in a 2-quart casserole. Bake at 350° for 1 hour uncovered.

Yield: 4 servings.

ENTREES

Butterfly Leg of Lamb on the Grill

1 (5-pound) butterfly leg of lamb
2 tablespoons prepared mustard
½ teaspoon salt
¼ teaspoon pepper
4 tablespoons brown sugar

2 tablespoons soy sauce
2 tablespoons olive oil
¼ clove garlic, crushed
½ cup lemon juice

Combine mustard, salt, pepper, brown sugar, soy sauce, oil, garlic, and lemon juice. Mix well. (You may wish to double the sauce.) Brush lamb with sauce and grill over medium to hot coals. Turn meat frequently and brush with sauce often. After about 30 minutes, meat should be rare. Baste with sauce, cover with foil, and allow to rest for 10 minutes before carving meat across grain.

Yield: 6 to 8 servings.

Ask butcher to butterfly lamb. Recipe may be cooked in a 450° oven for 35 minutes.

Veal Marsala

3 pounds veal, thinly sliced
⅔ cup Marsala wine
2 tablespoons parsley
Salt to taste
Pepper to taste

Garlic to taste
3 tablespoons butter
1 cup fresh mushrooms, sliced
6-8 slices Swiss cheese
Toast points

Marinate veal in wine, parsley, salt, pepper, and garlic for several hours. Drain veal and dry with paper towels, reserving marinade. Melt butter and sauté mushrooms. Remove mushrooms and sauté veal 2 minutes on each side. Pour reserved marinade over veal; add mushrooms. Top each slice of veal with a slice of cheese and cover until melted. Serve immediately over toast points.

Yield: 6 to 8 servings.

An electric skillet simplifies the preparation of this exceptional entreé.

Veal Scaloppine

1½ pounds veal slices
3 tablespoons flour
1 teaspoon salt
½ teaspoon pepper, freshly ground
3 tablespoons oil
½ cup mushrooms, sliced

1 clove garlic
1 lemon, sliced
¼ cup water
½ cup dry wine
Parsley to garnish
Hot cooked buttered noodles

Place each slice of veal between 2 pieces of wax paper. Pound each slice until paper thin. Combine flour, salt, and pepper. Dip veal into flour mixture and reserve. Sauté mushrooms in oil over medium heat. Add garlic and continue to sauté. Set mushrooms aside. In same skillet, brown veal on both sides. Remove garlic. Add mushrooms and lemon slices. Combine water and wine; and pour over veal. Simmer until meat is tender. Serve with noodles and garnish with parsley.

Yield: 4 servings.

Veal Paprikash

1 medium onion, chopped
3 tablespoons butter
1 pound veal steaks or cutlets,
   cubed
1 (10¾-ounce) can chicken broth
1 teaspoon paprika

Salt to taste
1 (8-ounce) can mushrooms
1 cup sour cream
Hot cooked rice or noodles
Parsley

Sauté onion in 1 tablespoon butter. Remove from skillet. Dredge veal in flour; brown in 2 tablespoons butter. Return onions to skillet; add broth and cook covered over low heat for 30 minutes. Add paprika, salt, and mushrooms. Cook 30 minutes longer. Stir in sour cream and serve immediately with parslied noodles or rice.

Yield: 4 servings.

Beef Tenderloin

1 (3 to 3½-pound) beef tenderloin,
  trimmed
8 tablespoons butter, softened

Worcestershire sauce, to taste
Garlic salt to taste
Seasoned salt to taste

Rub both sides of meat with butter. Sprinkle with Worcestershire sauce. Place in a shallow pan and season on one side with garlic salt and seasoned salt. Bake at 350° for 10 minutes, then broil for 5 minutes. Remove meat from oven and turn to other side. Season with garlic salt and seasoned salt. Bake, again, at 350° for 10 minutes and again, broil for 5 minutes. Remove meat from oven and wrap meat in foil with shiny side of foil on inside. Meat will be rare. Allow to rest 15 minutes before slicing.

Yield: 8 servings.

Stuffed Tenderloin of Beef

4 tablespoons butter
2 green onions, finely chopped
1 cup mushrooms, chopped
1 clove garlic, pressed
5 sprigs parsley, chopped
1 (3 to 3½-pound) filet of beef,
  trimmed

3 tablespoons bleu cheese,
  crumbled
Salt and pepper to taste
3 tablespoons butter, melted

Melt 4 tablespoons butter and sauté onions, mushrooms, garlic, and parsley. Set aside. Slit the tenderloin and stuff with the sautéed vegetables and bleu cheese. Close slit with toothpicks or number 8 thread. Season with salt and pepper; brush with melted butter. Grill over hot coals until beef is brown on outside. Remove to kitchen and loosely tent with foil. Allow to rest 1 hour or longer. Before serving, insert meat thermometer and cook at 350° until tenderloin is done as desired.

Yield: 8 servings.

Early in the day, grill the meat outside for a great charcoal flavor. Do the final cooking just before guests arrive. The result will be a delicious and impressive entreé.

Stuffed Flank Steak

¼ cup butter
2 tablespoons onion, chopped
3 tablespoons celery, chopped
¼ teaspoon salt
Dash of cayenne pepper
2 teaspoons parsley, chopped
1 cup stuffing mix or breadcrumbs

1 egg, slightly beaten
1 (1½-2 pound) flank steak
3 tablespoons vegetable oil
2 tablespoons flour
1 cup water
1 cup V-8 juice

In a large skillet, melt butter and lightly sauté onion and celery. Add salt, pepper, parsley, stuffing mix, and egg. Cut a pocket in the flank steak and fill with stuffing. Roll up steak and tie with poultry string. Heat vegetable oil in skillet. Sear steak on all sides and place in a deep casserole. Stir the flour, water, and V-8 juice into the pan drippings. Cook until slightly thickened. Pour over steak. Cover and bake at 250° for 1½ hours. Remove string. Slice and serve with gravy.

Yield: 6 servings.

Teriyaki Flank Steak on the Grill

1 (1¾ to 2-pound) flank steak
¾ cup vegetable oil
¼ cup soy sauce
¼ cup honey

2 tablespoons onion, chopped
2 tablespoons cider vinegar
1 clove garlic, minced
1½ teaspoon ground ginger

Place steak in a shallow pan. Mix together oil, soy sauce, honey, onion, vinegar, garlic, and ginger. Pour over steak and marinate in refrigerator 4 hours or over-night. Grill 5 inches from hot coals. For rare, cook 4 minutes on each side. Use marinade for basting. Slice thinly across grain.

Yield: 4 to 6 servings.

Marinated Eye of Round

1 (5-pound) eye of round
1 cup vegetable oil
½ cup vinegar
2 tablespoons seasoned salt

1 teaspoon tenderizer
1 tablespoon Worcestershire sauce
2 tablespoons onion, minced

Combine oil, vinegar, salt, tenderizer, Worcestershire sauce, and onion. Marinate meat in mixture for 48 hours in refrigerator. Bake uncovered at 450° for 30 minutes. Turn oven off and continue cooking roast for 2 hours. Meat will be cooked to medium. Serve warm or cold.

Yield: 10-12 servings.

Oriental Beef and Snow Peas

1 pound round steak
5 tablespoons soy sauce, divided
1 tablespoon sherry
4 teaspoons cornstarch
½ cup vegetable oil, divided

1 cup fresh snow peas, or 1
    (6-ounce) package frozen
1 clove garlic, crushed
¾ teaspoon sugar
Hot cooked rice

Cut meat into slices ¼ inch thick and 2 inches long. Combine 1 tablespoon soy sauce, sherry, and cornstarch; stir until cornstarch is dissolved. Coat beef with soy sauce mixture. Heat 6 tablespoons oil over high heat in wok or skillet. Add meat and stir fry until meat is browned. Remove meat and set aside. Pour remaining 2 tablespoons oil into wok, and stir fry snow peas over high heat 2 minutes. Add meat, garlic, remaining soy sauce, and sugar to skillet or wok; cook until thickened and bubbly. Serve over rice.

Yield: 4 servings.

Beef Burgundy

1½ pounds round steak
2 tablespoons vegetable oil
1 (16-ounce) can tomatoes, chopped
½ cup Burgundy wine
1 beef bouillon cube
1½ teaspoons salt
½ teaspoon basil

¼ teaspoon pepper
¼ teaspoon garlic salt
1 bay leaf
12 small whole white onions, peeled
6 medium carrots, peeled and cut
   diagonally into 1-inch slices
Hot cooked egg noodles

Cut steak into 1-inch cubes and brown in oil in a 3-quart Dutch oven, covered. Add tomatoes, wine, bouillon cube, salt, basil, pepper, garlic salt, and bay leaf. Cover and simmer 1 hour. Add onions and carrots. Replace cover and simmer 1 hour, or until vegetables and meat are tender. Remove bay leaf and serve over egg noodles.

Yield: 6 servings.

Glazed Corned Beef

1 (3½ to 4-pound) corned beef
1 medium onion, quartered
3 peppercorns
5 sprigs parsley, or 1 tablespoon
   dried

1 bay leaf
¼ cup prepared mustard
1½ teaspoons dry mustard
½ cup dark brown sugar

Place corned beef in a large Dutch oven. Add onion, peppercorns, parsley, and bay leaf. Cover with water. Simmer 1½-2 hours, covered. Remove from water and place in a baking dish. Combine prepared mustard and dry mustard. Spread mustards on corned beef, covering completely. Dredge beef in brown sugar, covering all sides. Bake at 350° for 30-45 minutes.

Yield: 4-6 servings.

Serve with steamed cabbage and glazed carrots.

Sweet and Sour Beef Stew

1½ pounds sirloin, cut into 1-inch cubes
2 tablespoons cooking oil
2 medium carrots, shredded (1 cup)
2 medium onions, sliced (1 cup)
1 (15-ounce) can tomato sauce
½ cup water
¼ cup brown sugar, packed
¼ cup vinegar
1 tablespoon Worcestershire sauce
1 teaspoon salt
1 tablespoon cold water
2 teaspoons cornstarch
Cooked yellow rice

In 3-quart saucepan brown meat, half at a time, in hot oil. In same saucepan combine meat, carrots, onions, tomato sauce, ½ cup water, brown sugar, vinegar, Worcestershire sauce, and salt. Cover and cook over low heat until meat is tender, about 1½ hours. Blend 1 tablespoon cold water with cornstarch; add to stew. Cook and stir until thickened and bubbly. Serve stew over yellow rice or noodles. Garnish with carrot curls and parsley.

Yield: 4 to 6 servings.

Company Stew

2 pounds round steak, cubed
4 medium onions, quartered
4-5 stalks celery, sliced
5 carrots, sliced
2 (8-ounce) cans water chestnuts, drained and sliced
1 pound mushrooms, sliced
1 pound green beans
1 (22-ounce) can tomatoes
1 cup Burgundy wine
2 teaspoons salt
2 tablespoons brown sugar
6 tablespoons tapioca

Combine meat, onions, celery, carrots, water chestnuts, mushrooms, beans, tomatoes, wine, salt, brown sugar, and tapioca in a large casserole with a tight fitting lid. Do Not Stir while cooking. Bake at 325° for 4-5 hours.

Yield: 6 servings.

Beef with Sherry

3 pounds stew beef, cut into cubes
2 (10¾-ounce) cans cream of
   mushroom soup
1 (1½-ounce) package onion soup
   mix

¾ cup sherry
Hot cooked rice or noodles

In a large casserole, combine beef, mushroom soup, onion soup mix, and sherry. Cover and bake at 350° for 3 hours. Serve over rice or noodles.

Yield: 6 servings.

Piccadillo

2 onions, chopped
1 green pepper, chopped
½ cup olive oil
1 pound ground beef
3 cloves garlic, minced
¾ teaspoon salt
¼ teaspoon pepper
¼ teaspoon garlic salt

1 (16-ounce) can tomatoes,
   chopped and drained
1 tablespoon brown sugar
¼ cup red wine
½ cup raisins
¼ cup green olives
1 tablespoon capers
Hot cooked rice

Brown onions and green pepper in olive oil. Add ground beef and brown. Add garlic, salt, pepper, and garlic salt. Stir well; add tomatoes, brown sugar, and red wine. Continue stirring until ingredients are blended. Remove from heat until 30 minutes before serving. Stir in raisins, olives, and capers. Simmer on lowest heat. Serve over rice.

Yield: 6 servings.

Recipe doubles easily.

Cheese-Stuffed Meat Roll

2 pounds extra lean ground beef
½ cup Italian style bread crumbs
1 egg
1 teaspoon salt
½ teaspoon pepper

½ teaspoon garlic powder
1 (8-ounce) can tomato sauce
1 (8-ounce) carton Ricotta cheese
4 ounces bleu cheese, crumbled

Combine beef, bread crumbs, egg, salt, pepper, garlic powder, and ½ can tomato sauce in medium bowl. Mix well. On wax paper, shape meat into a rectangle, ½ inch thick. Spread Ricotta cheese and crumbled bleu cheese on meat. Starting with short end, roll up jelly-roll fashion. Seal ends. Place in a shallow baking dish. Bake at 350° for 1 hour. Pour remaining tomato sauce over meat roll last 5 minutes of baking time. Let stand 15 minutes before slicing.

Yield: 6 to 8 servings.

Dutch Meat Loaf

1½ pounds ground beef
1 cup dry bread crumbs
1 medium onion, finely chopped
1½ teaspoons salt
¼ teaspoon pepper
1½ cups tomato sauce, divided

1 cup water
1 tablespoon prepared mustard
2 tablespoons vinegar
2 tablespoons brown sugar
Cooked egg noodles

Combine beef, bread crumbs, onion, salt, pepper, and ½ cup tomato sauce. Press into a 9 x 5 x 3-inch loaf pan. Combine 1 cup tomato sauce, water, mustard, vinegar, and brown sugar. Blend and pour ½ over loaf. Heat remainder for later. Bake at 350° for 1 hour. Let stand 10 minutes and invert on serving platter. Serve with noodles and reserved sauce.

Yield: 6 servings.

Tamale Pie

1 pound ground beef	½ cup water
2 medium onions, chopped	1 tablespoon chili powder
1 clove garlic, minced	1 tablespoon flour
1 whole pimento, chopped	2 tablespoons water
½ medium green pepper, chopped	1 cup ripe olives, chopped
½ cup mushrooms, chopped	2 cups sharp cheese, grated
2 (8-ounce) cans tomato sauce	2 cups corn chips, crushed

Brown beef and add chopped onions, garlic, pimento, green pepper, mushrooms, tomato sauce, ½ cup water, and chili powder. Simmer covered for 20 minutes (green pepper and onions will be slightly crispy). Make paste of 1 tablespoon flour and 2 tablespooons water. Stir into meat mixture and add olives. Layer ½ meat mixture, ½ grated cheese, and ½ crushed corn chips in a casserole dish. Repeat layers, ending with chips. Bake at 350° for 30 to 45 minutes.

Yield: 6 to 8 servings.

This dish is not too spicy and is enjoyed by children as well as adults.

Mushroom Basil Burger

¼ pound mushrooms, chopped	1 teaspoon basil leaves, crumbled
¼ cup onion, minced	¼ teaspoon pepper
1½ teaspoons salt	1½ pounds lean ground beef

Combine mushrooms, onion, salt, basil, pepper, and beef. Shape into 6 patties and grill outside, or broil in oven.

Yield: 6 servings.

Seminole Casserole

1 pound ground beef
¾ cup onion, chopped
1½ teaspoons salt
Pepper to taste
1 teaspoon garlic powder
1 teaspoon thyme
1 teaspoon oregano

½ small bay leaf
1 (16-ounce) can tomatoes
1 (10¾-ounce) can cream of
    mushroom soup
1 cup Minute rice
6 stuffed olives, sliced
½ cup Cheddar cheese, grated

Brown meat. Add onion and cook until tender. Drain thoroughly. Add salt, pepper, garlic powder, thyme, oregano, bay leaf, tomatoes, soup, and rice. Mix in half of the olives. Simmer for 5 minutes. Pour into a 2-quart casserole. Top with cheese and remaining olives. May be frozen at this point and thawed before baking. Bake at 350° for 25 minutes.

Yield: 4-6 servings.

Family Favorite Casserole

8 ounces egg noodles
1 tablespoon butter
1 pound lean ground beef
2 (8-ounce) cans tomato sauce
Salt to taste
8 ounces cottage cheese

8 ounces cream cheese
¼ cup sour cream
⅓ cup onion, minced
¼ cup green pepper, chopped
2 tablespoons butter, melted

Cook noodles and drain. Sauté beef in butter. Stir in tomato sauce. Remove from heat. Salt to taste. Combine cottage cheese, cream cheese, sour cream, onion, and green pepper. Layer in one 3-quart or two 1½-quart casseroles as follows: Noodles, cheese mixture, noodles, melted butter, and beef-tomato mixture. Chill at least 4 hours. Bake at 350° for 35 minutes.

Yield: 8 servings.

Homemade Pizza

Dough

1 package active dry yeast
⅔ cup lukewarm water
2 teaspoons sugar
½ teaspoon salt

1 tablespoon vegetable or olive oil
1½ cups flour
1 cup whole wheat flour
1 teaspoon oil

In the work bowl of a food processor fitted with a metal blade, dissolve yeast in warm water. Add sugar, salt, oil, and 1½ cups flour. Process for 15 seconds. Place work bowl in warm place and allow dough to rise 30 minutes. Add the whole wheat flour and process until a ball of dough forms. Remove dough and knead on floured surface for 1 minute. Lightly oil a 14-inch pizza pan. Roll out dough to fit and place in pan. Pinch a rim around edge.

Pizza Sauce

1 (6-ounce) can tomato paste
⅓ cup water
½ teaspoon garlic salt
2 teaspoons oregano

⅛ teaspoon pepper
1 to 2 tablespoons olive oil
¼ cup parsley, chopped

Combine tomato paste, water, garlic salt, oregano, pepper, olive oil, and parsley. Spread sauce on dough.

Topping

4 ounces mozzarella cheese,
  shredded
1 onion, thinly sliced
1 green pepper, thinly sliced
Fresh mushrooms, sliced

Pitted olives, sliced
Pepperoni, sliced
2 ounces Parmesan cheese, grated
¼ cup parsley, chopped

Sprinkle on mozzarella. Top with onion slices, green pepper slices, mushrooms, olives, and pepperoni. Top with Parmesan and parsley. Bake at 400° for 20 to 25 minutes.

Yield: 1 (14-inch) pizza.

Key West Hash

3 pounds Chorizo sausage, or
   Polish sausage
2 cloves garlic, minced
1 large onion, chopped
1 (16-ounce) can garbanzo beans,
   drained

⅓ cup green pepper, diced
1 (4-ounce) can tomato sauce
Hot cooked rice

Slice sausage and brown in a large skillet. Add garlic, onion, garbanzo beans, green pepper, and tomato sauce. Simmer 45 minutes, adding water if needed. Serve over white rice.

Yield: 6-8 servings.

Southern Baked Ham

1 (5 to 7-pound) cooked ham
¼ cup Dijon mustard
Whole cloves
⅓ cup apricot preserves, or orange
   marmalade

¼ cup maple syrup
1 cup red wine
⅓ cup cola drink
2 tablespoons cider vinegar

Preheat oven to 350°. Line baking pan with foil. Place ham in pan, fat side up; coat with mustard; stud with cloves. Mix preserves and syrup together and spread on ham. Combine wine, cola, and vinegar; pour over ham. Bake at 350° for 1 hour, basting every 15 minutes. Let rest for 15 minutes before serving.

Yield: 6 to 8 servings.

Barbequed Ham Slice

½ cup orange marmalade
2 tablespoons prepared mustard
1 teaspoon Worcestershire sauce

¼ cup water, or white wine
1 (2½ to 3-pound) fully cooked
  center sliced ham, 1-inch thick

Combine orange marmalade, mustard, Worcestershire sauce, and water or wine. Place ham in a shallow glass dish and cover with marinade. Refrigerate at least 1 hour. Remove ham from marinade and place on a heated grill. Cook approximately 30-45 minutes, turning frequently and basting with marinade.

Yield: 6 servings.

Grilled Lemon Ginger Pork Chops

½ cup vegetable oil
¾ cup soy sauce
2 teaspoons garlic powder
1 teaspoon black pepper, coarsely
  ground

1 tablespoon ginger, ground
Grated peel of 1 lemon
6-8 thick pork chops, trimmed

Combine oil, soy sauce, garlic powder, pepper, ginger, and lemon peel for marinade. Pierce pork chops on both sides with a fork. Marinate chops approximately 30 minutes before cooking on grill. Grill chops 8 minutes on one side; turn and grill 8 minutes on the remaining side.

Yield: 6 to 8 servings.

Layered Pork Chop Casserole

6 medium pork chops
5 tablespoons flour
1 teaspoon salt
¼ teaspoon pepper
1 tablespoon margarine
½ cup uncooked rice
6 tablespoons Dijon mustard
1 large onion, sliced

1 green pepper, cut into rings
2 tomatoes, sliced
1 (10½-ounce) can consommé
¼ cup water
½ cup sherry
⅛ teaspoon marjoram
⅛ teaspoon thyme

Trim excess fat from pork chops. Combine flour, salt, and pepper. Dredge chops in flour mixture and brown in margarine. Pour rice into a greased 8 x 11-inch casserole. Place pork chops over rice, and top each chop with 1 tablespoon mustard. Place an onion slice, green pepper ring, and tomato slice on each pork chop. Mix together consommé, water, sherry, marjoram, and thyme. Pour mixture over chops carefully. Cover tightly with foil. Bake at 350° for 1 hour.

Yield: 6 servings.

Marinated Pork Roast

½ cup dry sherry
½ cup soy sauce
2 cloves garlic, minced
1 teaspoon dry mustard

1 teaspoon thyme
1 teaspoon ground ginger
1 (4 to 5 pound) boneless pork loin
   roast

Make marinade by combining sherry, soy sauce, garlic, mustard, thyme, and ginger. Place pork loin in a large glass dish with marinade. Cover and refrigerate 2-3 hours or overnight. Remove roast and place on a rack in a shallow roasting pan. Reserve marinade. Roast pork uncovered at 325° for 3 hours or until meat thermometer reaches 175°. Baste with marinade during last hour of cooking time.

Yield: 8-10 servings

Curried Pork Chops

2 tablespoons butter, melted
1 tablespoon curry powder
4 thinly sliced pork chops

½ cup Cheddar cheese, grated
Chopped parsley
½ cup beer

Combine butter and curry powder in a skillet. Sauté pork chops over medium heat until done. Sprinkle with Cheddar cheese and parsley. Pour beer over chops and place under broiler until cheese melts. Serve immediately.

Yield: 2 servings.

Chinese Spareribs

½ cup dark corn syrup
½ cup pineapple juice
¼ cup soy sauce
2 tablespoons sherry

2 teaspoons ground ginger
¼ teaspoon dry mustard
⅛ teaspoon garlic powder
4 pounds lean spareribs, separated

Combine corn syrup, pineapple juice, soy sauce, sherry, ginger, mustard, and garlic powder. Pour into a large baking dish and add ribs. Cover and marinate overnight. Drain ribs and save marinade. Place in a shallow baking pan and cover with foil. Bake at 350° for 1 hour. Pour off liquid and bake 30 minutes longer uncovered. Baste frequently with marinade.

Yield: 4 servings.

The last 30 minutes of cooking time may be done on the grill.

Oven Barbequed Short Ribs

2 pounds short ribs
½ cup red wine
1 (8-ounce) can tomato sauce
2 tablespoons onion, chopped

1½ teaspoons salt
2 tablespoons wine vinegar
1 tablespoon prepared mustard
Dash of pepper

Trim excess fat from short ribs and rub hot skillet with fat. Brown ribs slowly on all sides; drain off fat. Combine wine, tomato sauce, onion, salt, wine vinegar, mustard, and pepper. Pour over ribs and cover tightly. Bake in a 300° oven for 1½-2 hours, or until meat is tender.

Yield: 4 servings.

Pork Barbecue-North Carolina Style

4 or 5 pound Boston butt, or fresh
  ham
1 large onion, chopped
3 tablespoons brown sugar
2 tablespoons dry mustard
¼ teaspoon red pepper

¼ teaspoon black pepper
1 cup vinegar
1½ cups water
½ cup catsup
½ cup Worcestershire sauce
1 teaspoon salt

Put meat in roaster. Mix onion, brown sugar, mustard, peppers, vinegar, water, catsup, Worcestershire sauce, and salt. Pour mixture over meat. Cover roaster and cook in a 325° oven for 5 to 6 hours or until meat is very tender. When meat is done, allow it and the drippings to cool. (You may wish to refrigerate to hasten the cooling.) Remove all fat and skin from the pork. Skim fat from sauce. Chop all lean meat and reheat in desired amount of sauce. If meat is to be frozen, pack in containers with some of the barbecue sauce. Reheat when ready to use.

Yield: 8 servings.

Tom Pate's Spicy Barbeque Sauce

½ cup butter
4 onions, minced
4 cloves garlic, minced
4 teaspoons Tabasco sauce
4 lemons, juiced and peelings
   grated

2 teaspoons chili powder
4 cups apple cider vinegar
32 ounces catsup
2 pounds brown sugar
1 (5-ounce) bottle Worcestershire
   sauce

Melt butter in saucepan. Sauté onion and garlic until light brown. Add Tabasco, lemon juice and peelings, chili powder, vinegar, catsup, brown sugar, and Worcestershire sauce. Cook over low heat 1 hour, stirring occasionally.

Yield: approximately 8 cups sauce.

Leftover sauce may be stored in refrigerator indefinitely. Always cook meat completely before using sauce.

Tom Pate's Eastern North Carolina Hot Sauce

1 gallon apple cider vinegar
5 ounces crushed red pepper

2 cloves garlic, minced
3-4 tablespoons salt

Mix vinegar, red pepper, garlic, and salt. Serve with any pork barbeque.

Yield: 1 gallon.

When it comes to catering a "pig pickin'," Tom Pate is the authority. Mr. Pate's reputation as one of North Carolina's finest outdoor cooks has reached all the way to Florida.

Barbeque Sauce

⅔ cup catsup
¼ cup apple cider vinegar
⅛ cup Worcestershire sauce
2 tablespoons brown sugar

Dash Tabasco sauce
Dash garlic powder
¼ teaspoon black pepper, coarsely
  ground

Mix catsup, vinegar, Worcestershire sauce, sugar, Tabasco sauce, garlic powder, and black pepper in saucepan. Simmer 20 minutes.

Yield: Approximately 1 cup.

Teriyaki Sauce

½ cup soy sauce
½ cup sugar
2 tablespoons sherry

1 small garlic clove, minced
1-inch piece ginger, crushed

Combine soy sauce, sugar, sherry, garlic, and ginger.

Yield: 1 cup.

Use as a marinade for beef, pork, or poultry.

Chicken and Artichoke Hearts

4 large chicken breasts, skinned,
  boned, and pounded
⅓ cup flour
5 tablespoons butter
10-12 fresh mushrooms, sliced
1 (15-ounce) can artichoke hearts,
  rinsed, drained, and halved
½ cup chicken broth
¼ cup white wine
Juice of ½ lemon or to taste
¼ teaspoon salt
⅛ teaspoon pepper

Dredge chicken in flour. Heat butter in skillet. Sauté chicken until golden brown on all sides and cooked through. Transfer to heated platter. Sauté mushrooms in skillet for 2 minutes. Stir in artichoke hearts, broth, wine, lemon juice, salt, and pepper. Cook over medium heat, stirring occasionally, until sauce is reduced slightly. Return chicken to skillet and warm through. Serve immediately.

Yield: 4 servings.

Veal scallops may be substituted for chicken.

Citrus Center Chicken

4-6 chicken breasts, skinned
Lemon-pepper seasoning
2 fresh oranges
1 cup sugar
½ teaspoon salt
½ cup white vinegar
¾ cup orange juice
2 teaspoons cornstarch

Sprinkle chicken with lemon-pepper and place in a single layer in a greased 9 x 13-inch baking dish. Grate 3 tablespoons orange peel and reserve. From the same orange, squeeze juice over chicken. In saucepan combine sugar, salt, vinegar, ¾ cup orange juice, and grated peel. Bring to a boil over medium heat, stirring often. Remove ¼ cup liquid and mix with cornstarch. Gradually add back to mixture in pan. Spoon 1 tablespoon of mixture over each piece of chicken. Bake at 350° for 30 minutes, uncovered. Pour remaining sauce over chicken and bake for 30 minutes more. Slice remaining orange for garnish.

Yield: 4-6 servings.

Cheese Stuffed Chicken Breasts

6 boneless chicken breasts
3 ounces cream cheese, softened
4 ounces bleu cheese
½ cup butter, softened
¼ teaspoon paprika
¼ teaspoon pepper
¼ teaspoon thyme
6 thin slices Swiss cheese
2 egg whites, beaten
½ cup flour
¼ teaspoon paprika
⅛ teaspoon pepper
1 cup cracker crumbs
¼ cup butter
¼ cup vegetable oil
6 lemon slices
¼ cup parsley, chopped

Slice through each breast and spread open to form a pocket. In bowl, combine cream cheese, bleu cheese, butter, paprika, pepper, and thyme. Mix thoroughly and divide into 4 parts. Mold into oval shape and wrap with Swiss cheese. Place cheese mixture into pocket in chicken breast. Secure with toothpick. Dip breast into egg whites, then roll in mixture of flour, paprika, and pepper. Dip into egg whites again, then roll in cracker crumbs. In skillet, melt butter and add oil. Sauté chicken breasts over medium heat until golden brown and completely cooked. Drain on paper towels. Before serving, garnish with lemon and parsley.

Yield: 4 servings.

Chicken Breast Marinade

½ cup soy sauce
½ cup sherry
1 cup pineapple juice
¼ cup red wine vinegar
1 tablespoon sugar
½ teaspoon garlic powder
2 pounds boneless chicken breasts

Mix soy sauce, sherry, pineapple juice, vinegar, sugar, and garlic powder. Pour over chicken and marinate 24 hours. Drain chicken and cook on grill, basting with marinade occasionally.

Yield: 4-6 servings.

May also be used on London broil or flank steak.

Chicken Piccata

6 chicken breasts, skinned and
   boned
⅓ cup flour
1½ teaspoons salt
½ teaspoon pepper

4 tablespoons butter
¼ cup lemon juice
1 lemon, thinly sliced
2 tablespoons parsley, chopped

Pound chicken breasts to ¼-inch thickness. Combine flour, salt, and pepper. Dredge chicken in flour mixture. Melt butter in a large skillet over medium heat. Cook chicken 3 to 4 minutes on each side, or until golden brown. Remove chicken and drain on paper towels. Transfer to a serving dish and keep warm. Add lemon juice and lemon slices to pan drippings in skillet. Cook until thoroughly heated. Pour lemon mixture over chicken and sprinkle with parsley. Garnish with additional parsley sprigs, if desired.

Yield: 6 servings.

Simple to prepare, but elegant enough to serve company.

Elegant Chicken

3 cups chicken, cooked, boned and
   cut into bite-size pieces
1 (6-ounce) package long grain and
   wild rice, cooked
1 (10-ounce) can cream of celery
   soup
1 (2-ounce) jar pimentos
1 cup mayonnaise

1 small onion, chopped and
   sautéed, if desired
2 (10-ounce) cans French-style
   green beans, drained
1 (8-ounce) can water chestnuts,
   sliced and drained
¼ teaspoon salt
⅛ teaspoon pepper

Combine chicken, rice, soup, pimentoes, mayonnaise, onion, green beans, water chestnuts, salt, and pepper. Pour into a greased 2½-quart casserole. Bake at 350° for 25-30 minutes.

Yield: 8 servings.

Button Mushroom Chicken with Snow Peas

2 tablespoons vegetable oil
½ teaspoon garlic, minced
1 medium fryer, or 4 breasts, boned
  and cut into 1½-inch cubes
1 teaspoon salt
2 cups snow peas
1 cup fresh button mushrooms, or 1
  (6-ounce) can mushrooms

1 (6-ounce) can bamboo shoots
½ cup celery, sliced
1 teaspoon soy sauce
¾ cup chicken broth
¼ teaspoon MSG (optional)
2 tablespoons cornstarch
2 tablespoons water
Hot cooked rice

Place oil in heated wok or skillet. Sauté garlic and chicken on high heat for 1 minute. Add salt, snow peas, mushrooms, bamboo shoots, and celery. Continue stir frying. Add soy sauce, broth, and MSG. Cook at low heat for 5 minutes. Make paste of cornstarch and water. Add to wok and mix at high heat until gravy thickens. Serve with rice.

Yield: 4 servings.

Lo-Cal Lemon Chicken Scallops

2 whole chicken breasts, skinned
  and boned
4 tablespoons fresh lemon juice
2 tablespoons Parmesan cheese,
  freshly grated

Pinch of ground nutmeg
Salt to taste
Pepper to taste

Cut chicken into 1-inch cubes. Marinate in lemon juice in a glass bowl for 15 minutes, at room temperature. Combine cheese, nutmeg, salt, and pepper in a plastic bag. Coat chicken in mixture. Spray a shallow baking dish with cooking spray. Arrange chicken in single layer. Bake uncovered at 475° for 4 minutes. Turn and bake 4 additional minutes.

Yield: 4 small servings, 115 calories each.

Poulet Grosse Pointe

6 chicken breasts
3 cups water
1 (9-ounce) can pitted ripe olives,
  sliced into rings
½ cup butter, divided
¾ pound fresh mushrooms, sliced
6 tablespoons flour
1½ teaspoons salt
¼ teaspoon pepper
1 cup heavy cream
¼ cup sherry
5 thin slices of toast, crusts
  removed and each cut into 4
  triangles
Paprika

Simmer chicken in 3 cups water, or enough to cover, for 30 minutes. Drain, reserving 2¾ cups chicken broth. Cool, skin, and bone chicken. Arrange in a 12 x 8 x 2-inch dish. Top with sliced olives. Heat 4 tablespoons butter in a skillet and sauté mushrooms. Remove from heat and stir in flour, salt, pepper, and broth. Gradually add cream. Return to heat; cook and stir until thickened. Add sherry and remove from heat. Pour sauce over chicken and olives. Lightly sauté toast triangles in 4 tablespoons butter. Arrange over top of chicken and sprinkle with paprika. Refrigerate until ready to cook. Remove chicken from refrigerator 1 hour ahead of baking time. Bake at 325° for 45 minutes.

Yield: 6 servings.

May prepare one day before serving.

Sesame Chicken

4 chicken breasts, skinned and
  boned
¼ cup sesame seeds
¼ cup soy sauce
3 tablespoons vegetable oil
2 tablespoons brown sugar
¼ teaspoon black pepper
3 cloves garlic, crushed
4 green onions, thinly sliced
½ teaspoon ground ginger
Hot cooked rice

Cut chicken into 1-inch cubes. Combine chicken, sesame seeds, soy sauce, vegetable oil, brown sugar, pepper, garlic, onions, and ginger. Cover and chill 1 to 4 hours. Pour into a 10 x 15-inch pan in a single layer. Broil 10 minutes, turn pieces, and broil 5 additional minutes. Serve over rice.

Yield: 4 servings.

Crab-Stuffed Chicken Breasts

6 chicken breasts, skinned and
boned
Salt to taste
Pepper to taste
½ cup onion, chopped
½ cup celery, chopped
3 tablespoons butter
3 tablespoons white wine
1 (6-ounce) can crabmeat, flaked

½ cup dry herbed stuffing mix
2 tablespoons flour
½ teaspoon paprika
2 tablespoons butter, melted
1 envelope Hollandaise sauce mix
¾ cup milk
2 tablespoons white wine
2 ounces Swiss cheese, shredded

Pound chicken to flatten. Sprinkle with salt and pepper. Sauté onion and celery in butter until tender. Remove from heat and add wine, crabmeat, and stuffing mix. Divide mixture among 6 breasts, roll up and secure with toothpicks. Combine flour and paprika. Coat chicken and place in a 9 x 13-inch baking dish. Drizzle with butter. Bake uncovered at 350° for 1 hour. Remove toothpicks and transfer to platter. Blend sauce mix and milk in pan. Cook and stir until thickened. Add wine and cheese, and cook over low heat until cheese is melted. Pour sauce over chicken and serve immediately.

Yield: 6 servings.

Easy Oven-Fried Chicken

½ cup margarine
1 fryer, cut up

1 cup Waverly Wafers crumbs
Lemon-pepper seasoning

Melt margarine. Dip chicken in margarine and roll in crumbs. Sprinkle on lemon-pepper. Place chicken in a 9 x 13-inch baking dish. Bake at 350° for 1 hour.

Yield: 4 servings.

LYCC Southern Fried Chicken

1 fryer, cut up
1 cup milk
½ teaspoon salt

¼ teaspoon pepper
1 cup flour
3 cups peanut oil

Marinate chicken in milk, salt, and pepper for 1 hour, turning once. Coat thoroughly in flour. Fry in very hot oil; legs, thighs, and wings for 10 minutes, breasts for 15 minutes, or until golden brown. Drain on paper towels.

Yield: 2 to 3 servings.

The Lakeland Yacht and Country Club was founded in 1924 during Florida's real estate boom. The Spanish-Mediterranean style club house was recently restored to its original appearance.

Chicken-Sausage Marengo

2 pounds sweet Italian sausage
2 tablespoons butter
2 tablespoons vegetable oil
2 medium fryers, skinned and cut
    into pieces
1 (1-pound, 12-ounce) can tomato
    puree
1 (6-ounce) can mushrooms, sliced
1 (8-ounce) can pitted ripe olives

¼ cup sweet pepper flakes
1 tablespoon parsley flakes
2 teaspoons celery flakes
1½ teaspoons Italian seasoning
1 teaspoon instant minced onion
½ teaspoon salt
¼ teaspoon ground black pepper
¼ teaspoon garlic powder
1 bay leaf

Slice sausage into 1½-inch pieces. Brown in a Dutch oven. Remove sausage to drain. Add butter and oil. Sauté chicken until browned. Remove chicken and pour off drippings. Drain mushrooms, reserve ½ cup of liquid; drain olives, reserve ¼ cup of liquid. Add tomato puree, mushrooms and ½ cup liquid, olives and ¼ cup liquid, pepper flakes, parsley flakes, celery flakes, Italian seasoning, minced onion, salt, pepper, garlic powder, and bay leaf. Return sausage and chicken to pan. Cover and simmer 30-40 minutes, or until chicken is tender. Remove bay leaf before serving.

Yield: 10-12 servings.

Old Fashioned Chicken Pie

1 (4 to 5-pound) chicken, cooked
2 eggs, hard-cooked
2¾ cups chicken stock
⅓ cup flour
2 cups flour, sifted
3 teaspoons baking powder

1 teaspoon salt
⅛ teaspoon nutmeg
½ cup shortening
1 egg, beaten
5 tablespoons water
1 tablespoon lemon juice

Remove chicken from bone and cut into bite-size pieces. Place in a lightly greased 9 x 13-inch baking dish. Slice eggs over chicken. In a saucepan, combine chicken stock and ⅓ cup flour. Bring to a boil, stirring constantly, and spoon over chicken. To make crust, combine 2 cups sifted flour, baking powder, salt, nutmeg, shortening, egg, water, and lemon juice. Knead dough and roll out on a lightly floured board. Line sides of baking dish with crust and top chicken mixture with crust. Slash vents in top. Bake in a 450° oven for 30 minutes.

Yield: 6-8 servings.

Add steamed vegetables of your choice for a meal-in-one.

Country Captain Chicken

1 teaspoon salt
½ teaspoon white pepper
6 chicken breasts, skinned
¼ cup vegetable oil
1 onion, chopped
2 green peppers, chopped
1 clove garlic, minced

2 teaspoons curry powder
1 (16-ounce) can tomatoes
½ teaspoon parsley, chopped
½ teaspoon dried thyme
¼ cup almonds, sliced and toasted
Hot cooked rice

Salt and pepper chicken. Brown in oil. Remove chicken and allow to drain. Sauté onions, peppers, garlic, and curry powder in same skillet. Add tomatoes with juice, parsley, and thyme. Cook over medium heat for 20 minutes. Arrange chicken in a 9 x 13-inch baking dish. Pour sauce over chicken and bake at 350° for 35-45 minutes. Sprinkle with toasted almonds and serve with rice.

Yield: 6 servings.

Prize-Winning Chicken Reuben

4 chicken breasts, skinned and
  boned
Salt to taste
Pepper to taste

16 ounces sauerkraut, well-drained
4 slices Swiss cheese
1 cup Thousand Island dressing
1 tablespoon parsley, chopped

Place chicken in a 2-quart greased casserole. Sprinkle with salt and pepper. Arrange ½ cup drained sauerkraut over each chicken breast. Top with Swiss cheese and then dressing. Cover and bake at 350° for 1 hour. Garnish with parsley.

Yield: 4 servings.

Ybor City Arroz Con Pollo

2 teaspoons oregano
½ teaspoon pepper
4 teaspoons salt, divided
2 chickens, cut up
½ cup oil
1 green pepper, cut into strips
1 cup onion, chopped
1 clove garlic, minced
1 bay leaf

1 teaspoon saffron
2 cups uncooked white rice
1 (1-pound, 12-ounce) can tomatoes
1 (10¾-ounce) can chicken broth
½ cup water
1 (10-ounce) package frozen peas
½ cup pimento stuffed olives,
  halved
1 (4-ounce) jar pimentos, diced

Combine oregano, pepper, and 2 teaspoons salt. Sprinkle on chicken and rub in. Let stand 10 minutes. In Dutch oven, brown chicken pieces in oil. Drain chicken. In same pan, sauté pepper, onion, and garlic. Add bay leaf, saffron, 2 teaspoons salt, and rice. Stir over medium heat 10 minutes, or until rice is browned. Add tomatoes and broth. Arrange chicken pieces on top of rice mixture. Cover and bake at 350° for 1 hour. Add ½ cup water. Do not stir. Sprinkle peas, olives, and pimentos on top. Cover and bake 20 minutes more. Let stand 10 minutes, covered, before serving.

Yield: 8-10 servings.

Ybor City is a historic district in Tampa, Florida. Once a world center for hand-rolled cigars, the city is enjoying a rebirth through restoration.

Almond Chicken

2 (2½-pound) fryers, skinned and
  cut into pieces
Salt to taste
1 cup flour
2 teaspoons salt
¼ teaspoon pepper
2 teaspoons paprika

2 eggs, slightly beaten
3 tablespoons milk
2 cups blanched almonds, finely
  chopped
2 tablespoons butter
2 tablespoons shortening
4 tablespoons butter, melted

Salt chicken. Combine flour, salt, pepper, and paprika. Coat chicken with mixture. Combine eggs and milk. Dip chicken into liquid and roll in almonds. Melt 2 tablespoons butter and shortening in large baking dish. Place chicken bone side down. Drizzle with 4 tablespoons melted butter. Bake at 400° for 1 hour.

Yield: 6-8 servings.

Chicken Parmigiana

1 cup packaged bread crumbs
¼ cup Parmesan cheese, grated
6-8 chicken breasts, skinned and
  boned
2 eggs, slightly beaten
2 tablespoons vegetable oil
1 small onion, minced
2 cloves garlic, crushed
1 (16-ounce) can tomatoes

1 (15-ounce) can tomato sauce
1½ teaspoons basil
½ teaspoon thyme
½ teaspoon onion salt
¼ teaspoon pepper
2 tablespoons butter
2 tablespoons olive oil
8 ounces mozzarella cheese, sliced
½ cup Parmesan cheese, grated

Combine breadcrumbs and ¼ cup Parmesan cheese. Dip chicken breasts into beaten egg and coat with crumb mixture. Set aside while preparing sauce. Heat oil in saucepan and sauté onion and garlic. Add tomatoes, tomato sauce, basil, thyme, onion salt, and pepper. Cover and simmer 15 minutes. In a separate pan, heat butter and olive oil. Brown chicken on all sides. Remove and place in a 9 x 13-inch baking dish. Top with mozzarella slices and pour sauce over all. Sprinkle with Parmesan cheese and bake at 350° for 30 minutes.

Yield: 6-8 servings.

Oriental Orange Chicken

2½ pounds of chicken breasts,
   skinned and boned
2 large navel oranges
3 tablespoons vegetable oil
1 teaspoon gingerroot, grated
¼ teaspoon hot sauce
4 green onions, cut into ¼-inch
   pieces

1 cup orange juice
⅓ cup soy sauce
¼ cup sugar
1½ tablespoons cornstarch
Hot cooked white rice
½ cup cashews

Cut chicken into 1-inch pieces. Grate 2 tablespoons orange peel and reserve. Peel and section the oranges. Coat sides of a preheated wok or skillet with oil. Allow to heat for 2 minutes at 325°. Stir fry chicken for 2 minutes, or until lightly browned. Remove and drain on paper towels. Stir fry orange peel, gingerroot, and hot sauce for 1½ minutes. Add chicken and stir fry 3 more minutes. Combine onions, orange juice, soy sauce, sugar, and cornstarch. Mix well and add to wok. Stir fry 3 minutes. Gently add orange sections and stir until heated. Serve over rice and top with cashews.

Yield: 6 servings.

Chicken In Sherry Sauce

4 chicken breasts, or 1 fryer, cut
   up
1 clove garlic, halved
Salt to taste
Pepper to taste
Paprika to taste

½ cup butter or margarine
1 (2-ounce) jar stuffed green olives,
   sliced
1 (4-ounce) jar mushrooms, sliced
1 cup sherry

Rub chicken with garlic halves. Sprinkle with salt, pepper, and paprika. Brown chicken in butter. Remove and arrange in a 9 x 13-inch baking dish. Top with olives and mushrooms. Slowly pour sherry around chicken. Cover and bake at 350° for 1 hour.

Yield: 4 servings.

Chicken Mexicali

1 (4-pound) chicken, cut up
4-5 cups water
1 tablespoon butter
1 medium onion, minced
2 green peppers, chopped
2 cloves garlic, minced
1 (15-ounce) can tomatoes
4 tablespoons parsley, chopped

8 ounces mushrooms, sliced
1 tablespoon oregano
½ teaspoon salt
1½ tablespoons chili powder
1 tablespoon cornstarch
⅓ cup water
1 (10-ounce) can enchilada sauce
Hot cooked white rice

Stew chicken in water 45 minutes, or until tender. Remove chicken to cool and reserve 2 cups of broth. Remove bones and cut chicken into cubes. Set aside. Melt butter in a large skillet and sauté onion, peppers, and garlic until tender. Add tomatoes, parsley, mushrooms, oregano, and reserved broth. Cook uncovered 15 minutes over medium heat. Combine salt, chili powder, cornstarch, and water. Stir into skillet and add chicken. Mix well. Transfer to a large casserole. Pour enchilada sauce over chicken mixture. Bake in preheated 400° oven 15 minutes, or until thoroughly heated. Serve over rice.

Yield: 6-8 servings.

Curry Glazed Chicken

2 tablespoons butter
¼ cup honey
3 tablespoons Dijon mustard
2 teaspoons curry powder, or to
taste

½ teaspoon salt
1 (2½-pound) chicken, cut up

Preheat oven to 375°. Place butter in a 9 x 13-inch baking dish and heat in oven until melted. Stir in honey, mustard, curry powder, and salt. Add chicken, turning to coat. Bake 20 minutes. Turn chicken over and continue baking 25 minutes longer.

Yield: 4 servings.

Chicken Tetrazzini

6 chicken breasts
2 tablespoons dried onion flakes
3 chicken bouillon cubes
8 ounces thin spaghetti
8 cups water
8 tablespoons butter or margarine
1 green pepper, finely chopped

1 (4-ounce) jar pimentos, diced
1 (8-ounce) can mushrooms, sliced
2 (10¾-ounce) cans cream of
  chicken soup
8 ounces sour cream
¾ cup sherry
1 cup Parmesan cheese

Cook chicken, onion flakes, and bouillon cubes in water for 45 minutes. Remove chicken and set aside. Prepare spaghetti in broth according to package directions, adding more water if necessary. In large skillet, melt butter and sauté pepper until soft. Remove from heat and stir in pimentos, mushrooms, soup, sour cream, and sherry. Skin chicken and cut into bite-size pieces. Add to sauce. Drain spaghetti and return to skillet. Pour sauce over spaghetti and mix well. Transfer to a 9 x 13-inch baking dish. Top with cheese. Bake at 350° for 30 minutes.

Yield: 10 servings.

Can be covered and refrigerated overnight or frozen up to 2 weeks.

Chicken Jambalaya

1 (3-pound) fryer, or 4 breasts,
  skinned and boned
3 tablespoons vegetable oil
1 cup green pepper, chopped
1 cup onion, chopped
1 clove garlic, minced
2 teaspoons salt

2 teaspoons Worcestershire sauce
¼ teaspoon thyme
¼ teaspoon Tabasco sauce
¼ teaspoon black pepper
3 cups chicken broth
1½ cups uncooked rice
1 (2-ounce) jar pimentos, chopped

Brown chicken in oil. Remove from skillet and set aside. Add pepper, onion, and garlic to pan drippings. Sauté 5 minutes over low heat. Add salt, Worcestershire sauce, thyme, Tabasco sauce, pepper, and broth. Simmer 10 minutes. Add rice and chicken. Cover and cook over low heat for 25 minutes. Stir with fork and cook 5 minutes longer. Garnish with pimentos.

Yield: 8 servings.

Chicken Mykonos

4 chicken breasts, skinned and
boned
1 egg
Dash salt
Dash pepper
½ cup flour
¾ cup vegetable oil
1 (16-ounce) can stewed tomatoes
1 teaspoon sweet basil
¾ teaspoon thyme
¾ teaspoon rosemary, crushed
¾ teaspoon marjoram
¼ teaspoon fresh ground pepper
Salt to taste
½ pound mushrooms, sliced
½ cup water
⅛ cup Ouzo, a Greek liqueur

Cut chicken into bite-size pieces. Dip into egg beaten with salt and pepper. Dredge in flour and fry pieces in hot oil over medium heat 5-10 minutes, or until a deep golden brown. Remove and set aside. Discard oil. Simmer stewed tomatoes over low heat. Add basil, thyme, rosemary, marjoram, pepper, and salt. Simmer 10 minutes. Add mushrooms and water, and cook until mixture thickens. Add chicken and cook 10 minutes, stirring occasionally. Add Ouzo and cook a few more minutes.

Yield: 4 servings.

Chinese Chicken

4 chicken breasts, skinned and
boned
2 tablespoons vegetable oil
1 red pepper, cut into strips
1 small onion, diced
1 cup celery, sliced diagonally
1 (5-ounce) can water chestnuts,
sliced
1 vegetable bouillon cube
½ teaspoon salt
⅓ cup water
2 tablespoons cornstarch
3 tablespoons soy sauce
Hot cooked rice

Cut chicken into strips and cook in hot oil for 3 minutes. Add pepper, onion, celery, water chestnuts, bouillon cube, salt, and water. Cover and simmer for 10 minutes. Combine cornstarch and soy sauce; stir into mixture. Cover and simmer 5 minutes. Serve over rice.

Yield: 4 servings.

Chicken Montmorency

1 (13-ounce) can black cherries
1 chicken bouillon cube
1 (3-pound) chicken, cut up
Salt to taste
Pepper to taste
Paprika to taste
3 tablespoons butter

1 tablespoon flour
1 teaspoon sugar
⅛ teaspoon allspice
½ teaspoon cinnamon
¼ teaspoon red food coloring
  (optional)

Drain cherries, reserving juice. Dissolve bouillon cube in reserved cherry juice. Sprinkle chicken with salt, pepper, and paprika. In heavy skillet, brown chicken in butter. Remove chicken. To pan drippings add flour, sugar, allspice, and cinnamon. Gradually add cherry liquid and food coloring. Return chicken to skillet, cover, and simmer 40 minutes. Gradually stir in cherries and cook an additional 5 minutes. Serve immediately.

Yield: 4 servings.

Chicken Cacciatore

1 (2½ to 3-pound) fryer, cut up
¼ cup olive oil
2 medium onions, chopped
2 cloves garlic, minced
1 (2-ounce) jar olives
1 (4-ounce) can mushrooms
1 (16-ounce) can tomatoes
1 (8-ounce) can tomato sauce

1 teaspoon salt
¼ teaspoon pepper
1 teaspoon oregano
½ teaspoon celery seed
1 bay leaf
¼ cup dry white wine
2 tablespoons cornstarch
2 tablespoons water

In a skillet, brown chicken pieces in oil. Remove and set aside. Sauté onions and garlic until tender. In bowl, combine olives, mushrooms, tomatoes, tomato sauce, salt, pepper, oregano, celery seed, and bay leaf. Return chicken to skillet. Pour tomato mixture over chicken. Cover and simmer 30 minutes. Stir in wine. Combine cornstarch and water. Stir into sauce. Simmer, uncovered, 15 minutes. Remove bay leaf and skim off fat before serving.

Yield: 4 servings.

Florida House Indian Chicken

1 (3 to 4-pound) fryer, cut up and
  skinned
¼ cup lemon juice
2 tablespoons honey
2 cups water
1 bay leaf
2 cloves garlic, crushed
1 medium onion, minced
¼ cup olive oil
2 tablespoons flour
1-2 tablespoons curry powder

½ teaspoon cinnamon
¼ teaspoon nutmeg
¾ cup apples, diced
¾ cup raisins
1 teaspoon honey
¾ cup yogurt, room temperature
2 tablespoons lemon juice
Hot cooked brown or white rice
Unsalted peanuts for garnish
Flaked coconut for garnish
Chutney for garnish

Marinate chicken in lemon juice and honey for 1 hour. Remove chicken from marinade and simmer chicken for 30 minutes in water and bay leaf, turning several times. Remove chicken and reserve broth. In skillet, sauté garlic and onion in olive oil. Discard garlic. Add flour and stir until browned. Stir in 1½ cups chicken broth until smooth. Add curry powder, cinnamon, nutmeg, apples, raisins, honey, and chicken. Simmer 5 minutes. Add more chicken stock if sauce is too thick. Remove from heat. Stir in yogurt and lemon juice. Serve over rice. Garnish with condiments of your choice.

Yield: 4-6 servings.

This recipe comes from Rhea Chiles, wife of U. S. Senator Lawton Chiles, who is a native of Lakeland. Rhea brought southern hospitality to Washington, D. C. when she founded Florida House. This lovely building welcomes Florida residents with, of course, Florida orange juice.

Grilled Duck Breasts

4 whole duck breasts, skinned and
  boned
2 cups milk

Nature's Seasoning or Everglades
  Seasoning
8 strips bacon

Place duck breasts in milk for 30 minutes. Remove and season both sides of breasts heavily. Place 2 breast halves together. Wrap with 2 strips of bacon completely covering breast, securing with toothpicks. Grill 5 minutes on each side to cook meat medium-rare.

Yield: 4 servings.

Florida Quail

8 quail
Salt to taste
Pepper to taste
½ cup flour
4 tablespoons butter
1 clove garlic, finely chopped
1 medium onion, thinly sliced

1 pound fresh whole mushrooms
1 cup chicken broth
½ teaspoon thyme
½ teaspoon parsley, chopped
1 bay leaf
¼ cup white wine

Split quail down back. Sprinkle with salt and pepper. Coat with flour. Melt butter in skillet and brown quail. Remove quail and add garlic, onion, and mushrooms. Sauté until mushrooms are cooked. Stir in broth, thyme, parsley, bay leaf, and wine. Place quail and liquid in roasting pan. Cover tightly and bake at 350° for 1½ hours or until tender. Baste occasionally.

Yield: 4 servings.

Stuffed Cornish Hens with Orange Sauce

4 Cornish Game Hens
1 (6-ounce) box long grain and wild
    rice
½ cup mushrooms, sliced

½ cup almonds, slivered
Salt to taste
Pepper to taste
2 tablespoons butter

Clean hens and set aside. Cook rice according to directions. Add mushrooms and almonds to rice. Stuff mixture into each hen cavity and secure legs. Sprinkle birds with salt and pepper. Dot with ½ tablespoon butter. Bake at 325° for 1 hour. If hens weigh more than 1 pound, 6 ounces, bake 15-30 minutes longer. Serve with warm orange sauce.

Orange Sauce

1 cup light brown sugar, firmly
    packed
2 tablespoons cornstarch
½ teaspoon salt

½ cup water
4 tablespoons orange peel, grated
2 cups fresh orange juice

Combine sugar, cornstarch, and salt in a saucepan. Stir in water, orange peel, and juice. Cook over low heat, stirring constantly, until thickened and transparent.

Yield: 4 servings.

Trout Italiano

6 trout fillets (6 to 8-ounces each)　　½ cup butter, browned
1 cup olive oil　　　　　　　　　　　¾-1 cup Italian breadcrumbs
½ teaspoon salt　　　　　　　　　　1 lemon, sliced thinly
¼ teaspoon pepper　　　　　　　　　½ cup fresh parsley, chopped

Place fillets in a single layer in a baking dish. Cover with olive oil. Marinate 1 hour in refrigerator. Drain off olive oil. Sprinkle with salt and pepper. Add browned butter. Bake 10 minutes in a preheated 400° oven. Turn fillets and sprinkle generously with breadcrumbs. Bake 10 minutes more, or until fillets flake easily. Garnish with lemon slices and parsley.

Yield: 6 servings.

Bass, red snapper, grouper, or flounder may be substituted for trout.

Grouper Almandine

6 fillets of grouper, 8 ounces each　　1 cup butter, divided
Salt to taste　　　　　　　　　　　1 cup almonds, sliced
Pepper to taste　　　　　　　　　　2 lemons
Flour for dredging

Wipe fillets with damp cloth. Salt, pepper, and dredge in flour. Sauté in ½ cup butter 5 minutes. Place in casserole and set aside. To make Almandine sauce, sauté almonds in ½ cup butter until lightly browned. Spoon almonds over grouper and squeeze juice of one lemon over top. Just before serving, place in a 375° oven 5-10 minutes, or until browned. Garnish with lemon slices.

Yield: 6 servings.

Red snapper or scamp may be substituted for grouper.

Grilled Florida Snapper

2½-3 pounds snapper fillets
½ teaspoon black pepper
½ cup lemon juice

½ teaspoon garlic powder
⅓ cup Worcestershire sauce
Ice cubes

Place snapper fillets in a large glass dish. Sprinkle with pepper, lemon juice, garlic powder, and Worcestershire sauce. Add several ice cubes on top and allow to marinate in refrigerator 3 hours. After fish has marinated, heat the grill. Cover grill rack with a layer of aluminum foil. Punch small holes throughout foil with a toothpick. Space holes ½-inch apart to allow heat to pass through. Coat the foil with vegetable oil. Place fillets on prepared rack and baste heavily with sauce. Do not turn fish. Baste every 8-10 minutes. Leave cover on grill except when basting. Length of cooking time varies with thickness of fish. Check after 20 minutes. Thicker fillets may take 30-40 minutes. Serve with extra sauce, warmed.

Basting Sauce

½ cup Worcestershire sauce
2 lemons squeezed
2 cloves garlic, minced

¼ cup butter
1½ teaspoons black pepper

Combine Worcestershire sauce, lemon juice, garlic, butter, and pepper.

Yield: 6 servings.

The recipe works best with large fillets and doubles easily to serve more guests.

Fish Milano

2 pounds thick fillets of sole or
   flounder
1 cup mozzarella cheese, shredded
1 large tomato, thinly sliced

½ teaspoon oregano
¼ teaspoon garlic powder
Salt and pepper to taste

Preheat oven to 375°. Grease a large baking dish. Rinse fillets in salted water and pat dry. Arrange in a single layer in dish. Layer with cheese and tomato slices. Sprinkle with oregano, garlic powder, salt, and pepper. Bake approximately 10 minutes, or until fish is opaque. Serve hot.

Yield: 4 servings.

Catch of the Day

2 pounds saltwater fish fillets
1 teaspoon salt
1 teaspoon paprika
2 tablespoons lemon juice

1 teaspoon onion, grated
¼ cup butter, melted
Pepper to taste

Place fish in a single layer in a lightly greased baking dish. Combine salt, paprika, lemon juice, onion, butter, and pepper. Pour over fillets. Bake at 350° for 20-25 minutes, or until fish flakes easily.

Yield: 4-6 servings.

A favorite recipe for men to prepare!

Smoked Mullet Romanoff

1 pound smoked mullet
8 ounces egg noodles
2 cups large curd cottage cheese
2 teaspoons Worcestershire sauce
1¼ cups sour cream

⅔ cup green onions, sliced
Dash of Tabasco
¼ teaspoon pepper
½ cup Parmesan cheese, grated

Flake the mullet, removing bones and skin. Set aside. Cook noodles according to package directions. Drain well and set aside. Combine mullet, cooked noodles, cottage cheese, Worcestershire sauce, sour cream, green onions, Tabasco, and pepper. Pour into a greased 2-quart shallow casserole. Sprinkle Parmesan cheese over top. Bake at 350° for 20-25 minutes.

Yield: 6 servings.

Tuna en Croute

2 (6½-ounce) cans tuna
10 ounces frozen peas, thawed
1 cup sharp cheddar cheese,
  shredded
1 cup celery, sliced
½ cup bread crumbs
¼ cup onion, chopped

¼ teaspoon salt
⅛ teaspoon pepper
1 cup mayonnaise
1 (8-ounce) can crescent rolls
1 tablespoon mayonnaise
1 teaspoon sesame seeds

Combine tuna, peas, cheese, celery, bread crumbs, onion, salt, pepper, and 1 cup mayonnaise. Spoon into a 10 x 6-inch baking dish. Separate dough into 4 rectangles and press perforations to seal. Cut dough into 4 x 8-inch strips. Make lattice over top of tuna mixture. Brush with 1 tablespoon of mayonnaise. Sprinkle with sesame seeds. Bake at 350° for 35-45 minutes. Serve with Cool Cucumber Sauce.

Cool Cucumber Sauce

½ cup mayonnaise
½ cup sour cream
½ cup cucumber, chopped
1 tablespoon chives, chopped

1 teaspoon parsley, chopped
¼ teaspoon salt
¼ teaspoon dried dill weed

Combine mayonnaise, sour cream, cucumber, chives, parsley, salt, and dill weed. Chill.

Yield: 6 servings.

Poached Salmon with Dill Sauce

½ onion, thinly sliced
4 salmon steaks
1 teaspoon peppercorns
1 bay leaf

1 teaspoon salt
1 lemon (reserve ½ for garnish)
Parsley (optional)

Line bottom of large skillet with onion. Top with salmon and add enough water to cover. Add peppercorns, bay leaf, and salt. Squeeze ½ lemon into pan and add lemon half. Simmer uncovered 10 minutes or until salmon is flaky. Carefully lift from pan and drain. To serve, place poached salmon on platter and garnish with parsley and lemon slices. Pass dill sauce separately.

Dill Sauce

1 cup sour cream
1 lemon, juiced

2 green onions, chopped
½ teaspoon dill weed

Combine sour cream, lemon juice, onion, and dill weed in a small saucepan. Heat until just warm.

Yield: 4 servings.

Grilled Gulf Shrimp

⅓ cup oil
⅓ cup sherry or sake
⅓ cup soy sauce

1 pound medium-large shrimp in shells

Combine oil, sherry, and soy sauce. Marinate shrimp in mixture 2-3 hours in refrigerator, turning occasionally. Cook over hot coals 2-3 minutes each side, basting with leftover marinade. It may be necessary to cook shrimp on a screen to prevent them from falling through grids. Serve in shells.

Yield: 4-6 servings.

Messy, but delicious!

Shrimp Elegante

1 (14-ounce) can artichoke hearts,
  drained and quartered
1½ pounds shrimp, cooked and
  shelled
2 tablespoons butter

¼ pound mushrooms, sliced
¼ cup Parmesan cheese
¼ teaspoon paprika
Parsley for garnish

Arrange artichoke hearts in the bottom of a greased 9 x 11-inch baking dish. Layer shrimp over artichokes. Set aside. Sauté mushrooms in 2 tablespoons butter. Spoon mushrooms over shrimp. Pour sauce over shrimp mixture. Sprinkle with Parmesan cheese and paprika. Bake at 375° for 20-30 minutes. Garnish with parsley.

Sauce

4 tablespoons butter
4 tablespoons flour
¾ cup milk
¾ cup heavy cream

Salt and pepper to taste
¼ cup dry sherry
1 tablespoon Worcestershire sauce

Melt butter, stir in flour, gradually add milk and cream, stirring constantly. Cook until thickened and smooth. Season with salt and pepper to taste. Add sherry and Worcestershire sauce.

Yield: 6 servings.

May be made 24 hours ahead of time.

Butter Fried Shrimp

¼ cup butter
1 clove garlic, minced
¼ cup flour
¼ cup Parmesan cheese, grated

2 tablespoons parsley, minced
1 pound large shrimp, shelled and
  deveined

Melt butter in a large skillet and sauté garlic for 2-3 minutes. Combine flour, Parmesan cheese, and parsley. Coat shrimp in flour mixture, and fry in butter 3-5 minutes, until batter is lightly browned.

Yield: 3 servings.

Shrimp Florentine

2 (10-ounce) packages frozen
    spinach, cooked and drained
½ cup almonds
½ cup onion, chopped
2 tablespoons butter
¼ cup butter, melted
2 tablespoons oil
½ cup flour
2 cups milk

1 cup evaporated milk
4 tablespoons sherry
2 tablespoons cream cheese
1 cup Old English cheese, cubed (or
    mild Cheddar)
Dash hot sauce
2 pounds shrimp, cooked and
    cleaned
1½ cups buttered bread crumbs

Place well-drained spinach in a greased casserole. Sauté almonds and onions in 2 tablespoons butter. Add almonds and onions to spinach and mix. Set aside. Make sauce by mixing ¼ cup melted butter, oil, and flour in a saucepan. Combine milk and evaporated milk and add to saucepan. Cook over medium heat, stirring constantly. When sauce begins to thicken, reduce heat to low. Add sherry, cream cheese, and Old English cheese. Stir until melted. Add hot sauce and shrimp. Cook 5 minutes. Pour mixture over spinach and top with breadcrumbs. Bake at 325° for 20 minutes.

Yield: 6 servings

An elegant choice to prepare in advance and bake just before guests arrive.

Barbequed Shrimp

2 pounds medium shrimp
1 cup olive oil
¼ cup chili sauce
1 teaspoon salt

1 teaspoon oregano
½ teaspoon hot pepper sauce
2 cloves garlic, minced
3 tablespoons lemon juice

Shell and devein shrimp leaving tails on. Combine olive oil, chili sauce, salt, oregano, hot pepper sauce, garlic, and lemon juice. Add shrimp and marinate at room temperature 1 hour. Skewer shrimp and grill 8 inches over gray coals, 5 minutes for each side.

Yield: 4 servings.

Sherry Garlic Shrimp

1½ pounds large shrimp, shelled
   and deveined
½ cup olive oil
3 tablespoons dry sherry
2-3 large cloves garlic, crushed

½ teaspoon thyme, crumbled
¼ teaspoon salt
⅛ teaspoon crushed red pepper
2 lemons, cut into wedges
4 parsley sprigs

Arrange shrimp in a single layer, slightly apart, in a shallow greased baking dish. Combine olive oil, sherry, garlic, thyme, salt, and red pepper. Pour over shrimp. Bake in a preheated 400° oven for four minutes, turn shrimp over and bake 4-6 minutes more. Shrimp will be ready when pink, firm, and barely opaque. Serve with pan juices. Garnish with lemon wedges and parsley sprigs.

Yield: 4 servings.

Shrimp with Feta Sauce

½ cup onion, minced
1½ tablespoons butter
1½ tablespoons oil
½ cup dry white wine
4 ripe tomatoes, peeled, seeded,
   and chopped
1 small clove garlic, minced
1 teaspoon salt

¼ teaspoon freshly ground pepper
¾ teaspoon oregano
4 ounces feta cheese, crumbled
1 pound large uncooked shrimp,
   shelled and deveined
Cooked spinach noodles
½ cup fresh parsley, chopped

In a heavy skillet, sauté onion in butter and oil until soft. Add wine, tomatoes, garlic, salt, pepper, and oregano. Simmer until sauce is slightly thickened. Stir in feta cheese and simmer 10-15 minutes longer. Just before serving, add shrimp to simmering sauce and cook 5 minutes, or until shrimp are just tender. Be careful not to overcook. Serve over spinach noodles and garnish heavily with parsley for color.

Yield: 4-6 servings.

Crusty French bread and a crisp green salad complete the meal.

Shrimp Cacciatore

½ cup butter
3 cloves garlic, minced
2 tablespoons olive oil
24 large shrimp, peeled and
   deveined
4 tablespoons parsley, chopped
½ cup green onions, chopped

1 cup mushrooms, chopped
4 tablespoons white wine
2 tablespoons lemon juice
1 cup tomato sauce
Salt to taste
Pepper to taste
Cooked rice or pasta

Heat butter, garlic, and olive oil in skillet. Add shrimp and sauté on both sides 3-4 minutes, or until done. Remove shrimp and set aside. Sauté parsley, onions, and mushrooms in same skillet. Add wine, lemon juice, and tomato sauce, stirring to blend. Add shrimp and heat thoroughly. Salt and pepper to taste. Serve over rice or pasta.

Yield: 4 servings.

Layered Shrimp Supreme

2 (10-ounce) packages frozen
   chopped spinach
2 (10¾-ounce) cans cream of
   mushroom soup
1 cup sour cream

½ pound fresh mushrooms, sautéed
½ cup Parmesan cheese, grated
1½ pounds shrimp, cooked and
   cleaned
¼ cup coconut, grated

Cook spinach according to package directions. Drain well. Set aside. Combine soups with sour cream. Add mushrooms, Parmesan cheese, and shrimp. Using a square casserole, layer half of spinach in bottom. Top with half shrimp mixture. Repeat layers. Sprinkle with coconut. Bake at 350° for 25-30 minutes.

Yield: 6 servings.

Recipe may be frozen.

Scallops Baked with Herbs

3 pounds fresh scallops, cleaned
4 tablespoons butter
¼ cup dry white wine
½ cup parsley, chopped
5 tablespoons chives, chopped

1 clove garlic, minced
6 shallots, peeled and chopped
2 teaspoons dried basil
1 teaspoon salt
¼ teaspoon black pepper

Divide scallops among 8 individual ramekins. Melt butter and mix with wine. Combine parsley and chives. Set aside 2 tablespoons and add rest to butter mixture. Add garlic, shallots, basil, salt, and pepper. Pour over scallops and cover with foil. At this point, scallops may be refrigerated up to 4 hours. Preheat oven to 425°. Bake 10 minutes or until liquid is frothy. Sprinkle with reserved parsley mixture and serve.

Yield: 8 servings.

A very special company dish when served in scallop shells.

Crab Newburg

2 cups crabmeat
½ cup butter
Juice of 1 lemon
2 tablespoons flour
2 cups heavy cream
¾ teaspoon salt
¼ teaspoon pepper

Pinch of cloves
½ teaspoon paprika
½ cup dry sherry
4 eggs, beaten well
1 tablespoon brandy
4-6 slices bread, for toast points

In a large, heavy skillet sauté crabmeat in butter for 1 minute. Add lemon juice and slowly blend in flour. While stirring, gradually add cream, salt, pepper, cloves, and paprika. Simmer 5 minutes. Remove from heat and pour in sherry. Carefully add beaten eggs, stirring constantly. Return to heat and add brandy, continuing to stir until thoroughly heated. Spoon over toast points and serve immediately.

Yield: 4-6 servings.

Five-Star Jambalaya

⅓ cup butter
4 pounds chicken, skinned and
   cut-up
1 pound cooked ham, cut in ½-inch
   cubes
⅓ cup flour
2 tablespoons vegetable oil
1 large onion, chopped
2 stalks celery, sliced
1 green pepper, chopped
1 red pepper, chopped
1 clove garlic, minced
½ teaspoon pepper
½ teaspoon thyme

¼ teaspoon red pepper, crushed
3 sprigs parsley, chopped
1 bay leaf
1 (1-pound, 12-ounce) can
   tomatoes, undrained
1 cup water
12 ounces tomato juice
1 pound shrimp, shelled and
   deveined
1 teaspoon gumbo filé powder
Cooked rice for 8 servings
½ cup parsley, chopped
Hot sauce to taste (optional)

In a 6-quart Dutch oven, melt butter over medium heat. Sauté chicken pieces until golden brown. Remove chicken and set aside. Add ham cubes to Dutch oven and sauté 5 minutes. Remove ham. Make a roux by stirring flour into oil used to brown chicken and ham. Stir until flour turns light brown. Remove from heat. In a skillet, heat vegetable oil and sauté onion, celery, green pepper, red pepper, and garlic. Cook until onion is golden. Add these vegetables to the Dutch oven. Stir in pepper, thyme, crushed red pepper, parsley, bay leaf, tomatoes and water. Crush tomatoes with a fork. Bring to a boil, stirring constantly. Return chicken and ham to pan. Add tomato juice. Cover and simmer 40 minutes. Stir in shrimp and simmer 5 minutes. Using a slotted spoon, remove chicken, ham, and shrimp to a heated serving platter. Keep warm. Bring sauce to a boil and add filé powder, stirring constantly. When thickened, remove from heat. Spoon rice around chicken, ham, and shrimp on platter and sprinkle with parsley. Pour ½ cup sauce over chicken mixture. Pass remaining sauce separately.

Yield: 8 servings.

Seafood Pie

1 (6-ounce) can crabmeat, flaked	2 tablespoons flour
2 (6-ounce) cans shrimp	2 (9-inch) pie shells, unbaked
½ cup celery, chopped	1 cup mayonnaise
½ cup green onions, chopped	1 cup dry white wine
8 ounces Swiss cheese, grated	4 eggs, beaten slightly

Mix crabmeat, shrimp, celery, and onion. Dredge cheese in flour. Add cheese to seafood mixture. Divide equally between 2 pie shells. Combine mayonnaise, wine, and eggs. Pour over seafood mixture. Bake at 350° for 35-40 minutes.

Yield: 2 pies.

After baking, the pies may be cooled, wrapped, and frozen. Before serving, remove from freezer for 1 hour, then bake at 300° for 15 minutes.

Simple Seafood Pilaf

¾ cup uncooked rice	1 (6-ounce) can crabmeat, drained
2 tablespoons butter	1 (7-ounce) can shrimp, drained
1 (3-ounce) can sliced mushrooms	¼ cup dry sherry
1 (10½-ounce) can chicken broth	2 tablespoons pimentoes, chopped
¼ cup green onions, chopped	

Brown rice in butter in a skillet for 5 minutes. Add mushrooms with liquid, chicken broth, green onions, crabmeat, shrimp, sherry, and pimentoes. Pour into a 1½-quart casserole. Cover and bake at 350° for 55 minutes. Uncover during the last 5 minutes and fluff with a fork.

Yield: 4 servings.

BREADS

Standard Yeast Rolls

1 package active dry yeast
3 tablespoons warm water, 105° -
   115°
1 cup milk, scalded
½ cup butter

¼ cup sugar
½ teaspoon salt
2 eggs, beaten well
3¾ cups flour

Dissolve yeast in water and set aside. Combine hot milk, butter, sugar, and salt. Cool to lukewarm. Add eggs and dissolved yeast. Stir in 2 cups flour and beat mixture well. Add remaining flour and mix thoroughly. Do not knead. Cover and chill dough in refrigerator for several hours or overnight. To make dinner rolls, shape into small balls, approximately ¾-inch in diameter. Grease muffin tins and place 3 balls into each tin. Allow to rise in a draft-free location until doubled in volume, about 45-60 minutes. Bake in a preheated 375° oven 15 minutes or until lightly browned.

Yield: 2 dozen rolls.

Rolls may be frozen after baking. This basic recipe may be varied in many ways. The Butter Pecan Rolls recipe which follows is one example.

Butter Pecan Rolls

1 cup brown sugar, divided
1 tablespoon water
1 tablespoon butter
½ cup pecans, coarsely chopped

½ standard yeast roll recipe
2 tablespoons butter, softened
3 tablespoons butter, melted

Combine ½ cup brown sugar, water, and 1 tablespoon butter in a small saucepan. Cook over low heat until sugar melts. Pour into a 10½ x 6½-inch pan. Sprinkle nuts over mixture and set aside. Roll bread dough into an 8 x 12-inch rectangle on a lightly floured board. Spread with 2 tablespoons of softened butter and sprinkle with remaining ½ cup brown sugar. Roll dough up jelly roll fashion. Cut into 1-inch slices and place over sugar and pecan mixture. Brush tops with remaining melted butter. Cover and allow to rise until doubled in volume. Bake in a 375° oven approximately 30 minutes.

Yield: 12 rolls.

English Muffin Loaf

1 cup warm water
1 package active dry yeast
1 tablespoon sugar
3 cups flour (all purpose or bread)

1 teaspoon salt
2 tablespoons butter
White cornmeal

Combine water, yeast, and sugar in a measuring cup. Wait 5 minutes, or until yeast activates and foams. Place 2½ cups flour, salt, and butter in food processor workbowl with metal blade. Turn on/off 4-5 times to cut-in butter. Pour yeast mixture through top of feed tube. Turn on/off 4-5 times. Turn processor on for 15 seconds, until dough forms a ball. Touch dough, and if sticky and wet, add ¼ cup more flour. Turn on/off to mix in flour. Touch again. If still tacky, add final ¼ cup of flour. Knead dough by turning food processor on until dough balls up again. Run food processor 45-60 seconds to knead. Turn dough into a greased bowl. Turn over to grease all dough surfaces. Cover and allow to rise until doubled, approximately 1 hour. Punch down and allow to rest 10-15 minutes. Place in a greased 8-inch round cake pan dusted generously with cornmeal. Dust top of dough with cornmeal. Cover and allow to rise until doubled, approximately 1 hour. Bake in a preheated 375° oven for 30-35 minutes. Cool 10 minutes in pan. Turn out onto rack to complete cooling.

Yield: 1 loaf.

If yeast does not get frothy after 5-10 minutes, discard and start over with a new package. This procedure is known as "proofing the yeast."

Whole Wheat Rolls

2 packages active dry yeast
½ cup warm water
Pinch of sugar
½ cup sugar
1¾ cups milk, scalded
1 tablespoon salt
3 tablespoons shortening

4 cups whole wheat flour, stirred
   and divided
3 cups all purpose flour, sifted and
   divided
2 eggs, beaten
½ cup butter, melted

Soften yeast in water with pinch of sugar. Set aside. In a large bowl, combine sugar, milk, salt, and shortening. Add 1 cup whole wheat flour and 1 cup all purpose flour, beating well. Pour yeast in and add eggs, mixing well. Stir in the remaining 3 cups of whole wheat and 2 cups of all purpose flour. If necessary, knead in flour with hands. Place in a greased bowl, turn dough over, and cover. Refrigerate until 2½ hours before serving. Shape into cloverleaf, Parkerhouse, or other shapes. Place on a greased baking sheet and brush with melted butter. Allow rolls to rise in a draft-free spot until doubled in size, approximately 1½ hours. Bake in a preheated 375° oven 15 minutes. Brush with additional butter.

Yield: 4 dozen rolls.

These are delicious dinner rolls with a healthy wheat flavor. For a lighter textured roll, use 3 packages of yeast in ¾ cup of water and continue to follow recipe.

Herb Cheese Loaf

1 (16-ounce) loaf crusty bread
½ cup butter, melted
2 cloves garlic, minced
2 tablespoons fresh parsley, minced

5 ounces Monterey Jack cheese,
   sliced
6 tablespoons Parmesan cheese,
   grated

Thickly slice bread, not cutting through completely. Combine butter, garlic, and parsley. Brush butter mixture on both sides of each slice. Insert Monterey Jack cheese between bread slices. Sprinkle with Parmesan cheese. Wrap in foil and place on rack over hot coals 12-15 minutes, turning every 5 minutes or bake in a 400° oven for 20 minutes.

Yield: 1 loaf.

Cheese Casserole Bread

1 package active dry yeast
2 tablespoons sugar
1 cup warm water
2¾ cups flour
3 tablespoons dry milk solids

1 teaspoon salt
2 tablespoons vegetable oil
1 cup sharp Cheddar cheese, cubed
1 tablespoon sesame seeds

Combine yeast and sugar with water. Set aside. Fit food processor with metal blade. Measure 1¾ cups flour, dry milk solids, salt, and vegetable oil into workbowl. Process until mixed, about 5 seconds. Turn on processor and add water/yeast mixture all at once through feed tube. Process 30 seconds. Add remaining flour, ½ cup at a time, processing 10 seconds after each addition. Pour half of batter into a greased 1½-quart casserole. Sprinkle cheese on top. Pour remaining batter over cheese. Stir gently to mix. Sprinkle top with sesame seeds. Cover lightly and set in a draft-free place to rise until doubled, about 45 minutes. Bake in a preheated 375° oven 25-30 minutes, or until lightly browned. Cool 10 minutes in casserole, and then turn out onto a wire rack.

Yield: 1 loaf.

This moist yeast bread requires no kneading and only one time to rise. Serve while it's still warm and there will be no leftovers.

Red Onion Loaf

1 loaf French bread, unsliced
½ cup mayonnaise
½ cup red onion, chopped

½ cup Parmesan cheese, freshly
   grated

Cut bread in half horizontally. Combine mayonnaise, onion, and Parmesan cheese. Spread mixture over bread halves. Place on baking sheet and bake at 350° for 15 minutes. Slice and serve.

Yield: 6-8 servings.

Refrigerator Bran Rolls

1 cup shortening or margarine
¾ cup sugar
1½ teaspoons salt
1 cup boiling water
1 cup bran cereal

2 packages active dry yeast
1 cup warm water, 105° - 115°
2 eggs, beaten well
6 cups flour, sifted

Combine shortening, sugar, and salt. Pour boiling water over shortening mixture. Stir until shortening is melted. Add cereal and mix well. Set aside to cool. In a separate bowl, dissolve the yeast in the warm water. Stir dissolved yeast and eggs into cooled cereal mixture. Add flour and mix until thoroughly combined. Beat batter and pour into a large greased bowl. Lightly grease the top of the batter, cover, and refrigerate at least 24 hours. Remove dough from refrigerator 2 hours before serving. Roll out dough on a lightly floured board. Cut with a 3-inch biscuit cutter and fold over to make Parkerhouse rolls. Cover with a light cloth and allow to rise until doubled in size, approximately 1 hour. Bake at 425° for 15-20 minutes.

Yield: 3-4 dozen rolls.

Best Buttermilk Biscuits

4 cups self-rising flour
1 cup vegetable shortening
2 cups buttermilk

Place flour in mixing bowl. Cut in shortening. Add buttermilk and mix well. Dough will be sticky. Flour hands and bread board. Pat dough into a circle ¾-inch thick. Cut dough with a biscuit cutter. Place on an ungreased baking sheet. Bake in a preheated 400° oven 15-20 minutes, or until golden brown.

Yield: 2 dozen biscuits (depending on size).

Delicious with butter or stuffed with ham for a special ham biscuit.

Popovers

2 eggs	¼ teaspoon salt
1 cup milk	1 tablespoon shortening, melted
1 cup flour	

Preheat greased popover pans in 425° oven. Using mixer, beat eggs and combine with milk. Sift flour and salt together. Add sifted ingredients to eggs and milk. Add shortening and beat until smooth. Fill hot popover pans two-thirds full. Bake at 425° for 10-15 minutes, or until popovers are puffed and begin to brown. Reduce heat to 350° and bake 15 minutes longer. Popovers should be a dark golden brown. Serve warm with butter, or cool completely and fill with chicken salad.

Yield: 6-8 popovers.

Cooled popovers are delicious filled with a chocolate filling and served as dessert.

Spoon Bread

2 cups water	1 cup milk
1 cup white cornmeal	3 eggs, well beaten
1 teaspoon salt	2-3 tablespoons butter or
1 teaspoon sugar	margarine, melted

Combine water, cornmeal, salt, and sugar in a large saucepan. Boil 5 minutes, stirring constantly. Remove from heat. Stir in milk, eggs, and butter. Mix well. Pour batter into a preheated greased 2-quart casserole dish. Bake in a preheated 400° oven for 50 minutes, or until the top is firm and brown. Cut into squares and serve hot.

Yield: 6 servings.

Corny Cornbread

1 (8.5-ounce) can cream-style corn
1 cup self-rising white cornmeal
1 cup sour cream

2 eggs, beaten
½ cup vegetable oil

Combine corn, cornmeal, sour cream, and eggs. Add oil and stir until just moistened. Pour into a lightly greased 9-inch baking pan. Bake in a preheated 400° oven 15-20 minutes, or until lightly browned.

Yield: 6-8 servings.

Mexican Muffins

2 cups corn flakes
1 cup flour
3 teaspoons baking powder
½ teaspoon salt
¼ cup sugar
1 egg, beaten

½ cup vegetable oil
½ cup milk
½ cup whole kernel corn, drained
2 tablespoons green pepper, chopped
2 tablespoons pimento, chopped

Slightly crush corn flakes and set aside. Sift together flour, baking powder, salt, and sugar. Combine egg, oil, milk, corn, green pepper, and pimento. Add egg mixture to dry ingredients, stirring carefully until combined. Fold in corn flake crumbs. Fill greased muffin tins ⅔ full. Bake in a preheated 400° oven for 20 minutes.

Yield: 12 muffins.

Purple Plum Pecan Bread

2 cups purple prune plums
  (Northwestern)
1 cup butter
2 cups sugar
1 teaspoon vanilla extract
4 eggs
3 cups flour

1 teaspoon salt
1 teaspoon cream of tartar
½ teaspoon baking soda
¾ cup plain yogurt
1 teaspoon lemon peel, grated
1 cup pecans, chopped

Cut plums into ½-inch pieces, leaving peel on. Set aside. Cream butter, sugar, and vanilla until fluffy. Add eggs, one at a time, beating well after each. Sift together flour, salt, cream of tartar, and baking soda. Combine yogurt and lemon peel. Add flour mixture and yogurt mixture alternately to creamed butter and sugar. Blend well. Gently stir in plums and pecans. Divide into 2 greased 9 x 5-inch loaf pans. Bake at 350° for 50-55 minutes.

Yield: 2 loaves.

Attractive and delicious bread for coffee or afternoon tea.

Strawberry Jam Loaf

1 cup butter, softened
1½ cups sugar
4 eggs, beaten
1 teaspoon vanilla extract
3 cups flour
¾ teaspoon cream of tartar
½ teaspoon soda

½ teaspoon salt
1 cup sour cream
1 cup strawberry preserves
½ teaspoon lemon juice
¾ cup pecans, chopped
Red food coloring, optional

Cream together butter, sugar, eggs, and vanilla extract. Set aside. Blend flour, cream of tartar, soda, and salt. Add dry ingredients to creamed ingredients, blending well. Stir in sour cream, strawberry preserves, lemon juice, pecans, and food coloring. Pour into 2 greased 9 x 5-inch loaf pans. Bake at 325° for 55-60 minutes.

Yield: 2 loaves.

Artichoke Spice Bread

¾ cup currants
1 (14-ounce) can artichoke hearts,
  or 1½ cups artichoke pulp
1½ cups sugar
½ cup vegetable oil
¼ cup orange juice
3 eggs
2 cups flour

1 teaspoon baking powder
1 teaspoon baking soda
½ teaspoon nutmeg
½ teaspoon cinnamon
½ teaspoon ground cloves
½ teaspoon salt
¾ cup walnuts, chopped

Wash currants and allow to drain. Set aside. Drain artichoke hearts and chop in food processor or blender. Combine the artichoke hearts, sugar, oil, orange juice, and eggs in mixer. Blend thoroughly. Sift flour, baking powder, soda, nutmeg, cinnamon, cloves, and salt together. Add to artichoke mixture, blending well. Stir in walnuts and currants. Pour into 2 greased 9 x 5-inch loaf pans and bake at 350° for 40-45 minutes. A greased bundt or tube pan may also be used, baking at 350° for 1 hour.

Yield: 2 loaves.

Toasted Coconut Loaf

Peel of 1 lemon
1 cup sugar
2¾ cups flour
1 teaspoon salt
1 tablespoon plus 1 teaspoon
  baking powder

1¼ cups shredded coconut, toasted
  and cooled
1½ cups milk
1 egg, beaten
2 tablespoons vegetable oil
1½ teaspoons coconut extract

Using food processor with metal blade, process lemon peel and sugar until peel is finely chopped. Add flour, salt, and baking powder. Turn on/off several times to mix well. Add coconut and mix well by turning on/off. In a 2-cup measuring cup, combine milk, egg, oil, and extract. Add to dry ingredients with machine running. As soon as all liquid is added, stop machine. Do not overmix. Pour batter into a lightly oiled 9 x 5-inch loaf pan. Bake in a 350° preheated oven for 55-60 minutes. Cool 10 minutes in pan and then invert on rack to cool completely.

Yield: 1 loaf.

Tropical Fruit Bread

3 cups flour
2 cups sugar
1 teaspoon baking soda
1 teaspoon salt
1 teaspoon cinnamon
1 cup pecans, chopped

3 eggs, beaten
1½ cups vegetable oil
2 cups mashed bananas
1 (8-ounce) can crushed pineapple,
    drained
2 teaspoons vanilla extract

Combine flour, sugar, baking soda, salt, and cinnamon. Stir in pecans and set aside. Mix together the eggs, vegetable oil, bananas, pineapple, and vanilla extract. Add to dry ingredients, stirring just until batter is moistened. Spoon batter into 2 greased and floured 9 x 3-inch loaf pans. Bake at 350° for 1 hour, or until done. Cool 10 minutes before removing from pans. Remove to wire racks to cool completely.

Yield: 2 loaves.

Date Pecan Bread

1 cup dates, chopped
1 cup boiling water
1⅔ cups flour
¼ teaspoon salt
1 teaspoon baking soda

½ cup butter
1 cup sugar
1 teaspoon vanilla extract
1 egg
1 cup pecans, chopped

Cover dates with boiling water. Allow to cool. Sift flour, salt, and baking soda together. Set aside. Cream butter, sugar, and vanilla. Add egg and beat well. Add dates and water to creamed butter mixture. Stir in flour mixture and pecans. Pour batter into 2 greased 7½ x 3½-inch pans lined with wax paper. Bake in a preheated 350° oven 40-50 minutes. Cool 5 minutes in pan. Turn onto cooling rack and remove wax paper. Cool to room temperature and wrap tightly in foil. Refrigerate 24 hours before serving for maximum flavor. Bread freezes well. To serve, slice and spread with cream cheese.

Yield: 2 loaves.

Pineapple Wheat Muffins

¾ cup all purpose flour
¾ cup whole wheat flour
⅔ cup wheat germ
½ cup sugar
½ cup coconut
½ cup nuts, chopped
1½ teaspoons baking soda

½ teaspoon salt
1 cup plain yogurt
2 eggs, beaten
¼ cup vegetable oil
1 (8-ounce) can crushed pineapple,
    well-drained

Combine all purpose flour, whole wheat flour, wheat germ, sugar, coconut, nuts, baking soda, and salt. Set aside. Combine yogurt, eggs, and oil. Add to dry ingredients. Stir lightly until just combined. Fold in pineapple. Spoon into greased muffin tins. Bake at 400° for 15-20 minutes.

Yield: 18 muffins.

Nutritious and delicious muffins!

Pecan Mini-Muffins

2 eggs, slightly beaten
1 cup brown sugar
½ cup flour

½ teaspoon baking powder
½ teaspoon salt
1 cup pecans, chopped

Mix eggs and sugar. Sift flour, baking powder, and salt 3-4 times. Add to egg mixture. Stir in pecans gently. Blend until batter is just moistened. Spoon into greased miniature muffin tins. Bake at 350° for 12-15 minutes.

Yield: 24 miniature muffins.

These muffins make delicious hors d'oeuvres filled with turkey slices and cranberry sauce.

Sugar-Crusted Muffins

2 eggs, beaten
½ cup milk
¼ cup applesauce
¼ cup butter, melted
2 cups flour

½ cup raisins
¼ cup sugar
1 teaspoon baking powder
½ teaspoon salt
½ teaspoon cinnamon

Topping

¼ cup sugar
¾ teaspoon cinnamon

¼ cup butter, melted

Preheat oven to 400°. Grease bottom only of 12 muffin cups. Combine eggs, milk, applesauce, and ¼ cup butter. Stir in flour, raisins, ¼ cup sugar, baking powder, salt, and ½ teaspoon cinnamon. Stir until just moistened. (Batter will be lumpy). Fill muffin cups ⅔ full. Bake until golden brown, 20-25 minutes. Mix together remaining ¼ cup sugar and ¾ teaspoon cinnamon. Dip tops of warm muffins into remaining ¼ cup butter, and then into sugar mixture.

Yield: 12 muffins.

Lemon Refreshers

1 cup flour
1 teaspoon baking powder
¼ teaspoon salt
½ cup butter, softened
½ cup sugar

2 eggs, separated
3 tablespoons lemon juice
1 tablespoon lemon rind, grated
2 tablespoons sugar
¼ teaspoon cinnamon

Combine flour, baking powder, and salt. Set aside. Beat butter until creamy. Gradually add sugar, beating until light and fluffy. Beat in egg yolks. Add dry ingredients to creamed mixture alternately with lemon juice. Mix until just combined. Beat egg whites until stiff, and stir in lemon rind gently. Fold egg whites into batter. Spoon batter into greased muffin tins, filling ¾ full. Combine sugar and cinnamon. Top each muffin with ½ teaspoon sugar mixture. Bake at 375° for 20-25 minutes.

Yield: 12 muffins.

Bits of Sunshine

1 cup margarine
8 ounces sharp Cheddar cheese, grated

1 cup sour cream
2 cups self-rising flour

Melt margarine and remove from heat. Add grated cheese. Stir and cool 2 minutes. Add sour cream and mix well. Stir in flour. Fill greased miniature muffin pans ⅔ full. Bake at 350° for 20-25 minutes.

Yield: 48 miniature muffins.

Easy to make cheese biscuits—very rich in taste!

Sticky Buns

1 pound frozen bread dough
½ cup dark brown sugar
½ cup light corn syrup
¼ cup butter

¾ cup pecan halves
¼ cup sugar
1 teaspoon ground cinnamon

Thaw bread dough to room temperature. Using a large ovenproof skillet or casserole, combine brown sugar, corn syrup, and butter over medium heat. Bring to a boil, stirring constantly. Reduce heat and simmer 1 minute. Remove from heat and cool briefly. Place pecan halves, flat side up, in bottom of skillet. Roll dough into a 16 x 2-inch rectangle on a lightly floured board. Combine sugar and cinnamon and sprinkle over dough. Roll-up tightly from long side, pinching seams to seal. Cut into 16 (1-inch) slices and place ½-inch apart in skillet. Arrange buns evenly to ensure even cooking. Cover and allow to rise in a warm place for 30 minutes, or until doubled. Bake in a preheated 375° oven for 15-20 minutes, or until golden brown. Invert onto serving dish and allow all caramel to drain over buns. Serve warm.

Yield: 16 buns.

Old-Fashioned Waffles

2 cups flour
2 heaping teaspoons baking powder
½ teaspoon salt

2 cups milk
1 cup butter, melted
3 eggs, separated

Sift flour, baking powder, and salt together. Slowly stir in milk, beating well. Add butter, mixing thoroughly. Whisk egg yolks and add to mixture. Beat egg whites until soft peaks form and fold in gently. Cook in waffle iron until golden brown. Serve with warm syrup.

Yield: 10-12 waffles.

These waffles are very rich in flavor, but light in texture. Delicious!

Overnight French Toast

8 slices French bread, ¾-inch thick
4 eggs, beaten
1 cup milk
1 tablespoon sugar
¼ teaspoon nutmeg

⅛ teaspoon salt
2 tablespoons orange juice
½ teaspoon vanilla extract
2-4 tablespoons butter
Confectioners' sugar

Place bread in a 9 x 13-inch baking dish. Combine eggs, milk, sugar, nutmeg, salt, orange juice, and vanilla extract. Beat well. Pour mixture over bread slices. Turn slices over to coat evenly. Cover and refrigerate overnight. To serve, sauté in butter 4 minutes on each side. Sprinkle with confectioners' sugar.

Yield: 4 servings.

Orange Marmalade Spread

1 tablespoon orange peel, grated   2 tablespoons orange juice
8 ounces cream cheese   ½ cup pecans, chopped
½ cup orange marmalade

Using a food processor, or blender, grate orange peel, add cream cheese and process until smooth. Add marmalade, orange juice, and nuts. Process until combined.

Yield: 1 cup.

Serve with nut breads or sweet crackers. May be used on butter flavored cookies for children. Won $100 in a recipe contest.

Honey-Orange Butter

½ cup butter, softened
¾ cup honey
½ teaspoon orange rind, grated

Cream butter until light and fluffy. Slowly add honey and beat well. Add orange rind and mix well. Cover and refrigerate several hours.

Yield: 1⅓ cups.

Serve with biscuits, waffles, or pancakes.

DESSERTS

Apple Nut Cake

1½ cups oil
1½ cups sugar
½ cup light brown sugar, firmly
  packed
3 eggs
3 cups flour
2 teaspoons cinnamon
1 teaspoon baking soda

½ teaspoon nutmeg
½ teaspoon salt
1 cup walnuts, coarsely chopped
3½ cups (about 2 pounds) tart
  apples, peeled and coarsely
  chopped (Granny Smith variety
  recommended)
2 teaspoons vanilla extract

Combine oil, sugar, and brown sugar. Blend well. Add eggs, one at a time, blending after each addition. Sift together flour, cinnamon, baking soda, nutmeg, and salt. Add to sugar mixture, blending well. Fold in nuts, apples, and vanilla extract. Pour into a generously greased and floured 10-inch tube pan. Bake at 325° for 1 ¾ hours. Cool in pan 10 minutes. Remove from pan and glaze.

Glaze

3 tablespoons butter
3 tablespoons light brown sugar
3 tablespoons sugar

3 tablespoons whipping cream
¼ teaspoon vanilla extract

Combine butter, brown sugar, sugar, cream, and vanilla extract in saucepan. Bring to boil over medium heat. Let boil one minute. Pour over warm cake.

Yield: 1 (10-inch) tube cake.

Apple Pecan Coffee Cake

2 teaspoons vanilla extract
3 eggs
1¼ cups oil
2 cups sugar
1 teaspoon salt

3 cups apples, chopped
3 cups flour
1 teaspoon baking soda
1 cup pecans, chopped

Mix vanilla extract, eggs, oil, sugar, and salt. Blend in apples, flour, baking soda, and pecans. Pour batter into an ungreased 9 x 13-inch pan. Bake at 350° for 1 hour. While cake is baking, make icing.

Icing

½ cup butter
1 cup brown sugar
1 cup evaporated milk

Bring butter, brown sugar, and evaporated milk to boil. Continue boiling for 3 to 4 minutes. Pour warm icing over warm cake. Cut into squares to serve.

Yield: 1 (9 x 13-inch) coffee cake.

Coconut Pound Cake

1 cup butter or margarine, softened
½ cup shortening
2¾ cups sugar
5 eggs
3 cups flour
1 teaspoon baking powder

½ teaspoon salt
1 cup milk
1 teaspoon coconut flavoring
1 teaspoon vanilla extract
1 (3½-ounce) can coconut

With electric mixer, cream butter and shortening with sugar. Add eggs, one at a time, mixing well after each addition. Combine flour, baking powder, and salt. Blend into butter mixture alternately with milk. Stir in coconut flavoring and vanilla extract. Fold in coconut. Pour into a well-greased 10-inch tube pan. Do not preheat oven. Put in a cold oven and bake at 325° for 1¼ hours, or until done. Cool for 15 minutes, remove from pan and cool completely.

Yield: 1 (10-inch) tube cake.

Cream Cheese Pound Cake

1½ cups butter, softened	3 cups flour
8 ounces cream cheese, softened	1 teaspoon vanilla extract
3 cups sugar	¾ teaspoon almond flavoring
6 eggs	

Cream butter and cream cheese. Blend in sugar. Add eggs one at a time, beating well. Add flour, vanilla extract, and almond flavoring a little at a time, and blend until smooth. Pour into a greased and floured tube pan. (Do not use a Bundt pan.) Bake at 325° for 1 hour 10 minutes. Cool in pan 10-15 minutes, then invert on platter.

Yield: 1 tube cake.

Consider serving this delicious cake with fresh peaches and Amaretto.

Chocolate Pound Cake With Caramel Glaze

1 cup butter, softened	5 tablespoons cocoa
½ cup shortening	¼ teaspoon salt
3 cups sugar	½ teaspoon baking powder
5 eggs	1 cup milk
3 cups flour	1 teaspoon vanilla extract

Cream butter, shortening, and sugar. Add eggs, one at a time, and blend well. Sift together flour, cocoa, salt, and baking powder. Add alternately with milk and vanilla extract. Pour into a greased and floured tube pan. Bake at 325° for 1½ to 2 hours. While cake cools, make glaze.

Glaze

½ cup margarine	2-3 cups confectioners' sugar,
1 cup brown sugar	sifted
¼ cup milk	

Stir margarine and sugar in saucepan over medium heat until sugar melts. Slowly add milk. Remove from heat. Add confectioners' sugar, ½ cup at a time, until spreading consistency. Drizzle on cake.

Yield: 1 tube cake.

Chocolate Sour Cream Cake

3 squares unsweetened chocolate
½ cup water
1 cup sour cream
2 cups sifted cake flour
1½ teaspoons baking powder
1 teaspoon baking soda
1 teaspoon salt

⅔ cup butter
⅔ cup light brown sugar, firmly
   packed
1 cup sugar
3 eggs
2 teaspoons vanilla extract

Stir chocolate and water in saucepan over very low heat until chocolate is melted. Cool thoroughly, then add sour cream, mixing well. Sift together flour, baking powder, soda, and salt. Set aside. Cream butter and sugars. Add eggs, one at a time, mixing well after each addition. Beat in vanilla extract. Alternately, add flour and sour cream mixture, mixing well after each addition. Pour batter into 2 greased (9-inch) pans which have been lined on bottoms with wax paper. Bake at 350° for 30-40 minutes. Cool cake in pans for 10 minutes, then remove from pans and cool on racks. Frost with butter frosting or chocolate butter frosting.

Butter Frosting

½ cup butter, softened
1 (16-ounce) box confectioners'
   sugar

1 teaspoon vanilla extract
1 (5-ounce) can evaporated milk
4 tablespoons cocoa (optional)

Whip butter. Add sugar, vanilla extract, and 2-3 tablespoons of evaporated milk. Whip until fluffy. Add more milk, one tablespoon at a time, until desired spreading consistency. For chocolate icing, stir in cocoa.

Yield: One 9-inch layer cake.

Chocolate Cinnamon Cake

½ cup shortening
½ cup butter or margarine
1 cup water
4 tablespoons cocoa
2 cups sugar
2 cups flour

1 teaspoon cinnamon
¼ teaspoon salt
½ cup buttermilk
1 teaspoon baking soda
2 eggs
1 tablespoon vanilla extract

Combine shortening, butter, water, and cocoa in saucepan. Bring to a boil, stirring constantly. Remove from heat. In a large mixing bowl, combine sugar, flour, cinnamon, and salt. Mix buttermilk and soda and add to dry ingredients. Stir eggs and vanilla extract into flour and buttermilk mixture. Add hot mixture and beat two minutes with electric mixer at medium speed. Pour into a greased and floured 9 x 13-inch baking pan. Bake at 325° for 40-50 minutes. Prepare icing while cake is baking.

Icing

4 tablespoons cocoa
½ cup butter or margarine
1 tablespoon vanilla extract

6 tablespoons milk
1 box confectioners' sugar, sifted
½ cup walnuts, chopped (optional)

Combine cocoa, margarine, and vanilla extract in a saucepan. Bring to boil. Add confectioners' sugar and milk; beat two minutes with electric mixer at medium speed. Pour over cake. Garnish with walnuts, if desired.

Yield: 1 (9 x 13-inch) cake.

Chocolate Coca-Cola Cake

2 cups flour	½ cup buttermilk
2 cups sugar	1 teaspoon baking soda
1 cup butter	2 eggs
3 tablespoons cocoa	1 teaspoon vanilla extract
1 cup Coca-Cola	1½ cups miniature marshmallows

Sift together flour and sugar. Melt butter in saucepan. Add cocoa and Coca-Cola. Heat to boiling; boil one minute. Add to flour and sugar. Stir in buttermilk and baking soda. Add eggs and vanilla extract and stir until smooth. Stir in marshmallows. Pour into a 9 x 13-inch greased pan. Bake at 350° for 40-45 minutes. While cake is baking, prepare icing.

Icing

½ cup butter	1 teaspoon vanilla extract
3 tablespoons cocoa	1 cup pecans, chopped
6 tablespoons Coca-Cola	
1 (16-ounce) box confectioners' sugar	

Mix butter, cocoa, and Coca-Cola in saucepan and bring to boil. Stir in sugar, vanilla extract, and pecans. Spread on warm cake.

Yield: 1 (9 x 13-inch) cake.

Mississippi Mud Cake

1 cup butter	2 cups sugar
½ cup cocoa	Dash salt
4 eggs, beaten	2 teaspoons vanilla extract
1½ cups flour	1½ cups pecans, chopped

Melt butter. Add cocoa and eggs. Mix. Add flour, sugar, salt, vanilla extract, and pecans. Mix well. Pour into a greased and floured 9 x 13-inch pan. Spread evenly. Bake at 350° for 30-35 minutes. While cake is baking, prepare topping.

Topping

½ cup butter, melted	½ cup milk
1 (16-ounce) box confectioners' sugar	½ teaspoon vanilla extract
½ cup cocoa	1 (6¼-ounce) bag miniature marshmallows

Combine butter, confectioners' sugar, cocoa, milk, and vanilla extract. Mix well. When cake is removed from oven, immediately sprinkle marshmallows over top of cake. Spread topping over melted marshmallows. Cool and cut into squares.

Yield: 1 (9 x 13-inch) cake.

All Occasion Cake

4 eggs, beaten	1 cup milk
2 cups sugar	½ cup margarine
2 cups flour	1 teaspoon vanilla extract
2 teaspoons baking powder	5 tablespoons cocoa (optional)

Combine eggs and sugar. Mix in flour and baking powder. Set aside. Heat milk; stir in margarine until melted. Add to flour and egg mixture. Stir in vanilla extract. (Stir in cocoa for a chocolate cake). Pour batter into a greased and floured pan. Bake at 350° for about 25 minutes.

Yield: 2 (9-inch) round cakes or 24 cupcakes or 1 tube cake.

There is no need to buy cake mixes with this quick and easy recipe. Top with your favorite frosting or fresh strawberries.

Brown Sugar Cake With Glaze

3 cups flour
1 teaspoon baking soda
1 cup butter
3 cups brown sugar, packed

4 eggs
1½ teaspoons maple flavoring
1 cup buttermilk

Sift together flour and baking soda, set aside. Cream together butter and sugar. Add eggs, one at a time. In measuring cup mix together maple flavoring and buttermilk. Alternately, add flour and buttermilk to mixture, starting and ending with flour. Bake in a greased bundt pan at 325° for 45-50 minutes. Cool completely. Invert on cake plate.

Glaze

¼ cup margarine
½ cup brown sugar
⅛ cup milk

1-1½ cups confectioners' sugar, sifted

Stir margarine and sugar in saucepan over medium heat until sugar melts. Slowly add milk. Remove from heat. Add confectioners' sugar, ½ cup at a time, until spreading consistency. Drizzle on cake.

Yield: 1 bundt cake.

Queen's Cake

1 cup boiling water	1 teaspoon vanilla extract
1 cup dates, chopped	1½ cups flour, sifted
1 teaspoon baking soda	1 teaspoon baking powder
1 cup sugar	½ teaspoon salt
⅓ cup butter	⅓ cup nuts, chopped
1 egg	

Pour boiling water over dates and baking soda. Set aside. Cream together sugar and butter. Beat egg and add to butter mixture along with vanilla extract. Sift flour, baking powder, and salt into butter mixture. Mix well. Add the date mixture and the nuts. Blend well and pour into a greased and floured 9 x 13-inch pan. Bake at 350° for 35 minutes. Cool completely then prepare frosting.

Frosting

⅔ cup cream	⅓ cup coconut
⅔ cup light brown sugar	⅓ cup nuts, chopped
¼ cup butter	

Bring cream, light brown sugar, and butter to boil, stirring constantly. Continue cooking and stirring for 3-5 minutes. Spread immediately on cake. Top with coconut and nuts.

Yield: 1 (9 x 13-inch) cake.

It is said that this is the only cake Queen Elizabeth II bakes herself. In return for sharing it with the public, the Queen asks that each time that it is made, 10 pence be donated to charity.

Hummingbird Cake

3 cups flour
2 cups sugar
1 teaspoon baking soda
1 teaspoon salt
1 teaspoon cinnamon
3 eggs, beaten

1 cup vegetable oil
1½ teaspoons vanilla extract
1 (8-ounce) can crushed pineapple
1 cup pecans, chopped
2 cups bananas, mashed

Combine flour, sugar, baking soda, salt, and cinnamon in a large mixing bowl. Add eggs and oil and stir just until dry ingredients are moistened. Stir in vanilla extract, canned pineapple with juice, pecans, and bananas. Spoon batter into 3 greased and floured 9-inch round cake pans. Bake at 350° for 25-30 minutes. Cool in pans 10 minutes. Remove and cool completely. Frost top, sides, and between layers.

Frosting

8 ounces cream cheese, softened
½ cup butter or margarine, softened
1 (16-ounce) box confectioners' sugar, sifted

1 teaspoon vanilla extract
½ cup pecans, chopped and divided

With electric mixer, beat cream cheese and butter until smooth. Add confectioners' sugar and vanilla extract; beat until light and fluffy. Stir in ¼ cup pecans. Sprinkle remaining ¼ cup pecans on top of frosted cake.

Yield: 1 (3-layer) cake.

Italian Cream Cake

½ cup butter
½ cup shortening
2 cups sugar
5 eggs, separated
2 cups flour

1 teaspoon baking soda
1 cup buttermilk
1 teaspoon vanilla extract
1 (3½-ounce) can coconut
1 cup pecans, chopped

Cream together butter, shortening, and sugar. Add egg yolks, one at a time, beating after each addition. Combine flour and soda and add to mixture alternately with buttermilk. Stir in vanilla extract, coconut, and pecans. Beat egg whites until stiff and fold into batter. Pour into 3 greased and floured 9-inch round cake pans. Bake at 350° for 25-30 minutes. Cool in pans 10 minutes, then remove and cool completely before frosting.

Frosting

8 ounces cream cheese, softened
½ cup butter
1 (16-ounce) box confectioners'
sugar

1 teaspoon vanilla extract
½ cup pecans, chopped (optional)
½ cup coconut (optional)

Beat cream cheese and butter. Gradually add sugar, beating well. Add vanilla extract. Add pecans and coconut if desired.

Yield: 1 (3-layer) cake.

Angel Pie

4 eggs, separated
¼ teaspoon cream of tartar
Pinch of salt
1½ cups sugar, divided
3 tablespoons fresh lemon juice

1 tablespoon lemon rind, grated
½ teaspoon salt
1 pint heavy cream
1 tablespoon sugar

Beat together egg whites, cream of tartar, and pinch of salt until stiff but not dry. Gradually beat in 1 cup sugar, a tablespoon at a time, until thoroughly blended. Spread meringue over bottom and up sides of a buttered 10-inch pie pan. Bake at 300° for 1 hour. Cool about 2 hours. (Crust will fall). Beat together egg yolks, ½ cup sugar, lemon juice, lemon rind, and ½ teaspoon salt. Cook mixture in double boiler, stirring until thickened. Cool slightly. Whip the cream with 1 tablespoon sugar. Combine half of the whipped cream with the lemon mixture. Pour into cooled meringue shell. Spread remaining whipped cream on lemon filling. Chill. Top with grated lemon rind if desired.

Yield: 8 servings.

Butterscotch Pie

½ cup butter
3 eggs, separated (reserve whites
  for meringue)
1 tablespoon vanilla extract
2 cups milk

¾ cup sugar
¾ cup brown sugar
6 tablespoons flour
1 (9-inch) pie shell, baked
Classic Meringue (see index)

Brown the butter in a large saucepan. Beat egg yolks slightly. Add a small amount of butter to egg yolks, then add all of the egg yolks to the butter. Stir in vanilla and milk. Combine sugar, brown sugar, and flour. Add to butter mixture. Cook over medium heat, stirring constantly until thickened. Cool. Pour into pie shell. Prepare meringue according to Classic Meringue. (See index.) Spread over filling. Bake at 350° for 10-12 minutes or until meringue is slightly browned. Cool, then refrigerate.

Yield: 8 servings.

Luscious Caramel Banana Pie

1 (14-ounce) can sweetened
   condensed milk
2-3 bananas
1 (9-inch) graham cracker crust

1 cup heavy cream
¼ cup confectioners' sugar
2 (1⅛-ounce) English toffee candy
   bars, crumbled

Pour condensed milk into an 8-inch pie plate. Cover plate with foil. Pour about ¼-inch hot water into a 2 quart shallow casserole. Place covered pie plate in casserole. Bake at 425° for 1 hour and 20 minutes or until milk is thick and caramel colored. (Add more water to casserole as needed.) Remove foil when done and set aside. Slice bananas and place on bottom of crust. Spread caramel mixture over bananas. Cool for at least 30 minutes. Combine cream and confectioners' sugar in mixing bowl. Beat until fluffy. Spread over caramel layer. Sprinkle with crumbled candy. Chill at least 3 hours or overnight.

Yield: 8 servings.

Strawberry Bavarian Pie

1 envelope unflavored gelatin
¼ cup warm water
¾ cup sugar, divided
⅛ teaspoon salt
3 egg yolks, beaten
1¼ cups milk
1 teaspoon vanilla extract

1 cup strawberries, pureed
Red food coloring
1 cup heavy cream, whipped
1 (9-inch) pie shell, baked
1 cup strawberries, sliced to
   garnish

Soften gelatin in warm water. In saucepan combine gelatin, ½ cup sugar, salt, egg yolks, and milk. Cook over medium heat, stirring constantly, until custard coats spoon. Stir in vanilla. Refrigerate until partially set. Then beat custard until just smooth. Add pureed strawberries. Beat egg whites, gradually adding ¼ cup sugar, until stiff. Fold into custard. Add several drops red food coloring and blend. Fold in whipped cream. Spread in pie crust. Chill until set. Garnish with sliced strawberries.

Yield: 8 servings.

For a variation, prepare with a chocolate wafer crust.

Heavenly Chocolate Pie

3 tablespoons cornstarch
3 tablespoons cocoa
1 cup plus 1 tablespoon sugar
½ cup butter or margarine
¼ teaspoon salt
1 (5.3-ounce) can evaporated milk
1 cup milk

1 teaspoon vanilla extract
2 eggs, separated (save whites for
   meringue)
1 (9-inch) pie crust, baked
Classic Meringue (see index)
Chocolate curls to garnish

Combine cornstarch, cocoa, sugar, butter, salt, evaporated milk, milk, and vanilla in a double boiler. Cook slowly until the mixture begins to thicken. Remove from heat. Add beaten egg yolks and continue to cook until thickened. Pour into baked pie crust. Top with Classic Meringue (see index) or with sweetened whipped cream. Cool completely. Refrigerate until ready to serve.

Yield: 8 servings.

This pie filling is delicious as a pudding for parfaits or as a filling for popovers.

Brownie Fudge Pie

¼ cup butter
¾ cup brown sugar, firmly packed
1 (12-ounce) package semi-sweet
   chocolate chips
3 eggs, beaten
¼ cup flour

1 cup pecans, coarsely chopped
1 teaspoon vanilla extract
1 (9-inch) pie shell
Whipped cream or ice cream for
   topping

Melt butter, brown sugar, and chocolate chips in double boiler. Cool. Add beaten eggs. Combine flour with nuts and add to chocolate mixture. Stir in vanilla. Pour into pie shell. Bake at 375° for 30-35 minutes. Cool and refrigerate several hours before serving. Top with whipped cream or ice cream if desired.

Yield: 8-10 servings.

No Ordinary Chocolate Pie

Meringue crust

4 egg whites
¼ teaspoon cream of tartar
1 cup sugar

Combine egg whites and cream of tartar; beat until stiff but not dry. Add sugar gradually, beating well. Make a "crust" with the mixture in a greased 10-inch (deep dished) glass pie plate. Bake at 275° for 1 hour. Cool to room temperature.

Filling

(6-ounce) package semi-sweet
   chocolate chips
2 egg whites
1 pint heavy cream, divided

6 egg yolks
2 tablespoons sugar
Shaved chocolate to garnish

Melt chocolate chips in double boiler or microwave. Beat egg whites until stiff. In a separate bowl beat ½ pint (8-ounces) of heavy cream until stiff. Add egg yolks one at a time to cooled melted chocolate. Fold in the egg whites and the whipped cream until mixture is smooth and all one color. Pour into meringue crust and refrigerate one hour. Whip the remaining ½ pint of heavy cream with sugar. Spread on top of pie. Garnish with shaved chocolate if desired.

Yield: 1 (10-inch) pie.

Cranberry Meringue Pie

2¼ cups sugar
¾ cup water
4 cups fresh cranberries
3 tablespoons cornstarch
½ teaspoon almond extract

¼ teaspoon salt
3 eggs, separated (save whites for
  meringue)
1 (9-inch) pie shell, baked
Classic Meringue (see index)

In a large saucepan combine sugar and water. Heat to a boil. Add cranberries and reduce heat. Cook until berries pop (10-12 minutes), stirring often. Remove from heat. Combine cornstarch, almond extract, salt, and egg yolks. Add 2 tablespoons hot cranberry mixture to egg mixture. Add all of the egg mixture to the cranberries in the saucepan. Return to low heat and cook, stirring constantly, until mixture is translucent and begins to boil. Pour into a pie shell. Prepare meringue according to Classic Meringue (see index), substituting ½ teaspoon almond extract for vanilla. Spread over filling. Bake at 350° for 10-15 minutes. Cool and refrigerate.

Yield: 10 servings (only 280 calories per serving).

Classic Key Lime Pie

3 eggs, separated (save whites for
  meringue)
1 (14-ounce) can sweetened
  condensed milk
½ cup Key lime juice

Rind of a Key lime, grated
1 (9-inch) graham cracker crust,
  baked and cooled
Classic Meringue (see index)

Blend egg yolks with sweetened condensed milk, lime juice, and lime rind. Pour into graham cracker crust. Top with Classic Meringue (See index). Bake at 350° for 10-12 minutes until meringue is browned. Cool, then chill.

Yield: 8 servings.

Coconut Cream Pie

¾ cup sugar
⅓ cup flour
¼ teaspoon salt
2 cups milk
3 eggs, separated (save whites for meringue)

3 tablespoons butter
1 teaspoon vanilla extract
1½ cups shredded coconut
1 (9-inch) deep pie shell, baked
Classic Meringue (see index)
⅓ cup shredded coconut

Combine sugar, flour, and salt in saucepan. Stir in milk and mix well. Cook, stirring constantly over medium heat until thickened. Remove from heat. Beat in egg yolks. Cook 2 more minutes. Remove from heat and add butter and vanilla. Stir in 1½ cups coconut. Pour into pie shell. Prepare meringue according to Classic Meringue. (See Index). Spread over filling. Sprinkle ⅓ cup coconut over meringue. Bake at 350° for 12-15 minutes. Cool completely then refrigerate.

Yield: 8 servings.

Coconut Ice Box Pie

3 eggs, separated
¼ teaspoon salt
1 teaspoon vanilla extract
¾ cup sugar, divided
1 envelope unflavored gelatin

¼ cup milk
1 cup heavy cream, whipped
¾ cup coconut
1 (9-inch) pie shell, baked and cooled

Beat egg yolks with salt, vanilla, and half of the sugar. Combine gelatin and milk in bowl. Place bowl in a pan of very hot water, and stir gelatin until it is dissolved. Add egg yolk mixture to gelatin. Fold in whipped cream. Beat egg whites with other half of sugar, and fold into mixture. Add coconut. Pour into pie shell. Refrigerate until firm.

Yield: 8 servings.

Will keep several days in refrigerator or will freeze. Fresh coconut is best.

Peppermint-Fudge Ribbon Pie

Fudge Sauce

2 tablespoons butter
2 (1-ounce) squares unsweetened
chocolate

1 cup sugar
1 (5.3 ounce) can evaporated milk
1 teaspoon vanilla extract

Combine butter, chocolate, sugar, and evaporated milk in saucepan. Cook and stir until thickened. Add vanilla. Cool completely.

Pie

2 pints peppermint ice cream,
softened
1 (9-inch) pie shell, baked

Classic Meringue (see index)
Peppermint candy, crushed for
garnish

Soften ice cream. Spread 1 pint in pie shell. Cover with half of the cooled fudge sauce. Repeat layers. Freeze overnight. Prepare meringue according to Classic Meringue. (See index.) Spread over pie. Garnish with crushed candy. Bake at 375° for 5-6 minutes. Serve immediately. Freeze leftovers.

Yield: 6-8 servings.

Malt Shop Pie

1 pint vanilla ice cream, softened
½ cup malted milk balls, crushed
2 tablespoons milk
1 (9-inch) graham cracker crust
3 tablespoons instant chocolate-
flavored malted milk powder

3 tablespoons marshmallow
topping
1 cup heavy cream
Crushed malted milk balls for
topping

Blend softened ice cream, malted milk balls, and 1 tablespoon milk. Spread in graham cracker crust and freeze. Combine malted milk powder, marshmallow topping, and 1 tablespoon milk. Add cream and beat until soft peaks form. Spread over ice cream layer. Freeze until firm. Sprinkle with crushed malted milk balls.

Yield: 8 servings.

Mocha Meringue Pie

2 egg whites
½ teaspoon baking powder
Pinch of salt
¾ cup sugar
1 cup chocolate wafer crumbs
½ cup pecans, chopped

1 teaspoon vanilla extract
Coffee ice cream, softened
½ cup confectioners' sugar
1 cup heavy cream
Sweet chocolate curls to garnish
½ cup Kahlúa

Have egg whites at room temperature. Beat until frothy. Add baking powder and beat slightly. Gradually add salt and sugar. Continue beating until stiff and glossy. Fold in chocolate wafer crumbs, pecans, and vanilla. Make a "crust" with the meringue mixture in a buttered 9-inch pie pan. Bake at 350° for 30 minutes. Cool. Spread ice cream over crust. Cover and freeze overnight. Remove pie from freezer. Combine confectioners' sugar and cream; beat until light and spread on pie. Garnish with chocolate curls. Pour 1 tablespoon Kahlúa over each slice when served.

Yield: 8 servings.

Standard Pie Crust

1½ cups flour, sifted
½ teaspoon salt

½ cup vegetable shortening
4-5 tablespoons cold water

Sift flour and salt together. Cut in shortening until it looks like cornmeal. Sprinkle water 1 tablespoon at a time over flour mixture. Gently blend and form into a ball. Flatten on a lightly floured board. Roll from center to outside edges until ⅛-inch thick. Transfer to pie plate and trim excess 1-inch beyond edge. Fold excess pastry under and flute edges. For recipes with prebaked crusts, prick bottom and sides of crust with fork and bake at 450° for 10-12 minutes. Do not prick pastry if filling and crust are baked together.

Yield: 1 (8 or 9-inch) crust, or 4-6 tart shells.

Graham Cracker Crust

1½ cups graham cracker crumbs   **⅓ cup butter, melted**
⅓ cup light brown sugar   **½ teaspoon ground cinnamon**

Thoroughly combine graham cracker crumbs, sugar, butter, and cinnamon. Firmly press mixture into a buttered 9-inch pie pan. Crust may be baked at 375° for 6-8 minutes to lightly brown. Cool before filling. For an unbaked crust, chill 45 minutes before filling.

Yield: 1 (9-inch) crust.

To shape the crumb crust evenly, place crumbs in center of a 9-inch pie plate and press an 8-inch pie plate firmly into the mixture.

Classic Meringue for Topping Pies

3 egg whites, at room temperature   **¼ teaspoon cream of tartar**
½ teaspoon vanilla extract   **5-6 tablespoons sugar**

Beat egg whites with vanilla and cream of tartar until soft peaks form. Add sugar, one tablespoon at a time, continuing to beat until stiff peaks form, the mixture is glossy, and the sugar is completely dissolved. Spread meringue over pie filling. Be careful to seal meringue to edges of pastry. For meringue to mound its highest, be sure the bowl and beaters are clean of grease. Egg whites should be at room temperature and without a speck of egg yolk.

Amaretto Cheesecake

1½ cups graham cracker crumbs
2 tablespoons sugar
1 teaspoon cinnamon
6 tablespoons butter or margarine, melted
24 ounces cream cheese, softened
1 cup sugar
4 eggs
½ cup Amaretto
8 ounces sour cream
4 teaspoons sugar
1½ tablespoons Amaretto
¼ cup sliced almonds, toasted, for garnish
1 (1-ounce) square semi-sweet chocolate, grated, for garnish

Combine graham cracker crumbs, sugar, cinnamon, and melted butter. Mix well. Firmly press mixture into bottom and ½-inch up the sides of a 9-inch springform pan. Beat cream cheese with electric mixer until light and fluffy. Gradually add 1 cup sugar, mixing well. Add eggs, one at a time, beating well after each addition. Stir in ½ cup Amaretto; pour mixture onto crust in pan. Bake at 375° for 45 to 50 minutes until set. Combine sour cream, 4 teaspoons sugar, and 1½ tablespoons Amaretto. Stir well and spoon over cheesecake. Bake at 500° for 5 minutes. Cool to room temperature, then refrigerate 24 to 48 hours to let flavors ripen. Garnish with almonds and chocolate.

Yield: 1 (9-inch) cake.

Chocolate Mousse

1 (6-ounce) package semi-sweet chocolate chips
2 eggs
3 tablespoons strong hot coffee
1 tablespoon rum
¾ cup milk, scalded
Whipped cream for garnish
Shaved chocolate for garnish

Place chocolate chips, eggs, coffee, rum, and milk in blender and blend at high speed for 2 minutes. Pour into custard cups or dessert glasses and chill for several hours. This dessert may be made a day ahead. Garnish with whipped cream or shaved chocolate if desired.

Yield: 4 servings.

Cointreau or brandy may be substituted for rum.

Strawberry Mousse

1½ cups low-fat milk
1½ cups frozen unsweetened
  strawberries, halved

4-5 tablespoons sugar
2 teaspoons vanilla extract
Whole fresh berries for garnish

Using a food processor, process milk 3-5 minutes until doubled in volume. When thickened, add the berries through the feed tube while machine is still running. Add sugar and vanilla extract. Continue processing until mixture is a uniform pink color. Spoon into individual dishes and garnish with a whole berry. Serve immediately. Freeze leftovers.

Yield: 4-6 servings.

Peach Ladyfinger Trifle

24 ladyfingers
1 cup peach preserves
4 tablespoons Amaretto
6 cups fresh peaches, sliced
2 (3¾-ounce) packages instant
  vanilla pudding

4 tablespoons sugar
1 pint whipping cream
Toasted slivered almonds

Split ladyfingers and spread with peach preserves. Reassemble and arrange on bottom of a 124-ounce trifle bowl. Sprinkle with Amaretto. Arrange peaches on top of ladyfingers. Make pudding according to package directions. Pour pudding over peaches. Refrigerate several hours. Just before serving beat together sugar and whipping cream until stiff. Spread over pudding. Sprinkle toasted slivered almonds over whipped cream.

Yield: 12 servings.

Seasonal fresh fruits and other preserves may be substituted for peaches.

Strawberries Jubilee

½ cup butter
1 quart strawberries, halved
¼ cup sugar
3 tablespoons orange liqueur
1 teaspoon grated lime peel

¼ cup brandy
Vanilla ice cream or pound cake
   slices
Mint leaves for garnish

In microwave, melt butter in a large shallow dish. Add strawberries and cook 1 minute. Stir in sugar, liqueur, and lime peel. Cook 2 minutes, stirring gently. Heat brandy in a long-handled pan until warm. Ignite and pour over strawberries. Serve hot over ice cream or pound cake slices. Garnish with mint leaves.

Yield: 8 servings.

This recipe may be made on stove top by increasing cooking time 2-3 minutes.

Fudge Truffle Cake

8 ounces semi-sweet chocolate
1 cup sugar
1 cup unsalted butter
½ cup brewed coffee
4 eggs, beaten
1 cup heavy cream

¼ cup confectioners' sugar
½ teaspoon vanilla extract
Chocolate curls for garnish
Fresh strawberries, cherries, or
   raspberries for garnish

Melt chocolate, sugar, and butter in the top of a double boiler. Allow to cool. Add coffee and eggs, beating well. Pour the batter into a buttered and foil-lined 8½-inch springform pan. Bake at 350° for 30-40 minutes or until top forms a crust. Cool and refrigerate overnight. Cake may be frozen at this point. When ready to serve, whip the cream with the confectioners' sugar and vanilla extract until soft peaks form. Slice the cake into pie-shaped wedges and top with whipped cream. Garnish with chocolate curls and fruit. Refrigerate leftovers.

Yield: 8-10 servings.

This elegant dessert may also be presented as a whole cake topped with whipped cream, chocolate, curls, and fruit.

Chocolate Coeur À La Crème

2 ounces semi-sweet chocolate
   chips
8 ounces cream cheese, room
   temperature

1¼ cups whipping cream, divided
⅔ cup confectioners' sugar, sifted
1 teaspoon vanilla extract

Melt chocolate chips in microwave; cool. Beat cream cheese until light and fluffy. Gradually add ¼ cup whipping cream and beat until smooth. Mix in sugar, vanilla extract, and melted chocolate. In another bowl, whip remaining 1 cup cream until soft peaks form. Gently fold into cream cheese mixture. Line a 4-cup coeur à la creme mold with dampened cheesecloth, extending enough over edges to overlap filled mold. Pour mixture into mold and set on a rack placed over a pan. Refrigerate 8 hours or overnight. Just before serving, pull back cheesecloth, invert mold onto platter, and remove all cheesecloth. Serve with raspberry sauce.

Raspberry Sauce

1 (10-ounce) package frozen
   sweetened raspberries, thawed
2 tablespoons confectioners' sugar

Puree raspberries in food processor. Strain through sieve to remove seeds. Stir in sugar.

Yield: 6-8 servings.

Grasshopper Tarts

Shells

1 (6-ounce) package semi-sweet
  chocolate chips
2 tablespoons shortening

Heat chocolate chips and shortening over medium heat, stirring constantly until chocolate is melted. Line 12 muffin cups with paper liners. Swirl 1 tablespoon chocolate mixture in each cup with back of spoon to coat bottom and sides. Refrigerate shells until hard. Carefully remove paper liners and place chocolate cups in muffin tin.

Filling

32 large marshmallows
½ cup milk
¼ cup Creme de Menthe
3 tablespoons white Creme de
  Cacao

1½ cups heavy cream
Few drops of green food coloring,
  if desired
Whipped cream for garnish
Shaved chocolate for garnish

Heat marshmallows and milk over medium heat, stirring constantly until marshmallows are melted. Refrigerate until thickened. Stir in Creme de Menthe and Creme de Cacao. Beat cream until stiff. Fold into marshmallow mixture. Fold in food coloring. Pour into chocolate shells. Chill thoroughly or freeze. Serve with whipped cream and shaved chocolate if desired.

Yield: 12 tarts.

Chocolate Meringue Torte

Meringue

3 egg whites
½ teaspoon cream of tartar
¾ cup sugar

¾ cup pecans, finely chopped
Brown paper

Beat egg whites until frothy. Add cream of tartar and continue beating until soft peaks form. Slowly add sugar while continuing beating until stiff peaks form. Gently fold in half of the pecans. Cut 2 (8-inch) circles from brown paper. Put paper circles on baking sheet and spread one half of meringue on each. Sprinkle each meringue circle with remaining pecans. Bake at 275° for 45 minutes. Turn off oven and leave meringue in oven with door closed for an additional 45 minutes.

Chocolate Filling

1 pint whipping cream
1 cup chocolate syrup, divided
1 teaspoon vanilla extract

Beat whipping cream until stiff. Gently fold in ¾ cup syrup and vanilla extract. To assemble torte, spread one half of filling on top of one meringue. Top with second meringue and top with remaining filling. Drizzle top with remaining chocolate syrup. Freeze. Wrap in foil and return to freezer. Let stand at room temperature 20 minutes before serving.

Yield: 8 servings.

Oreo Crowd Pleaser

1 (20-ounce) package Oreos,
  crushed
½ gallon vanilla ice cream, softened

1 (12-ounce) container frozen
  whipped topping, softened

Save enough of the crushed Oreos to be used as topping. Mix remaining Oreos, ice cream, and frozen whipped topping thoroughly. Spread mixture into a 9 x 13-inch pan. Top with reserved crushed cookies. Freeze until firm. Cut into squares and serve.

Yield: 12 servings.

Tennessee Toddy Ice Cream

1 (16-ounce) can sweet red cherries,
    pitted and halved
½ cup bourbon
½ gallon vanilla ice cream
2 dozen coconut macaroons,
    crumbled
1 cup pecans
1 (16-ounce) container frozen
    whipped topping

Combine cherries and their juice with bourbon; refrigerate overnight. Soften ice cream and add to cherry mixture. Mix well. Add macaroons, pecans, and thawed frozen whipped topping and stir until well blended. Place in freezer. Stir several times so that cherries do not sink to bottom.

Yield: 12-16 servings.

Frozen Peanut Butter Squares

½ cup butter or margarine
2 cups graham cracker crumbs
¼ cup sugar
8 ounces cream cheese, softened
⅔ cup extra crunchy peanut butter
2 cups confectioners' sugar
1 cup milk
1 (16-ounce) container frozen
    whipped topping

Melt butter and combine with graham cracker crumbs and sugar. Press into a 9 x 13-inch baking pan. Blend cream cheese, peanut butter, and confectioners' sugar. Slowly add the milk, blending well. Fold in whipped topping. Pour into crust and freeze. Cut into squares to serve.

Yield: 15 servings.

Café Jamaica

1 teaspoon instant coffee	½ cup whipping cream
6 tablespoons dark rum	Chocolate curls for garnish
1 quart coffee ice cream, softened	Sliced strawberries for color

Dissolve instant coffee in rum. Blend rum-coffee mixture into ice cream with a fork. Place in a covered container and return to freezer. (It will not freeze completely firm.) Just before serving, whip cream and ripple it gently through ice cream. Serve in individual sherbet dishes. If desired, garnish with chocolate curls or sliced strawberries to add color.

Yield: 6-8 servings.

Frozen Lemon Pudding

3 egg yolks	¼ teaspoon salt
⅓ cup lemon juice	1 cup whipping cream
1 cup sugar, divided	3 egg whites
1 teaspoon grated lemon rind	Vanilla wafer crumbs

Cook egg yolks, lemon juice, ½ cup of sugar, lemon rind, and salt in double boiler until thickened. Cool. Whip cream and fold into lemon mixture. Beat egg whites, gradually adding remaining ½ cup of sugar, until stiff, and fold into mixture. Sprinkle vanilla wafer crumbs in bottom of an 8 x 8-inch square dish. Pour mixture into dish and sprinkle more crumbs on top. Freeze 4 hours or until solid.

Yield: 6-8 servings.

May be used as a frozen pie filling with a graham cracker crust.

Pecan Pie Bars

Crust

1 cup butter, melted
2 cups flour
1 cup light brown sugar

½ teaspoon cinnamon
¼ teaspoon nutmeg

Mix together butter, flour, brown sugar, cinnamon, and nutmeg. Spread into a 9 x 13-inch pan. Bake at 350° for 12-15 minutes. Cool.

Filling

4 eggs, slightly beaten
¼ cup flour
1 (3½-ounce) can coconut
3 cups dark brown sugar

2 cups pecans, chopped
1 teaspoon salt
1 teaspoon vanilla extract
Confectioners' sugar

Lower oven temperature to 325°. Combine eggs, flour, coconut, brown sugar, pecans, salt, and vanilla extract. Spread over crust. Bake 40-45 minutes or until firm. Sprinkle with confectioners' sugar. Cool. Refrigerate until firm. Cut into bars.

Yield: 4 dozen.

Peppermint Party Brownies

4 eggs
2 cups sugar
1 cup cocoa
1 cup flour

½ teaspoon peppermint extract
1 teaspoon vanilla extract
1 cup butter, melted

Whisk eggs and sugar until well blended. Add cocoa and flour; mix well. Stir in peppermint extract, vanilla extract, and butter. Spread into a greased 11 x 17-inch pan. Bake at 350° for 15 minutes. Do not overbake. Cool.

Frosting

2¾ cups confectioners' sugar
½ cup butter
½ teaspoon peppermint extract

Milk
3 drops green food coloring

Cream confectioners' sugar and butter until creamy. Add peppermint extract and enough milk to obtain desired icing consistency. Food coloring may be added if desired. Frost cooled brownies.

Glaze

2 (1-ounce) squares of unsweetened
   chocolate
2 tablespoons butter

Melt chocolate and butter in a double boiler or microwave. Brush on frosted brownies with a pastry brush. Chill 10 minutes before cutting into 2 x ½-inch fingers.

Yield: Approximately 60 brownies.

Chocolate Toffee Squares

2 cups flour
½ cup butter, softened
1½ cups light brown sugar

1 cup pecans, chopped
⅔ cup butter
1 cup semi-sweet chocolate chips

Combine flour, ½ cup softened butter, and 1 cup light brown sugar. Beat with electric mixer 2-3 minutes. Press into a 9 x 13-inch pan and sprinkle with pecans. Combine ⅔ cup butter and the remaining ½ cup light brown sugar in a saucepan. Cook over medium heat, stirring constantly until bubbly. Pour over pecans. Bake at 350° for 20 minutes. Remove from oven and sprinkle with chocolate chips. After chips melt, spread evenly to frost. Cool. Cut into small squares. Very rich!

Yield: 48 squares.

Caramel Chocolate Brownies

1 (14-ounce) bag caramels
⅔ cup evaporated milk, divided
1 box German chocolate cake mix
¾ cup butter, melted

1 cup pecans, chopped
1 (6-ounce) package semi-sweet
 chocolate chips

Melt caramels with ⅓ cup evaporated milk in double boiler, stirring until smooth. Set aside. Combine cake mix, melted butter, remaining ⅓ cup evaporated milk and nuts. Press half of cake mixture into a greased 9 x 13-inch pan. Bake at 350° for 6 minutes. Sprinkle chocolate chips on top, then cover evenly with caramel mixture. Dribble remaining cake mixture on top. Bake 20 minutes. Cool 30 minutes. Chill 1 hour before cutting into squares.

Yield: 48 brownies.

Lime Bars

1 cup flour	½ teaspoon baking powder
½ cup butter, softened	¼ teaspoon salt
¼ cup confectioners' sugar	1 teaspoon grated lime peel
2 large eggs	2 tablespoons fresh lime juice
1 cup sugar	

Beat together flour, butter, and confectioners' sugar until blended. Press into bottom of an 8-inch square pan. Bake at 350° until golden, about 20 minutes. (Leave oven on.) Beat together eggs, sugar, baking powder, salt, lime peel, and lime juice until ivory colored. Pour over hot crust. Bake at 350° until edges are browned, about 25-30 minutes. Cool and cut into 2-inch squares.

Yield: 16 squares.

Captain's Bars

½ cup cake flour	1 cup sugar
¾ teaspoon baking powder	2 eggs, well beaten
½ teaspoon salt	¼ cup milk
⅓ cup shortening	1 teaspoon vanilla extract
2 (1-ounce) squares unsweetened	1 cup walnuts, chopped
chocolate, melted	

Sift together flour, baking powder, and salt. Set aside. Add shortening to melted chocolate and stir until smooth. Gradually add sugar to eggs, then blend in chocolate mixture. Stir in flour mixture; blend in milk, vanilla extract, and walnuts. Pour into a greased 8-inch square pan and bake at 325° for 40-50 minutes. Cool. Cut into squares.

Yield: 16 bars.

All purpose flour may be substituted for cake flour by using ½ cup, less 2 tablespoons.

Cookie Madam Butterscotch Cheesecake Bars

6 tablespoons butter or margarine
1 (12-ounce) package butterscotch
  morsels
2 cups graham cracker crumbs
1 cup chopped nuts

8 ounces cream cheese
1 (14-ounce) can condensed milk
1 egg
1 teaspoon vanilla extract

Preheat oven to 350° if using metal baking pan, or 325° if using glass baking dish. Place butter and morsels in a greased 9 x 13-inch baking pan. Heat in oven about 3 minutes or until butter and morsels are melted. Watch carefully that butter does not burn. Remove from oven and stir in crumbs and nuts. Reserve 1 cup of crumbs for topping, and press remainder into bottom of pan. In a bowl, beat cream cheese, condensed milk, egg, and vanilla extract until blended. Pour over crumb mixture in pan. Sprinkle reserved 1 cup of crumb mixture on top. Bake 25 to 30 minutes, or until toothpick comes out clean.

Yield: 16 squares.

Traditional Sugar Cookie Cutouts

1 cup butter, softened
1½ cups confectioners' sugar
1 egg
1 teaspoon vanilla extract
½-¾ teaspoon almond extract

2½ cups flour
1 teaspoon baking soda
1 teaspoon cream of tartar
Granulated sugar

Cream butter, sugar, egg, vanilla, and almond extract. Combine flour, baking soda, and cream of tartar. Add to creamed mixture, blending well. Cover and refrigerate 2-3 hours, or overnight. Roll out dough on a lightly floured board, about ⅛-inch thick. Cut into desired shapes and carefully transfer to a lightly greased baking sheet. Sprinkle with granulated sugar. Bake in a preheated 375° oven for 7-9 minutes.

Yield: 4-5 dozen.

If cookies are to be frosted omit the granulated sugar sprinkled on top.

Molasses Sugar Cookies

⅔ cup cooking oil
1 cup sugar
1 egg
¼ cup molasses
2 teaspoons baking soda
½ teaspoon ground cloves

½ teaspoon ground ginger
1 teaspoon ground cinnamon
2 cups flour, sifted
½ teaspoon salt
Granulated sugar for rolling

Combine oil and sugar. Add egg and molasses. Beat well. Sift together baking soda, cloves, ginger, cinnamon, flour, and salt. Mix with other ingredients and chill overnight. Form into 1-inch balls and roll in granulated sugar. Place on a greased cookie sheet about 2-inches apart. Bake at 375° for 8-10 minutes.

Yield: 12 dozen small cookies.

Cocoa Kisses

1 cup margarine
⅔ cup sugar
1 teaspoon vanilla extract
½ cup cocoa

1⅔ cups flour
1 cup pecans, chopped
1 (9-ounce) package Hershey's
    Kisses, unwrapped

Cream together margarine, sugar, and vanilla extract until fluffy. Gradually blend in cocoa and flour. Stir in nuts. Refrigerate dough at least 30 minutes. Mold one rounded teaspoon of dough around each Kiss and roll into a ball. Place on cookie sheets about 1-inch apart. Bake at 375° for 10-12 minutes. Be careful not to overcook. Cool.

Yield: 4 dozen.

After Dinner Cookies

1 cup vanilla wafer crumbs
¾ cup pecans, finely chopped
1 cup confectioners' sugar
2 tablespoons light corn syrup

⅓ cup green Creme de Menthe
Additional confectioners' sugar for
  rolling

Combine vanilla wafer crumbs, pecans, and sugar in medium size bowl. Add corn syrup and Creme de Menthe. Mix well. Dough will be stiff. Roll into small balls, ¾-inch in diameter. Moisten hands if dough tends to stick to them. (Balls may be frozen at this point.) Roll in additional confectioners' sugar. Store in an airtight container. (Be sure to thaw completely before rolling in sugar.)

Yield: 4 dozen.

Cherry Pecan Slices

2¼ cups flour
1 cup butter, softened
1 egg
2 tablespoons milk

1 teaspoon vanilla extract
1 cup confectioners' sugar
2 cups whole candied red cherries
1 cup pecan halves

In a large bowl combine flour, butter, egg, milk, vanilla extract, and confectioners' sugar. Blend well. Stir in cherries and pecans carefully. Chill dough 1 hour. Shape dough into two 10-inch rolls and wrap in plastic wrap. Chill 1-2 hours until firm. Cut rolls into ¼-inch slices. Place on ungreased cookie sheets. Bake at 400° for 7 minutes. Watch carefully. Edges should be golden brown. Cool on wire racks.

Yield: 75 cookies.

Chocolate Chip Kisses

2 egg whites
⅛ teaspoon cream of tartar
⅛ teaspoon salt
1 teaspoon vanilla extract

¾ cup sugar
½ cup semi-sweet chocolate chips
¼ cup nuts, chopped

Beat egg whites, cream of tartar, and salt in small bowl until soft peaks form. Add vanilla. Add sugar gradually, beating until stiff. Fold in chocolate chips and nuts. Cut brown wrapping paper to fit baking sheets. Drop mixture by teaspoonfuls onto ungreased paper, about 2 inches apart. Bake at 300° for 25 minutes, until dry. Let cool slightly before removing from paper. Cool completely on rack. Store in airtight containers.

Yield: 3 dozen.

Peanut Butter-Chocolate Chip Crispies

½ cup butter, softened
⅓ cup peanut butter
⅔ cup sugar
⅓ cup brown sugar, packed
1 egg
½ teaspoon vanilla extract

1 cup flour
½ teaspoon baking soda
¼ teaspoon salt
1 cup semi-sweet chocolate chips
2 cups Rice Krispies cereal,
    crushed to equal 1 cup

Cream butter and peanut butter with sugars. Add egg and vanilla extract; mix until blended. Combine flour, baking soda, and salt. Add to creamed mixture and mix well. Stir in chips and cereal. Drop by level tablespoonfuls onto greased cookie sheets. Bake at 350° for 8-10 minutes. Bottoms should be lightly browned. Let stand 1 minute on cookie sheet before removing.
Yield: 4½ dozen.

Brownie Spoon Cupcakes

4 ounces semi-sweet chocolate
1 cup butter
1 pinch salt
1¾ cups sugar

1 cup flour, sifted
4 large eggs
1 tablespoon vanilla extract

Melt chocolate, butter, and salt in double boiler or microwave. Combine sugar, flour, and eggs. Add chocolate to flour mixture. Stir in vanilla extract. Line small or medium cupcake tins with paper. Fill cups ⅔ full with mixture. Bake at 325° for 25-30 minutes for medium cupcakes or 15 minutes for small cupcakes. Cupcakes will fall after removal from oven.

Icing

4 tablespoons butter
2 cups confectioners' sugar
2-3 tablespoons milk

Combine butter and confectioners' sugar. Add milk, one tablespoon at a time, to obtain desired spreading consistency. Fill center of cupcakes with icing while cupcakes are still warm.

Yield: 48 small cupcakes or 24 medium cupcakes.

Rich enough to eat with a spoon!

Caramel-Pecan Turtle Candy

1 pound caramels
2 tablespoons milk
2 cups pecans, chopped
Parchment paper

1 (12-ounce) package semi-sweet
 chocolate chips
¼ bar paraffin

Melt caramels with milk in microwave, stirring frequently. When mixture is fully melted, add pecans and mix well. Place parchment paper on cookie sheet. Drop caramel-nut mixture by teaspoonfuls onto parchment sheet. Place in freezer and harden completely. Melt chocolate chips and paraffin in double boiler. Remove candy pieces from freezer and drop one at a time into melted chocolate. Coat well. Use two forks to retrieve candy from chocolate mixture; let excess chocolate drip off. Place coated candy back on parchment and return to freezer to harden. (If candy is to be used soon, it may be stored at room temperature. Box it between layers of waxed paper.)

Yield: 36 pieces.

Kraft caramels may be used but commercial caramel bought at a candy supply store is preferable.

Brandy Balls

1 (6-ounce) package semi-sweet
 chocolate chips
3 tablespoons light corn syrup
½ cup brandy or rum
2½ cups vanilla wafers, finely
 crushed

¾ cup nuts, finely chopped
¼ cup confectioners' sugar
Additional sugar for rolling

Melt chocolate over low heat in double boiler or in microwave. Remove from heat and add corn syrup and brandy. Combine vanilla wafers, nuts, and confectioners' sugar. Add chocolate mixture and mix well. Let stand 30 minutes. Form into small balls and roll in confectioners' or granulated sugar.

Yield: 4 dozen.

White Cranberry-Almond Fudge

8 ounces cream cheese
2 (16-ounce) boxes confectioners' sugar
1 teaspoon almond extract
1 cup almonds, chopped
1 cup fresh cranberries

Cream the cheese and sugar until fluffy. Beat in extract. Knead in almonds. Press half the mixture in a 9-inch square pan. Place cranberries evenly over mixture. Cover with remaining mixture and press level. Cut into squares and store in refrigerator.

Yield: 64 squares.

Microwave Peanut Brittle

1 cup peanuts
1 cup sugar
½ cup light corn syrup
¼ teaspoon salt
1 teaspoon butter
1 teaspoon vanilla extract
1 teaspoon baking soda

Stir peanuts, sugar, light corn syrup, and salt into a 1½ quart casserole. Cook 8 minutes on high in microwave, stirring well after 4 minutes. Add butter and vanilla extract and cook 1 minute longer on high. Add baking soda and quickly stir until light and foamy. Immediately pour onto a lightly buttered baking sheet. Spread thinly. When cool break into pieces and store in an airtight container.

Yield: 6-8 servings.

Easy Peanut Butter Fudge

½ cup butter
1 pound light brown sugar
½ cup milk
¾ cup peanut butter

1 teaspoon vanilla extract
1 (16-ounce) box confectioners'
   sugar

Melt butter in a large saucepan. Add brown sugar and milk. Melt on low heat. Mix in peanut butter and add vanilla extract. Beat in confectioners' sugar until smooth. Pour into a 9 x 13-inch pan and chill. Cut into pieces.

Yield: 100 squares.

Rocky Road Fudge

1 (6-ounce) package semi-sweet
   chocolate chips
½ cup butter, softened
2 cups sugar
⅔ cup evaporated milk

1 cup miniature marshmallows
½ cup miniature marshmallows,
   frozen
1 teaspoon vanilla extract
1 cup walnuts, chopped

Stir together chocolate chips and butter in a large mixing bowl. Combine sugar, milk, and 1 cup marshmallows in large saucepan. Bring to a boil over medium heat and boil exactly 5 minutes, stirring constantly. Pour over chocolate chips and butter and blend well until mixture begins to thicken. Stir in ½ cup frozen marshmallows, vanilla extract, and walnuts. Pour into lightly greased 8-inch square pan. Chill until firm. Cut into bite-sized squares.

Yield: 64 squares.

Chocolate Dipped Strawberries

9 ounces milk chocolate
1 (1-ounce) square unsweetened
   chocolate

2 tablespoons vegetable oil
2 quarts fresh strawberries
Toothpicks

Heat milk chocolate, unsweetened chocolate, and oil in double boiler until melted. Place toothpicks in strawberries and dip into chocolate mixture. Stick toothpicks into styrofoam until chocolate sets. Strawberries may be placed in refrigerator to harden.

Yield: 2 quarts strawberries.

Elegant addition to a holiday buffet.

Chocolate Pretzels

1 (6-ounce) package semi-sweet
   chocolate chips
2 tablespoons corn syrup

2 tablespoons shortening
1½ teaspoons water
25-30 (3-inch) twisted pretzels

Combine chocolate chips, corn syrup, shortening, and water in double boiler. Stir frequently until mixture melts and is smooth. Remove from heat. Using 2 forks, dip each pretzel into chocolate mixture. Let pretzels cool on racks with waxed paper underneath. Chill 10 minutes in refrigerator. Let stand at room temperature for 1 hour. Store in covered container.

Yield: 25-30 pretzels.

This quick and easy recipe is a great holiday gift idea! It is easy to double the quantity.

Acknowledgments
Contributors and Testers

Debbie Akers
Honey Allen
Sandra Allen
Moira Allsopp
Betsy Anderson
Joan Anderson
Linda Anderson
Barbara Andrews
Ruth Arthur
Gale Artigliere
Michelle Badcock
Anne Balmond
Joyce Barclay
Lisa Rogers Bare
Diane Barendse
Carol Jenkins Barnett
Bena Bayless
Tom Bayless
Edie Baylis
Ann Caroline Bean
Peggy Beck
Sharon Becker
Carolyn Belcher
Richard Berquist
Olive Betheo
Cheryl Black
Juanita Black
Pat Blalock
Lamar Blanton
Sue Blanton
Becky Blue
Gail Bonnichsen
Jean Boone
Judy Bopp
Trish Bredbenner
Annie Laurie Brennan
Pauline Brennan
Kitty Brooks
Merrill Brown
Mary Jane Bryan
Jane Bryant
Lynda Buck
Jean Bunch
Virginia Caldwell
Anne Calhoun
Dolores Campbell
Helen Cannon
Jean Cantlin
Karen Cardman
Susie Carr
Donna Cassidy

Melissa Causey
Jesse Chappell
Cindy Chase
Pam Chase
Dianne Claussen
Beverly Clements
Kathleen Coffman
Sue Coleman
Dottie Collins
Kathy Cook
Cookie Madam
Nancy Cox
Susan Cox
Jan Craig
Denise Crenshaw
Barbara Cutrell
Cathy Dalton
Bill Daughtrey
Liz Daughtrey
Penny Davey
Fleta Dean
Mary Ann DeLoach
Anna Maria DiCesare
Lin Docherty
Donna Doran
Nancy Dotson
Barbara DuBose
Tommie DuBose
Bootie Dukes
Elsie Durrence
Connie Dutch
Bob Eanett
Darlene Eanett
Bonnie Edwards
Jim Edwards
Helen Ehlenbeck
Leonette Ehlenbeck
Linda Einisman
Dan Elkin
Sandra Ellington
Pat Engle
Ansley Evans
Julie Evans
Lynne Fargher
Marche Farnsworth
Carol Fear
Martha Ann Ferguson
Susan Ficquette
Nancy Fisher
Betsy Fordyce
Judy Fortin

Patty Fouts
Anne Furr
Tracy Gaines
Sheri Geiger
Grace Graper
Mona Green
Susan Gustashaw
Susan Guiterrez
Tammy Haer
Carolyn Harper
Judy Harris
Rebecca Harris
Diane Harvey
Sue Harwell
Felicia Hauseman
Dawn Hawkins
Joyce Hazenzall
Doris Heath
Janet Henderson
Rosa Hernandez
Linda Herold
Maud Hester
Barbara Higginbotham
Jacki Hill
Pat Hill
Ann Hilliard
Lyn Holcom
Virginia Hollon
Courtney Holmes
Gail Holmes
Margaret Holmes
Debbie Hooks
Ann Horning
Cindy Howard
Harriet Huggins
Cynthia Hutton
Dotty Ivey
Barbara Jackson
Becky Jackson
Elizabeth Jacobs
Lana Jacobs
Chris Jacobsen
Mary Jacobsen
Roddy Jennings
Chris Johnson
Julie Johnson
Martha Jones
Debe Jordan
Jody Kane
Kay Kelley
Bev Kelly

Acknowledgments continued

Beth Kennedy
Nancy Dew Kibler
Nell Kibler
Sandy Kibler
Mary Lu Kiley
Claudia Kittleson
Melinda Knight
Colleen Kremer
Linda Laborde
Lakeland Yacht and
    Country Club
Kiki Lesley
Jane Lewers
Grace Lewis
Debbie Liles
Bev Lindsey
Carole Little
Sheila Lotterhos
Mary Jane Lowe
Gloria Lunz
Carolee Lyons
Doris Lyons
Kim Lyons
Neil Lyons
Pat Lyons
Linda Magnusen
Juanita Marshall
Gail Maenza
Beverly Mansfield
Beth Martin
Cindy Martin
Gladys Martin
Beth Mason
Sally Mawhinney
Aleene Mayo
Carolyn McCarthy
Virginia McClurg
Kaye McConnell
Margy McKee
Peggy McKeel
Thomas McKewen
Anne McLaughlin
Betty Ann McNeill
Beth McSween
Pat Meland
Bobby Miller
Diane Miller
Nancy Miller
Sharon Miller
Carol Minnotte
Piper Mislovic
Zuma Mollison
Ada Maria Montero

Cecelia Moore
Kem Moore
Kathy Mullens
Fran Munson
Bennie Jo Murray
Beth Myers
Greg Myers
Marjorie Myers
Martha Nicolette
Junis Nunez
Sandi Opalinski
Park Place Café
Virginia Peacock
Ann Peddy
Jeanette Penkert
Sally Petcoff
Stephanie Peterson
Cheryl Philpot
Linda Pipping
Petra Platt
Jolene Poppell
Prema Rao
Doris Ann Reavis
Vicki Reddick
Donna Reed
Connie Renz
Belinda Roberts
Carole Roberts
Marjorie Roberts
Jamie Robinson
Marie Rumph
Kim Ruthven
Becky Sandusky
Sarah Sandusky
Lyn Scott
Corinne Sherwood
Joy Sherwood
Kathy Sherwood
Suzanne Siegel
Leslie Sikora
Deborah Sims
Nancy Simpson
Shellie Sinclair
Betsy Sklenicka
Eileen Smith
Robin Smith
Janet Snapp
Dee Socia
Sally Solomon
Sandra Solomon
Cindy Spear
Natalie Spresser
Missy Steadman

Mary Stephens
Peggy Stephens
Mary Stiles
Mike Stiles
Jo Stitzel
Patsy Stokes
Nettie Stone
Linda Swain
Eileen Sweet
Tonie Sweet
Olinda Sykes
Laura Taft
Bill Taggart
Nita Taggart
Colette Tarver
Susie Tart
Lucy Tavrides
Ruthellen Taylor
Cindy Terry
Brenda Thigpen
Betty Todd
Janie Towne
Freddie Trovillion
Doreen Venables
D. H. Viertel
Weezie Vreeland
Leslie Wallace
Pamela Walmsley
Cindi Ward
Nitzy Waters
Weebo Watkins
Betsy Watson
Judy Webb
Sharie Weeks
Judy Welch
Ann Wellman
Glyn Wheeler
Marianne Wheeler
Susan Wheeler
Andrea Whiteley
Linda Wilder
Sally Wilfong
Susan Willis
Margaret Wollett
Marge Woodard
Dana Woodsby
Bettie Wooten
Rob Wright
Evelyn Yarborough
Helen Yates
Frances Yeilding

Index

PALM COUNTRY
·Cuisine·

2020 Crystal Grove Drive
Lakeland, FL 33801

Please send me _____ copies of Palm Country Cuisine
at $14.95 each $ _____
add postage and handling at $2.00 each $ _____
add gift wrap (if desired) at $1.00 each $ _____
Florida residents add 5% sales tax at $.75 each $ _____
Total $ _____

Name _____
Address _____
City _____ State _____ Zip _____

Please make checks payable to **Palm Country Cuisine**. Proceeds will benefit the community through the Junior League of Greater Lakeland, Inc.

PALM COUNTRY
·Cuisine·

2020 Crystal Grove Drive
Lakeland, FL 33801

Please send me _____ copies of Palm Country Cuisine
at $14.95 each $ _____
add postage and handling at $2.00 each $ _____
add gift wrap (if desired) at $1.00 each $ _____
Florida residents add 5% sales tax at $.75 each $ _____
Total $ _____

Name _____
Address _____
City _____ State _____ Zip _____

Please make checks payable to **Palm Country Cuisine**. Proceeds will benefit the community through the Junior League of Greater Lakeland, Inc.

PALM COUNTRY
·Cuisine·

2020 Crystal Grove Drive
Lakeland, FL 33801

Please send me _____ copies of Palm Country Cuisine
at $14.95 each $ _____
add postage and handling at $2.00 each $ _____
add gift wrap (if desired) at $1.00 each $ _____
Florida residents add 5% sales tax at $.75 each $ _____
Total $ _____

Name _____
Address _____
City _____ State _____ Zip _____

Please make checks payable to **Palm Country Cuisine**. Proceeds will benefit the community through the Junior League of Greater Lakeland, Inc.

Please list any book stores or gift shops in your area
that you would like to handle this book.

_____

_____

_____

_____

_____

_____

Please list any book stores or gift shops in your area
that you would like to handle this book.

_____

_____

_____

_____

_____

Please list any book stores or gift shops in your area
that you would like to handle this book.

_____

_____

_____

_____

_____